Ted Hughes

For the first time, one volume surveys the life, works and critical reputation of one of the most significant British writers of the twentieth century: Ted Hughes.

This accessible guide to Hughes' writing provides a rich exploration of the complete range of his works. In this volume, Terry Gifford:

- offers clear and detailed discussions of Hughes' poetry, stories, plays, translations, essays and letters
- includes new biographical information, and previously unpublished archive material, especially on Hughes' environmentalism
- provides a comprehensive account of Hughes' critical reception, separated into the major themes that have interested readers and critics
- offers useful suggestions for further reading, and incorporates helpful cross-references between sections of the guide.

Part of the Routledge Guides to Literature series, *Ted Hughes* presents an accessible, fresh, and fascinating introduction to a major British writer whose work continues to be of crucial importance today.

Terry Gifford is a pioneering ecocritic and Ted Hughes scholar. He is co-author (with Neil Roberts) of *Ted Hughes: A Critical Study* (1981) and author of *Reconnecting With John Muir: Essays in Post-Pastoral Practice* (2006). He is Visiting Professor at the University of Chichester, UK, and Profesor Honorario at the Universidad de Alicante, Spain.

Routledge Guides to Literature

Editorial Advisory Board: Richard Bradford (University of Ulster at Coleraine), Shirley Chew (University of Leeds), Mick Gidley (University of Leeds), Jan Jedrzejewski (University of Ulster at Coleraine), Ed Larrissy (University of Leeds), Duncan Wu (St Catherine's College, University of Oxford).

Routledge Guides to Literature offer clear introductions to the most widely studied authors and texts. Each book engages with texts, contexts and criticism, highlighting the range of critical views and contextual factors that need to be taken into consideration in advanced studies of literary works. The series encourages informed but independent readings of texts by ranging as widely as possible across the contextual and critical issues relevant to the works examined, rather than presenting a single interpretation. Alongside general guides to texts and authors, the series includes 'Sourcebooks', which allow access to reprinted contextual and critical materials as well as annotated extracts of primary text.

Already available:*

Geoffrey Chaucer by Gillian Rudd
Ben Jonson by James Loxley
William Shakespeare's The Merchant of Venice: *A Sourcebook* edited by S. P.
  Cerasano
William Shakespeare's King Lear: *A Sourcebook* edited by Grace Ioppolo
William Shakespeare's Othello: *A Sourcebook* edited by Andrew Hadfield
William Shakespeare's Macbeth: *A Sourcebook* edited by Alexander Leggatt
William Shakespeare's Hamlet: *A Sourcebook* edited by Sean McEvoy
John Milton by Richard Bradford
John Milton's Paradise Lost: *A Sourcebook* edited by Margaret Kean
Alexander Pope by Paul Baines
Jonathan Swift's Gulliver's Travels: *A Sourcebook* edited by Roger D. Lund
Mary Wollstonecraft's A Vindication of the Rights of Woman: *A Sourcebook*
  edited by Adriana Craciun
Jane Austen by Robert P. Irvine
Jane Austen's Emma: *A Sourcebook* edited by Paula Byrne
Jane Austen's Pride and Prejudice: *A Sourcebook* edited by Robert Morrison
Byron by Caroline Franklin
Mary Shelley's Frankenstein: *A Sourcebook* edited by Timothy Morton
The Poems of John Keats: A Sourcebook edited by John Strachan
The Poems of Gerard Manley Hopkins: A Sourcebook edited by Alice Jenkins
Charles Dickens's David Copperfield: *A Sourcebook* edited by Richard J. Dunn
Charles Dickens's Bleak House: *A Sourcebook* edited by Janice M. Allan
Charles Dickens's Oliver Twist: *A Sourcebook* edited by Juliet John
Charles Dickens's A Tale of Two Cities: *A Sourcebook* edited by Ruth Glancy
Herman Melville's Moby-Dick: *A Sourcebook* edited by Michael J. Davey
Harriet Beecher Stowe's Uncle Tom's Cabin: *A Sourcebook* edited by Debra J.
  Rosenthal

* Some titles in this series were first published in the Routledge Literary Sourcebooks series, edited by Duncan Wu, or the Complete Critical Guide to Literature series, edited by Jan Jedrzejewski and Richard Bradford.

Ted Hughes

Terry Gifford

Routledge
Taylor & Francis Group

LONDON AND NEW YORK

First edition published 2009 by Routledge
2 Park Square, Milton Park, Abingdon, OX14 4RN

Simultaneously published in the USA and Canada
by Routledge
270 Madison Ave, New York, NY 10016

Routledge is an imprint of the Taylor & Francis Group, an informa business

© 2009 Terry Gifford

Typeset in Sabon and Gill Sans by
Taylor & Francis Books
Printed and bound in Great Britain by
CPI Antony Rowe, Chippenham, Wiltshire

British Library Cataloguing in Publication Data
A catalogue record for this book is available from the British Library

Library of Congress Cataloging in Publication Data
Gifford, Terry.
Ted Hughes / Terry Gifford. – 1st ed.
p. cm. – (Routledge guides to literature)
Includes bibliographical references and index.
1. Hughes, Ted, 1930–1998–Handbooks, manuals, etc. I. Title.
PR6058.U37Z6945 2008
823'.914 – dc22
2008027782

ISBN 10: 0-415-31188-8 (hbk)
ISBN 10: 0-415-31189-6 (pbk)
ISBN 10: 0-203-46321-8 (ebk)

ISBN 13: 978-0-415-31188-5 (hbk)
ISBN 13: 978-0-415-31189-2 (pbk)
ISBN 13: 978-0-203-46321-5 (ebk)

In memory of three pioneering American Hughes scholars and friends:

Fred Rue Jacobs, Len Scigaj and Diane Middlebrook

and for newborn Lewis Edwards

Contents

Acknowledgements

This book is dedicated to three special people who are much missed among the community of Ted Hughes scholars – Fred Rue Jacobs, Leonard M. Scigaj and Dianne Middlebrook – and to my newly born Kiwi grandson, Lewis Edwards. Keith Sagar first brought together a group of Ted Hughes scholars for a conference in Manchester, England, 1980. Beginning with the early kindnesses of Keith Sagar, the community of Hughes scholars have, for nearly forty years, generously exchanged information and arguments with me, including the three feisty, much-missed friends to whom this book is dedicated.

Fred Rue Jacobs, an enthusiastic Ted Hughes bibliophile, was the Librarian at Bakersfield College in a bleak part of California to which he gave much-appreciated eccentric and loving life. He became a friend of Ted Hughes, later visiting him annually when Fred came to England for treatments for his cancer at health farms in Devon. He was the first, and most serious, collector of Hughes material in the USA and the first scholar to write about Hughes's dramatic work. Every time I visited him at his small apartment I laid out my mat and sleeping bag on the floor of the 'Hughes shrine' (a room containing nothing but bookshelves and filing cabinets devoted to Hughes material) before Fred regaled me with stories and offered copies of the latest esoteric publications on Hughes that I had missed. When Hughes died of cancer, Fred was distraught that Hughes, private until the last, had not contacted him on the very subject on which Fred regarded himself as an expert and a survivor for at least twelve years. Fred's sheer enthusiasm for the work of Hughes and for documenting it, talking about it and loving its spirit, was a gift I felt privileged to have shared.

Len Scigaj came from Virginia Tech to every Ted Hughes conference with the unflinching seriousness of a tennis-player and scholar. He had a passion for getting things right, for going to the sources and checking them with Hughes directly. Len hated my quoting him in *Green Voices* 'out of context', but he brought me into his pioneering classes in ecocriticism at Virginia Tech and we talked long and hard about the works of Hughes on bicycle rides from his home. Len's students became the environmentalist activists on campus and Len marched with them on protests. Len felt the isolation of a committed teacher of the works of Hughes in 1990s America where the prejudices of Plath partisans held sway. More than anyone else in America at the time, Len tried to gain

xii   ACKNOWLEDGEMENTS

recognition for studies of the works of Hughes, at the Modern Language Association's annual conference, with publishers and with the growing number of ecocritics who appreciated writers concerned with the environment in all its forms and discourses. Len's sudden heart attack prevented him from taking satisfaction in some of the later signs of hope for Hughes studies in the USA.

Diane Middlebrook was one of a number of scholars who more recently came to the works of Hughes via those of Sylvia Plath. This was a significant development at Joanny Moulin's 2000 conference in Lyon where Diane gave a glimpse of her theory of the self-construction of the Ted Hughes biography in his works. Diane kindly organised my Hughes files at my house in Derbyshire, England, while going through them in preparation for her book, before we went to see *Alcestis* at Dean Clough in Halifax with Neil Roberts – a memorable and moving event for all of us. Diane brought fresh perspectives to our conferences and a gracious wit to what had been, for too long, mainly male conversations on the work of Hughes.

In the 1970s when I began serious research on the works of Ted Hughes I was grateful to Sheffield City Libraries who, through the wonderful resource of the British Library's Interlibrary Loans system, delivered into my hands rare limited editions and much more beyond my reach as a local secondary school teacher with a passion for the work of Hughes. The supportive role of a civic library in that era ought to be acknowledged, and its support for British readers of this book who do not have access to a university library should hopefully continue to be sustained.

Neil Roberts at Sheffield University took on my proposal for MA research on Hughes and when we became neighbours, with our young children playing in the same streets, Neil suggested, at the completion of my MA, that we write a book together. We were amused to find that Hughes himself wrote to Sagar that we probably wrote alternate chapters (which we did in first draft, but handed over to the other to rewrite, with the proviso that we both agreed on every final sentence) and that one of us was more right than the other (26. 2. 1979, BL ADD 78757, f. 18). Hughes took our royalties in permission fees and when *Ted Hughes: A Critical Study* (1981) went out of print we each received from Faber a royalty statement of minus £11. Thus are academics often financially rewarded. Fortunately the real rewards lie elsewhere, as these acknowledgements might suggest.

David Craig's encouragement and conversations as my PhD supervisor, mentor and climbing partner are not to be underestimated as a long-sustained influence on my work on Hughes, especially in relation to his critique of twentieth-century culture. The challenge and warmth of his friendship has sharpened many of the readings of Hughes's texts in this book.

The staff at Special Collections in the Robert W. Woodruff Library, Emory University, Atlanta, Georgia, USA make every visit a delight. Their enthusiasm for sharing their treasures led to their showing me not only an unsent letter, but a volume of my poems in Hughes's library – a sadly neglected influence yet to be pursued by Hughes scholars.

My parents, Edna and Dennis Gifford, will be pleased to see that I've been gainfully occupied during my retirement. This book benefits from their cuttings service.

ACKNOWLEDGEMENTS   xiii

Bruce and Chris at The Watts Russell Arms, Hopedale, Staffordshire, England, continue to provide the most convivial reading room in the world.

In addition, this book has benefited from information generously provided by: Al Alvarez, Carol Bere, John Billingsley, Rand Brandes, Brian Clarke, Ian Cook, Donald Crossley, Ian Dempster, Ed Douglas, Stephen Enniss, Seamus Heaney, Carol Hughes, Olwyn Hughes, Daniel Huws, Tim Kendal, Michael Martin, Leo Marx, Joanny Moulin, Christopher North, Richard Price, Neil Roberts, Keith Sagar, Ronald Schuchard, John Sewell, Dave Sissons, Ann Skea, Tim Supple and Daniel Weissbort.

Final thanks must go to my wife, Gill Round, who ... might have wished, before the computer crashed at precisely this point, that I was about to acknowledge her cracking the whip so lovingly over the years I have been working on this book.

The publisher and author would like to thank, for permission to reprint material under copyright, Faber and Faber and the estate of Ted Hughes.

Terry Gifford
Sella, Alicante, 2008

Introduction

Ted Hughes is already regarded as a major poet of the twentieth century. This book presents the evidence for his being read as a writer with huge significance for the future of the human species in the twenty-first century. Although the complete body of his work is still in the process of being archived and published, there is plenty of evidence for such a claim. We have a *Collected Poems*, together with selections of his essays, translations and letters which include useful annotations and notes. And the bulk of Hughes's papers are now available to scholars in two great libraries in Britain and America. Essentially a poet, the range of his work also includes stories, plays, translations, essays and letters. Within them is a body of work that Hughes called 'within hearing of children' that is not only of great educational value, but also essential for adult readers who wish to hear what Hughes has to say to the twenty-first century.

When we have learned to undo the artificial separations we have erected between forms of knowledge (the humanities and the sciences; art and activism, for example) we shall not only be able to appreciate the range of Hughes's interests, including esoteric forms of knowledge, in relation to his writing, but be able to reconnect the 'work' of the poet with his life's 'work' as supporter of educational broadcasting, the creative writing movement, local environmental activism and national campaigns against agricultural and industrial pollution. Hughes himself was deeply read, for example, in both astrology and the science of water pollution. He was also a literary historian, tracing the path Western culture has taken that led to our self-destructive separations of knowledge. So this book attempts to reconnect and cross-reference the 'whole work' of Ted Hughes, from all aspects of the life to the work and to its impact.

From the beginning Hughes possessed an amazingly coherent sense of the field he wanted to explore and articulate, first through poetry, and then quickly also through stories and plays. He knew that he needed to break with the conventional wisdom, preoccupations and modes of poetry that dominated in England when he began publishing his poetry. He felt that the Movement poets were avoiding the most urgent questions facing human beings in a post-industrial society. From the beginning his work was a radical attempt to challenge the taken-for-granted by addressing those urgent questions: What connected human nature, the inner lives of people, with the great forces of nature around them? How could people negotiate a relationship with the apparently battling life and death processes of the earth in which they had their home? How should a responsible, morally aware, decision-making animal find its home in the elemental and subtle dynamics of ecology? How could the observation of those dynamics in nature inform both the quality of unconscious life – its passions, fears and desires – and the conscious decisions of a species that is clearly on a path of self-destruction? What can the natural gift of the imagination do to engage with these questions? It is common to find critics speaking of the vision of Ted Hughes and it is true that a coherent body of insights into these questions can be articulated from reading his work. But in the writing itself the poet is conducting an enquiry with all the resources of language in its most subtle and sensitive mode. The poetry is an imaginative exploration that can only hint at answers to these questions. This gives us the enjoyment – and now the sense of urgent importance – of discussing our readings of this challenging and increasingly relevant work.

Of course, Hughes himself believed that the poet had a public duty to explore the most troubling questions of his time and to produce work that might have a healing function if the poet has faced up to the most dangerous risks, and kept his moral and linguistic focus. From his university studies in anthropology he understood the ancient discipline of the poet as shaman of his tribe. Hughes's personal experience, his wide reading and his studies of other poets, all gave him rich and sometimes painful resources with which to undertake the imaginative journeys that resulted in the poems, stories and plays. Our responsibility is to discuss them as clearly as we can in our search for their healing qualities and insights. Again, the parts of this book that attend to the life, the work and the criticism should all be seen as essential to our consideration of those key questions for our time that Hughes was imaginatively investigating on our behalf.

Some of the information presented here is published for the first time, especially on the environmental concerns and activities of Hughes. To read Elaine Feinstein's first and only biography one would hardly think of Ted Hughes as an environmental writer and activist. Frustrating in its errors as this biography is to the participants, it does represent a first attempt to chronicle the life to which Chapter 1 'Life and contexts' of this book is indebted. Restrictions of space have necessarily required much omission of detail in Chapter 1. For example, those interested in the competing claims of lovers will have to consult Feinstein. But if this book is, in part, the first 'green' biography, it also includes the first recent survey of the critical reception of the work in Chapter 3 'Criticism'. Again, apologies should be offered to those critics who might feel that their contributions to debates about Hughes's work have been overlooked or underplayed.

The readings of the works offered in Chapter 2 are intended to provide a starting point for the reader's own interpretation of the texts, not to substitute for them. As the Chapter 3 survey of critical positions demonstrates, there is always room for different theoretical frames of reference, for differences of emphasis, for identifying omissions and for downright disagreement. Hughes himself said, 'Finally, poems belong to readers – just as houses belong to those who live in them and not to the builders' (17. 3. 1975, BL ADD 78756, f. 20).

The only abbreviation used in this book is *Letters* for *Letters of Ted Hughes*, London: Faber & Faber, 2007. Cross-referencing between chapters is a feature of each volume in the Routledge Guides to Literature series. Cross-references appear in brackets and include a chapter title as well as the relevant page numbers in bold type, e.g. (see Life and contexts, **pp. 12–14**). References beginning 'MSS' are to manuscripts held in the Department of Special Collections of the Robert W. Woodruff Library, Emory University, Atlanta, Georgia, USA. References beginning 'BL' are from the Manuscript Department of the British Library, London.

1

Life and contexts

The childhood to undergraduate years (1930–56)

Two themes dominate the youth of Ted Hughes: his fascination with wildlife and his early sense of himself as a future writer and poet. Both might have been thought unlikely, given Hughes's upbringing in the two different industrial areas of first West Yorkshire and then South Yorkshire. But the young Hughes's sense of being most alive in the countryside (easily accessible from each of his two childhood homes), a supportive family and nurturing state schools provided him with opportunities that were to shape his life's work. All of his resources as a writer of poetry, fiction, literary studies, book reviews, translations, letters and children's works are aimed at exploring the tensions and connections between our inner nature and the external nature, in both of which Hughes believed that we must find a way to be at home. Hughes's constructions in his work of a range of figures such as the fox, the wodwo, Crow, the Iron Man, the moors, a river, Shakespeare's goddess, Alcestis, Sylvia Plath and himself are all observed with a naturalist's attention and a storyteller's sense of aiming his construction towards healing the gap between inner and outer nature. Hughes said that when writing for children he knew that there were fewer defences thrown up across that gap: 'the audience is still open' (Kazzer 1999: 193). It is clear that in his own childhood he was increasingly 'at home' within the family, the countryside, schooling and the connections between them.

The street into which Edward James Hughes was born on 17 August 1930 was a row of terraced houses in the West Yorkshire village of Mytholmroyd that looked out across an open square of waste land and up through fields to the moors beyond. (The first syllable of this village is not pronounced 'myth' (*pace* Greening 2007: ix); the 'y' is pronounced 'I'.) Number 1 Aspinal Street is on a corner and round its side it has an open arched entrance to a cobbled yard at the back of the house. One street further back behind the house was the canal, crossed by the bridge that gives access to the main road that runs through the Calder Valley, the natural corridor that contains Mytholmroyd, and west over the Pennines from the Yorkshire to the Lancashire textile industries. In this deeply cut valley, road, railway, river and canal run close together with factories and mills in between them. Terraced housing has crept up the sides of the valley, most notably at the steeply tiered town of Hebden Bridge, the centre of the nineteenth-century woollen industry that used water to power weaving looms. What had begun as a cottage industry in the higher villages above Hebden Bridge such as Heptonstall, where many small windows gave good light in the upper rooms of eighteenth-century cottages, developed into the centre of the industrial revolution with large mills and their tall chimneys, although industrial decline was well established by the time of Hughes's childhood in the Depression years of the 1930s.

The spirit of dogged survival in the people of West Yorkshire, that is evoked so strongly in *Remains of Elmet* (1979), is symbolised not just by the presence of the industrial past in the valley and the marginal, often abandoned, hill farms above, but by the monuments to the dead of the First World War that stand on the rim of the valley and the surprising number of huge square nonconformist chapels that, now disused, still litter the landscape. Hughes explains in his book about his earliest landscape that this area was known as Elmet. It was the last Celtic kingdom in England and was famed for its independence and resilience. The villages of the Calder Valley lost dramatic numbers of men in the First World War, but the population's ability to accept suffering had been sustained by the force of Methodism since John Wesley's preaching had first taken root here, seemingly in the bleak conditions of the landscape itself. In his introduction to *Remains of Elmet*, Hughes emphasises that growing up here, 'you could not fail to realise that cataclysms had happened ... Gradually, it dawned on you that you were living among the survivors, in the remains'. Hence the original title of his book, *Remains of Elmet*. A second version, which contained more poems about the resilience of local people, was simply titled *Elmet* (1994).

Hughes's mother Edith was a descendant of the Norman family named Ferrer (later Farrar), one of whom, Nicholas Ferrer, is the subject of a poem by Hughes. One of six children, Edith's sister Hilda lived at 13 Aspinal St and her brother Albert lived at 19 Aspinal St. Her brothers Tom and Walter also lived with their families in Mytholmroyd, so that Hughes grew up with a strong sense of a close family that he came to celebrate with the inclusion of several family poems in *Elmet*. (Mentioned in poems are uncle Albert: 1902–47, the brother of Hughes's mother Edith: 1898–1969, uncle Thomas: 1891–1951, uncle Walt: 1893–1976, and aunts Miriam: 1896–1915 and Hilda: 1908–2003). Because at least three sets of relatives had farms on the hillsides above the Calder Valley, the sense of family ownership of this landscape must have been strong. Edith must have given her children great self-confidence through allowing Ted to be taken on shooting and camping expeditions from the house by his brother Gerald, who was ten years older. Ted's sister Olwyn, who was two years older than him, came to play an important supportive role in his life, not only as a mentor through school and later as his literary agent, but by moving in and looking after his two children when his wife Sylvia Plath committed suicide. At school, Olwyn lent Ted the books of poetry she was studying in classes two years ahead of him, but it was their mother who first supported her children's early interest in literature by buying books to extend their reading experience. She herself loved poetry, Wordsworth especially, and made up stories for the children when they were small. That Edith had a matter of fact attitude towards the occasional appearance of the ghost of her elder sister Miriam, who had died young, would also be significant in Hughes's later interest in esoteric forms of knowledge. We also now know that Edith Hughes wrote at least one poem and a narrative of her childhood (Emory, Gerald Hughes collection). Ted was later to return the debt to his mother by taking her and his father into his Devon home for long periods as she became infirm, and also in his second and more personal homage to his childhood, *Elmet*.

Hughes's father, William Henry Hughes, was one of only seventeen men in a whole regiment of the Lancashire Fusiliers to have survived the battle of Gallipoli in the First World War. (Seventeen thousand, three hundred and forty-two members of his regiment did not return from the First World War.) He was saved by his paybook from a piece of shrapnel penetrating to his heart. The young boy heard his father calling out in his sleep in the nightmares that continued to haunt him. An able footballer, William's fitness was tested to exhaustion as he repeatedly carried back wounded men at Ypres, for which he was awarded the Distinguished Conduct Medal. He was a carpenter, who, after church on Sunday, once took Ted along the canal towpath to the pub near his mother's house to see the man who bit off rats' heads, as reconstructed in the story 'Sunday' in *Wodwo* (1967). In Hughes's writing his father is usually associated with the trauma of a survivor of the First World War. The horrors of his father's war came to be overlaid with the horrors that made such an impression on the imagination of Hughes himself in the aftermath of the Second World War when the images of the camps and the Japanese cities were finally made public.

With a group of other boys, Hughes played in the nearby woods, swam in the river and fished in the canal. For his fourth birthday he was given a simple animal identification book and Gerald taught him how to trap small animals before later taking Hughes on hunting trips in the woods and moors where Ted acted as retriever. Later Gerald taught him how to use a gun. In the story 'The Deadfall' that opens the collection *Difficulties of a Bridegroom* (1995), Hughes describes a camping trip with his brother to Crimsworth Dene as though it is autobiographical. Their purpose was shooting rabbits, but they discovered a dead young fox caught in a gamekeeper's trap. The story has a supernatural element that anticipates the even stronger fantasy element in the final one in the collection in which the narrator, sickened by his brother's relentless shooting of everything that moves, decides to quit himself, with weird consequences. But as young brothers they certainly do seem to have shot more than just rabbits, sometimes accompanied by their Uncle Walt, who appears in several poems, always closely associated with an intimate knowledge of this West Yorkshire landscape.

At the age of eight the family moved to Mexborough, a South Yorkshire mining village where, once again, a river ran behind the newspaper and tobacconist shop William ran on the main street. On the other side of the river was rolling farmland with ditches and copses, pheasants and partridges, rabbits and foxes, and a farm that Hughes came to know well. Rather than move to Mexborough, at the age of seventeen his brother left the family to become a gamekeeper in Devon, but Hughes became friends with the son of a gamekeeper on a nearby estate where they could roam the woods and lakes, learning to fish for pike. It was in the hollows and farms, parkland and ponds of this landscape that Hughes developed his adolescent study of wildlife, informed by the magazines easily available in his father's shop. At the age of fifteen his awareness of the destructiveness of his mode of engagement with the animals he had been trapping and shooting led to an imaginative interest in their inner lives and their habitats. At the same time he had registered the combined effects of silage and chemical pollution in the two rivers of his childhood:

> From my earliest days I was hooked on fish – but I lived by a river, the West Yorks Calder, that had no life in it at all. Straight industrial effluent. And the Don, in South Yorks, ... was worse. So my greening began you could say with everything that lay about me in my infancy.
> (Gifford 1995: 132)

Hughes added about his secondary school, Mexborough Grammar, that 'our school song was "By Don and Dearne" – both dead, crucified rivers' (T.H. to T.G., 17. 12. 1993, MSS 644, Box 54, FF1).

From the primary school down the road from the family corner shop, Hughes followed his sister in passing an exam at eleven years old to gain a place at Mexborough Grammar School. This school had a reputation for developing talented children from this area of the South Yorkshire coalfield. Here a series of inspirational teachers of English encouraged Hughes's original writing in a manner that was progressive for its time, when essays and analysis dominated the English secondary school curriculum. A class reading of *The Jungle Book* sent Hughes to the library at the age of thirteen to find Kipling's verse. He imitated and experimented in his own writing with the verse forms he encountered. 'It was in the fourth year [year 10] that the teachers began remarking on some of his poetry', said Vera Paley, his form teacher (*Sheffield Star* 20. 12. 1984). John Fisher, the charismatic English teacher Hughes revered, included his work in the school magazine and introduced Hughes to the work of Eliot and Hopkins. An interest in Yeats came via Celtic folktales, originally found in a children's encyclopaedia that his mother had bought for the home. At the same time Olwyn, who was to gain a Distinction in the Higher School Certificate for English Literature, and with what Hughes later called 'a marvellously precocious taste in poetry'(*Letters* 725), now became the school's prodigy and her brother's mentor. Hughes recalled that 'by sixteen I had no thought of becoming anything but a writer of some kind, certainly writing verse' (*Letters* 725). At the age of nineteen he had written the exquisite poem 'Song' for a Sixth Form girlfriend in the manner of the metaphysical poets. It was the earliest poem included in his first published collection.

In 1948 Mexborough Grammar School's development of Hughes led to his winning an Open Exhibition to Pembroke College Cambridge to read English, supported by John Fisher's sending some of Ted's poems to the college. First he had to do two years' National Service, much of it at Fylingdales radar station on the North Yorkshire moors, where he 'read and re-read Shakespeare and watched the grass grow' (Sagar 1975: 8). Having studied *King Lear* for A Level exams (together with Hardy's *The Woodlanders* and Shelley's *Adonais*, the latter learned by heart), the influence of Shakespeare's verse rhythms and phrasing were quite as strong on Hughes's early poetry as was his preoccupation with Shakespeare's themes in his later work. He also read Spenser and Milton aloud to himself while walking on the moors. By the time he went to university he knew most of the work of the Romantic poets and Robert Graves' *The White Goddess*, which he had received as a prize at Mexborough. Based upon the model provided by John Fisher, Hughes had high hopes that English at Cambridge would feed his growth as a writer.

This was not to be the case. At Cambridge Hughes immediately felt the isolation of a rather reserved grammar school boy among public school products who were in the majority. 'I was a quiet type, an outsider … (I lay low, because I felt, I suppose, that I was in enemy country. First two years, I didn't feel much social self-confidence.)' (BL ADD 78761, f. 61). The weekly essay of close analysis of texts became destructive rather than supportive of his deep appreciation of literature. The literary set, centred around King's College and the journal *Granta*, were deliberately exclusive and dilettante, with connections to literary life in London. Despite what he felt about himself, Hughes displayed a charismatic self-confidence that is attested to by the memoirs of fellow students at the time and he had the ability to be successful in the intensive system of essays, supervisions and exams. At the end of his second year he gained an upper second classification and one of his supervisors later wrote to tell him that she had learned more from him about Dylan Thomas than she could teach him about John Donne. Most of Hughes's friends were made in his second and third years and they can remember him quoting Blake and Hopkins by heart, singing ballads and living in his own slightly unconventional way. Some of these friends were made for life and his correspondence with them is now a major biographical source. One of them, Terence McCaughey, who was doing research on Scottish ballads at the time Hughes met him, became an Emeritus lecturer in Divinity at Trinity College, Dublin and was to officiate at Hughes's funeral service.

Blocked in the writing of his own poems by the hard rigour of dissecting and evaluating those of others, Hughes changed to study Archaeology and Anthropology for his third year. The turning point in making this decision was a famous dream that came at the end of a long night struggling to complete a critical essay. A fox appeared in his room in Cambridge and placed a bloody paw on the blank page in front of Hughes, leaving a blood-print and speaking the words, 'Stop this. You are destroying us.' Hughes often told this story in introducing the poem 'The Thought-Fox', written two years later. Hughes was not the only poet whose creativity was crushed by the spirit of the English course at that time. Brian Cox, a fellow grammar school entrant to Pembroke College and Cambridge English, only returned to writing poetry late in his life, writing in his memoir of Hughes, that at Pembroke, 'in those Leavis dominated years, so unsympathetic to the early work of young writers, I never found out he wrote verse' (1999: 32).

So the poet freed his creative spirit and came to deepen his knowledge of the folktales he had first read in the encyclopaedia his mother had bought him. The study of the role of myth in culture, and of the healing role of the shaman, bard, singer of songs, teller of tales in 'primitive' societies, came to inform his own work in crucial ways that are transparent from *Wodwo* to his work as Poet Laureate. He began to publish in Cambridge literary journals, including *Granta*, often using the pseudonym 'Daniel Hearing', and he gained a reputation as a serious poet that attracted the interest of other aspiring poets such as Peter Redgrove, who sought him out. Ironically, when he graduated he could not leave Cambridge behind him and returned at the weekends from the odd jobs he found in London to stay with friends who gravitated to a rented hut (until recently used for chickens) in the garden of St Botolph's rectory.

Hughes had a series of jobs after leaving university that were intended to sustain his real vocation to write poetry. His job in London Zoo was actually washing dishes rather than feeding the animals. He read novels for the J. Arthur Rank film company, summarising them for potential directors, but found that it affected his own work. Back in the hut one weekend his friends decided to start a literary magazine to be called the *St Botolph's Review* and a party was arranged to launch the first issue. It was hawked around the two female colleges on the day of the party and a copy was bought by an American Fulbright scholar at Newnham College called Sylvia Plath.

The Plath years (1956–63)

Sylvia Plath was born on 27 October 1932 into a spacious detached house in a leafy Boston street close to the Harvard Arboretum in a suburb called Jamaica Plain. Her father, Otto, had a Harvard University doctorate in Entomology and the year after she was born published his only book, *Bumblebees and Their Ways*. He had emigrated to America from Germany at the age of sixteen and her mother, Aurelia, was twenty-one years younger than him and was a second generation Austrian. The only thing Plath's childhood had in common with Hughes's was that she was also taken to Sunday School at the local non-conformist church. When Plath was eight years old her father died suddenly and she felt abandoned, saying to her mother, 'I'll never speak to God again.' As the elder of two children now brought up by her mother alone, she took on an ambition to be successful, first at school and then in sending out her stories for publication while still a schoolgirl. After an outstanding career at Smith College, Plath spent the early summer working in New York at the invitation of *Madamoiselle* magazine and returned to find that she had not been accepted on an end-of-summer short-story writing class at Harvard. Her depression led to her attempted suicide at the age of twenty-two. When she gained a Fulbright scholarship to study in England at Cambridge University, her hard work and undoubted flair had given her the academic success she desired, if only a fragile sense of self-confidence. At Cambridge she published poetry in a student magazine that was ridiculed by a friend of Hughes in another magazine. At the party to launch the *St Botolph's Review*, Hughes approached her and they discussed his friend's review of her poem until suddenly Hughes kissed her. He snatched her hairband and earrings to keep and in return she bit him so hard on the cheek that she drew blood.

Very quickly Hughes moved back to Cambridge from London to be close to Plath. They were married in London on 16 June 1956, secretly in order not to compromise Plath's scholarship, as she thought it would. (In fact, she had drawn the wrong conclusions from a requirement to notify the Fulbright authorities of her intention to marry.) Her mother was present at the wedding, but Hughes maintained the secrecy for a while with his own family. After a honeymoon in the quiet little fishing village of Benidorm in Spain (the little house they rented still sits among the tower blocks, opposite a pet shop), they found that it was perfectly possible for them to set up home together in Cambridge on the ground floor of 55 Eltisley Avenue. From a gate at the end of the street they could walk on the path through Granchester Meadows, where Hughes called up owls and Sylvia recited Chaucer to the bemused cows. Plath began to send out Hughes's poems for publication as well as her own and she submitted a collection of forty of his poems to an American competition for a first book. When he won, Harper Brothers published *The Hawk in the Rain* in 1957 to startlingly good reviews. Hughes later admitted that his exposure to American poetry had been a key to his recovery of his voice after his 'six years of bewilderment' between writing the poem 'Song' and 'The Thought-Fox'. Indeed, the remarkable degree of collaboration between the two talented poets, that began in Eltisley Avenue, should not be underestimated. Hughes set lists of titles for Plath to explore while she set readings in American poetry for him, and they exchanged dreams, and played with tarot cards and the Ouija board to find ideas for poems.

Unlike Hughes, Plath had always wanted a prestigious post in academia, and on the completion of her Fulbright she was offered a teaching post back at Smith College. So Hughes committed himself to a life in America and they moved into a flat in a large rambling house in Northampton, Massachusetts, 337 Elm Street, which is opposite Smith College and on a corner next to a park. But Plath soon realised that the work was too exhausting to leave energy for her writing and Hughes found himself unable to write, trapped in the isolation of the house, their poverty and his natural reserve. Plath's capacity for instant jealousy if she saw him talking to a female student was continued from their Cambridge days and by this time Hughes must have been acutely aware that Plath's inner fears led her to display what would now be called 'bi-polar' behaviour. He taught at the University of Massachusetts for a semester, but also realised that this was no help to his writing and at the end of the academic year the two poets resigned their posts to move into an apartment on the ninth floor of a house on Beacon Hill in the centre of Boston. At 9 Willow Street they began a freelance life together with views over the city from the Charles River to the northern reaches of the city beyond, towards Harvard. The poem '9 Willow Street' in *Birthday Letters* (1998) describes how what should have been a liberation for Plath, 'Freed from school / For the first time in your life', somehow became a cage. Hughes was finding it hard to understand and harder to tolerate Plath's volatile moods and repeated blockages that, in turn, created his own. 'Each of us was the stake / Impaling the other', he wrote in the poem that contains the desperate exclamation, 'What a waste!' It was clear that for both of them America was not a place in which they could work.

It was in America that Hughes first became 'properly aware' of ecological and conservation issues. He had been fishing on Cape Cod without realising, until he read about it in *The Nation* magazine, that 'the mackerel around Cape

Cod were radioactive'. US atomic waste had been dumped in the sea off Boston seven days a week for fourteen years and now the barrels were beginning to break up. 'And simultaneously, of course, Rachel Carson's book *Silent Spring* came out which suddenly revealed the whole of America as a poisoned land' (Gifford 1995: 131). With this 'changed idea of the world', which endorsed what he had seen of the early effects of silage on the River Don in the 1940s, Hughes brought back from America an awareness of the insidious effects of effluents on water quality that was to drive him to local environmental activism twenty years later. Meanwhile his preoccupation with the hubris of the human species' treatment of its home environment would come to dominate his poetry and stories. His old university friend Daniel Huws recalls that after his return from America Hughes 'was the first person I remember talking of the perils of factory farming and of additives to foods' (Huws 2007).

In January 1959 Hughes and Plath decided that they would return to England. But before doing so they planned a trip driving across America to California and back to spend the autumn at Yaddo, an artists' retreat in Saratoga Springs, New York State. Here they both found a surge of creative energy, Plath writing a third of the poems that would go into her first collection and Hughes working on a libretto for the *Bardo Thödol* or *The Tibetan Book of the Dead* with a Chinese composer. This work was never completed, but its influence can be found in the radio play 'The Wound' in *Wodwo* (1967) and in both *Crow* (1970) and *Cave Birds* (1978). Back in England, their need to decide where to live was given some urgency by Plath's pregnancy.

They were directed to a London flat to rent at 3 Chalcot Square by the poet W.S. Merwin and his wife Dido, whom they had met in Boston. This flat was so small that Hughes worked in the hallway at a borrowed card table, although on one morning he counted 104 interruptions from Plath. In March 1960 Hughes's second book *Lupercal* was published to immediate acclaim in the *Observer* from Al Alvarez, who was the most influential figure on the literary scene at the time. Readings, recordings and writing for the BBC were supplemented by an increasing number of invitations to write book reviews. Mr and Mrs Hughes were invited to dinner with T.S. Eliot and his wife, together with the poet Stephen Spender. In April Frieda Rebecca Hughes was born and the flat became obviously too small for a family, so they decided to start looking for a house outside London. They began what became a daily pattern of divided childcare so that Plath wrote in the mornings and Hughes in the afternoons. In October 1960 Plath's first collection *The Colossus* was published with an impact that disappointed her. By August 1961 she had finished her novel *The Bell Jar* and was again pregnant as they moved into the large house they had found in Devon – Court Green in the village of North Tawton.

Court Green is a thatched former rectory standing next to the village church. Attached to it are three acres of land including an apple orchard. Once again the couple divided the day, with Hughes undertaking renovations and gardening in the mornings while looking after Frieda. Now, although Plath delighted in their new country life, her comparative isolation intensified her depressions, and although Hughes was aware of this, he was also aware that she was writing her best poetry so far. Once again, Plath's jealousy surfaced when Hughes gave help to a local schoolgirl who was studying his work. In January 1962 Nicholas

Farrar Hughes was born during a long cold winter, but Plath managed to write a radio play for the BBC and Hughes began travelling to London more frequently to make recordings. Occasionally guests came to stay from London, such as the new tenants of 3 Chalcot Square, the poet David Wevill and his wife Assia, who stayed for a weekend in May.

That weekend Hughes fell in love with Assia. It is now clear that this was what she had intended would happen (Koren and Negev 2006: 86). During his visits to London in June he began an affair with Assia. Plath grew suspicious and during one of Hughes's London trips she burnt all the papers in his study, just as she had torn up his treasured *Complete Works of Shakespeare* earlier in London when Hughes was late home from a meeting at the BBC. On 9 July Plath picked up the phone to hear a male voice (actually a colleague of Assia's) asking to speak to Hughes. Plath suspected that she was being duped and, after Hughes finished the call, pulled the phone from its socket and asked him to leave the house. With her mother, who was by now visiting for the summer, she drove him to the station. In London Hughes moved between the houses of various friends, but in September Hughes and Plath visited Ireland together to find her a house to rent for the winter, staying with the poet Richard Murphy. However, this ended with Plath returning to Court Green alone as Hughes travelled on to visit the artist Barrie Cooke.

By December 1962 Plath had found a flat to rent in London at 23 Fitzroy Road where Yeats had once lived. With Hughes's help she established a home there as Hughes went back to Yorkshire for Christmas with his family. In January he returned to London and visited Plath regularly, joining a party on 14 January to launch *The Bell Jar*. In a timeline written in 1995 for Frieda, who asked what happened in her early life, Hughes wrote: 'Between her moving to London and her death, I visited about every other day' (MSS 1014, Box 2, FF1). But Plath's depression returned, for which her doctor treated her with anti-depressant drugs, not knowing, because of a different English name, that these had had a violently adverse effect on her when prescribed in America. In the coldest winter for a century, with no water from frozen pipes and no telephone, she sought help from friends who collected her to stay for a weekend. Saying that she felt much better and wanted to return home, she was driven back to her flat, where she put her children to bed, sealed their bedroom door and gassed herself. She was found dead on the morning of 11 February 1963 when an expected nurse could not gain entry and raised the alarm.

Al Alvarez, to whom Plath had read her last poems at his home nearby, believes that this was an attempted suicide that was tragically successful. Hughes believed that they would have been reconciled had this not happened: 'We ran out of time – by days, I think. So I shall always believe' (*Letters* 721). The extent of his devastation, from which he never really recovered, is expressed in a note written in May in response to condolences from one of Plath's room-mates at Smith: 'That's the end of my life. The rest is posthumous' (Smith College Plath papers, series 6, Hughes correspondence).

As the heir to his wife's estate, Hughes had the responsibility for publishing her work, a task that lasted for most of the rest of his life. Clearly a believer in her poetic genius, he had to integrate the startling poems, which she had been writing at more than one each day towards the end, into a second collection that she had already made in a working file. These later poems, which are now among her most famous works, were combined by Hughes with a selection from her file to make Plath's second collection *Ariel*, which was posthumously published in 1965. Hughes was subsequently accused by Plath's readers of distorting her plans for *Ariel* and with being slow to produce the *Collected Poems*, a collection of her stories, her letters and her journals. But it is perhaps understandable that coming to terms with her suicide, bringing up their children and developing his own relationships, while continuing his own writing, had both complicated his ability to edit her work and made her life and work a perpetual presence in his own life, as *Birthday Letters* showed. Nevertheless, in his lifetime Hughes succeeded in publishing Plath's complete works.

The Assia period (1963–69)

Assia Gutmann's father was of Russian Jewish origin, her mother was German and she was born in Germany on 15 May 1927 just before her family moved to Palestine for the duration of the Second World War. When it ended they all moved to Canada. The poet David Wevill was Assia's third husband, whom she first met on a ship from Canada to England when she was married to her second husband. She subsequently joined Wevill in Burma where he was teaching for two years and they married when he left for England. The Wevills applied to take over the Hughes's flat in Chalcot Square and the couples met a few times to discuss this in London. When she met Ted Hughes Assia was working in a well-paid job at an advertising company in London, as was her husband for a different company.

Assia has been described as 'predatory' and 'rapacious' by Al Alvarez (1999: 209) and glamorous, poised, sophisticated and seductive by others (Feinstein 2001: 136–37). In a collection of poems addressed to Assia, *Capriccio* (1990), published in an edition limited to fifty copies eight years before he died, Hughes opened one poem with the words, 'You thought of him as one for your collection'. Assia's boss remembers her discussing the seduction of Hughes before the weekend visit to Court Green, following which Assia sent him a blade of grass in an empty envelope, the kind of enigmatic gesture in which she specialised. In a letter to Plath's mother, written soon after Plath died, Hughes referred to his 'madness', as he did to two other friends (*Letters* 215). It seems that even as Hughes was involved in his relationship with Assia, he was well aware that he was mesmerised by her charismatic beauty and exotic charm. Many of the poems in *Capriccio* mythologise Assia's culturally rich European background with a mixture of icons and narratives from Hebrew, Russian and Celtic folktales that cast Assia as more witch than earth mother, that is, more Lilith than Inanna. The equivocal nature of their relationship for the next six years reflects Assia's strange attraction as he characterised it in *Capriccio* late in his life.

The house in which Plath had killed herself was still under lease and was the children's home, so it was here that Hughes now lived with the support of his aunt Hilda who moved down from Yorkshire for the first few months. Before moving back north Hilda hired a nanny to look after the children as Assia was still actually based at the flat of her ever-tolerant husband, moving between the two homes. In September 1963, when Hughes decided to move back to Court Green, Assia did not accompany him. Hughes's sister Olwyn gave up her job in Paris to look after the children in Devon while Hughes earned a living largely from writing book reviews, complaining in a letter to his brother in June 1964 that he could not settle to any serious work of his own. He wrote:

> I've had a great taste of womankind in the last two years – evidently I'm a sucker of some sort ... All I've ever been interested in is simplifying my existence so I could write and all I've ever done is so involve myself with other people that now I can't move without horrible consequences of all kinds, on all sides.
>
> (19. 6. 1963, MSS 854, Box 1, FF12)

But he admitted that he would be looking after the children full-time 'the minute I cease to be a sucker'. In March 1965 Assia gave birth to Hughes's daughter Shura in London, where Hughes had been visiting her regularly from Devon. When, in September, Olwyn moved out of Court Green after two years there, Assia moved in. Hughes invited his parents to move to Court Green with a view to house-sitting while he, Assia and the three children moved to Ireland for an unspecified period, thinking that the milder Devon climate would be good for his mother, who was suffering from severe asthma and arthritis.

From February 1966 what actually became a three month stay in Ireland with Assia and the children proved productive for Hughes's writing and by February 1967 he was completing the manuscript of *Wodwo* which would end a seven year gap since his second collection. Hughes's parents stayed on and having them living with him further inhibited Hughes's writing, together with the inevitable strains in relationships in the house arising partly from his father's dislike of Assia. While Assia and his father were at loggerheads, his mother's health was failing. Nevertheless, during this unsettled period Hughes was able to make two important contributions to opening up English poetry to international influences which were also to be significant in his own work. In 1965 with his old university friend Daniel Weissbort he founded the journal *Modern Poetry in Translation* which first introduced to English readers the European poets whose work Hughes went on to champion and absorb: Miroslav Holub from Czechoslovakia, Jámos Pilinsky from Hungary, Vasco Popa from Yugoslavia, Zbigniew Herbert from Poland and Yehudah Amichai from Israel. This journal coincided with Al Alvarez's influential series *Penguin Modern European Poets*. In 1967 Hughes was a co-director of the first International Poetry Festival at the Albert Hall, writing many of the programme notes himself and demonstrating his wide knowledge and appreciation of his internationally important contemporaries. Following the insularity of English poetry in the 1950s established by the Movement poets and characterised by Larkin's sneers at 'abroad', this was not just a huge reversal of attitudes, but a surprisingly popular one. Holub, for example, claimed that he became more widely read in Britain than at home. Poetry festivals and regular poetry reading venues sprang up throughout the country. Hughes had helped unlock access to forces that were to change the range of resources available to English poetry, not least in his own work. In the 1960s Hughes also persuaded his friend David Ross to begin what may have been the first environmentally conscious magazine, *Your Environment* (Huws 2007).

It was Hughes who decided that the tension between his parents and Assia should be resolved by her moving back to London where he would visit her frequently. So in 1968 Assia moved to Clapham Common and regained a job at the advertising company where she had worked previously. Hughes worked with her during his London visits on her translations for a book of poems by the Israeli poet Yehuda Amichai that came out that year. In 1968 Hughes began seeing the woman who would become his second wife, Carol Orchard, the daughter of a local man, Jack Orchard.

What is clear from the *Letters* (2007) is the generosity with which Hughes, from the earliest years, had himself sent off the manuscripts of young poets among his friends. For two years during this period Hughes served on the Arts Council's Literature Panel, urging the support of younger poets. Olwyn became his literary agent, beginning a long period of not only increasing his income from writing, but defending his interests and his privacy. Hughes started a collaboration with the theatre director Peter Brook, writing a distinctively original version of *Oedipus* (1969) and working on a film of *King Lear* with Brook. Hughes was also writing the series of radio talks for schools published in the book *Poetry in the Making* (1967) to be followed by the publication of his hugely influential children's story *The Iron Man* (1968). Following the publication of Plath's *Ariel* in 1965, her work and life-story accumulated interest into what was to become a cult status. Hughes gained unexpected royalties from the sales of *Ariel* which he invested for the future of Plath's children. Assia felt that she was increasingly regarded as the cause of Plath's death and she was haunted by the high-profile celebrity status of Plath in literary London. She tried for a while to do without Hughes, but this only resulted in her wanting his phone calls all the more. Friends who met them together in London found them to be deeply unhappy with each other.

In August 1968 Hughes took Assia and Shura with him on a reading tour through Germany and their relationship was uneasy. Nevertheless, following Assia's divorce, they decided to try to find a home of their own in which to live together. In March 1969 they travelled to Yorkshire and Northumberland to look for a possible home that was outside the spheres in which they had previously moved. They also house-hunted near Manchester where Hughes was booked to record a reading for BBC schools television. From there Assia took the train back to London while Hughes returned to Court Green. Assia's biographers report that she had liked all the houses they had seen and Hughes had found fault with all of them (Koren and Negev 2006: 199). But Hughes told his sister Olwyn that 'the houses, that they had seen in the rain, were all dismal. Assia was very depressed by the house hunt' (letter to T.G., 26. 1. 2008). Upon his return to Devon Hughes received a phone call from Assia which ended in her feeling that she lacked reassurance in their relationship. She was being treated by her doctor for serious depression and she relapsed into the isolated misery of her state prior to the trip with Hughes to Germany. She pulled a mattress up to the gas stove, gave Shura and herself sleeping pills and switched on the gas.

For two years Assia had been threatening to close friends that she would kill herself, but they took it as part of her rhetoric when depressed. Upon her death, her sister immediately returned to Hughes several manuscripts of Plath's that Assia had stolen as an investment for Shura's future. In a letter to her sister Hughes referred to Assia as his 'true wife'. For the last two years, in the writing hut that his father had built for him in the garden at Court Green, Hughes had been working on the *Crow* poems. What was now the last of those poems had been written on the train back from Manchester. When the book was published in 1970 its dedication read: 'In Memory of Assia and Shura'.

The deaths of Assia and Shura in March 1969 were followed in May by the death of Hughes's mother Edith in Yorkshire. Hughes returned to Yorkshire to live at Lumb Bank, Heptonstall, just below his parents' house, which he had bought on the day of his mother's funeral. Throughout this period Hughes had clearly used the writing of stories and poems for children as a therapeutic process in accordance with his belief in the healing power of imaginative literature for the maker and the reader. Beginning with *Meet My Folks!* in 1961 and ending with *The Iron Man* in 1968, this was a period in which Hughes published six books for children and only *Wodwo* (1967) for adults. What links his third major collection of poems for adults and the work for children is the development of the mythic voice which was to be the key to Hughes's next phase of work. This was to emerge from the stability of Hughes's second marriage.

From marriage to the Laureateship (1970–84)

Hughes returned to Devon in 1970 and married Carol Orchard, a nurse and the daughter of Jack Orchard who had lost his farm some years before. Carol immediately began the refurbishment of Court Green, which was to be Hughes's home for the rest of his life. The reception of *Crow* (1970) established Hughes as a major European poet in the tradition of those whose work he had been promoting to a traditionally parochial English audience through *Modern Poetry in Translation*. Hughes was invited to read in Israel and to work with Peter Brook on a play for the Shiraz-Persepolis Festival in Iran that resulted in Hughes inventing a language for the *Orghast* project in 1971. In 1976 Hughes visited Australia to read at the Adelaide Literary Festival, taking with him his father to stay with his older brother Gerald who had emigrated there in 1948.

After marriage to Carol, Hughes entered a period of major and remarkably varied productivity resulting, towards the end of the 1970s, in the publication, within two years of each other, of four significant and very different collections. The *Crow* project, which had been curtailed by Assia's death, was redeveloped into a new mythic narrative sequence that resulted in *Cave Birds* (1978). A long neglected idea for a film script was turned into the remarkable poetic narrative with an epilogue of enigmatic lyrics titled *Gaudete* (1977). A project that had been proposed to the photographer Fay Godwin in 1970 emerged as the collaborative book about the Calder Valley's landscape and culture, *Remains of Elmet* (1979). In 1973 Hughes had bought a farm of 95 acres called Moortown, five miles north of Court Green. It was run by Carol's father Jack with the help of Hughes and his wife. In 1979 Hughes published the diary poems of his work there in the collection titled *Moortown*, which also included mythic sequences published a little earlier by his and his sister Olwyn's co-owned Rainbow Press in limited editions, *Prometheus on his Crag* and *Adam and the Sacred Nine*, together with other poems. The farm was not sold until 1997, although Hughes's involvement in the farming there stopped with the death of Jack Orchard in 1976 that is recorded in some of the most moving poems in *Moortown*.

What should not be forgotten is the significance of a small body of poetry for children that emerged after a silent decade following *The Iron Man*. *Season Songs* (1976) celebrated the cycles of growth and decay in witty and formal poems that will continue to serve an important ecological function in education. This was followed by *Moon Bells* (1978) that was influential in schools at the time, and then by the major collection for children *Under the North Star* (1981). *What is the Truth?* (1984) is an entertaining and challenging series of narrative-linked poems that develops the imaginative enquiry of the prose stories from twenty years earlier that were collected in *How the Whale Became* (1963). 'The truth' was that God's Son realised that the earth, where all living things are sacred, is the best place to be. In 1972 Hughes wrote a long letter to *The Times Literary Supplement* proposing a plan for schoolchildren to plant trees in cooperation with local farmers. The language and vision is typical of the way Hughes thought of his potential educative influence in Britain: 'The method goes beyond biology and involves the children in the future of their trees – and automatically in the future of the whole living environment in a way that connects their creative responsibility and their deepest instincts' (*Times Literary Supplement* 17. 11. 1972).

In the 1970s Hughes continued editing the works of Sylvia Plath (his 1965 edition of *Ariel* had appeared three years after her death), culminating in the *Collected Poems* in 1981. He recognised Plath's talent for prose, as he indicated in his introduction to the collection *Johnny Panic and the Bible of Dreams* (1977). Hughes had allowed *The Bell Jar* to be published in America where it had become a bestseller and, after some doubts about the idea, he gave permission to Plath's mother, Aurelia Plath, to publish her daughter's letters to her as *Letters Home* (1975). Perhaps as a result of reading Plath's journals during this editing work Hughes began to quietly publish the first of the poems that would be included in *Birthday Letters*, 'You Hated Spain' (1979) and 'The Earthenware Head' (1980). But the popularity of Plath's work in America resulted in a backlash against Hughes as Plath became an iconic figure for the emerging feminist movement and Hughes was regarded simply as 'the murderer' of Plath, as the feminist poet Robin Morgan put it in one published poem. Such reductive and destructive prejudices stuck, especially among teachers, and sadly persist to this day. Hughes was barracked by feminists at readings in Australia and America. The name 'Hughes' on Plath's gravestone in Heptonstall cemetery began to be regularly chipped off whenever Hughes had it replaced. Even after these extreme reactions had subsided, a residual prejudice denied Hughes, during his lifetime, a place on the university or school curriculum in America, in stark contrast to the status and income derived from popularity in the American academy enjoyed by his friend Seamus Heaney.

Under the surface of a stable decade of poetic productivity and success, the 1970s were an emotionally turbulent period for Hughes. The decade had begun with Hughes falling out with his friend and supporter Al Alvarez who had published in the *Observer* newspaper the first extract from his memoir of Sylvia Plath's last years and weeks during which she had used Alvarez as a sounding-board for her final poems. Always protective of what privacy he could retrieve, Hughes objected in a letter to Alvarez that the effect of this publication on the children would be damaging. Alvarez had thought that he had been discreet in his piece but did not realise that Hughes had not explained to the children that their mother had committed suicide. In 1971 Hughes had reluctantly decided to send them away to school and he now brought them home for a week to explain this fact to them. Alvarez asked the newspaper to withdraw the planned second instalment of the memoir, but did publish what he had intended in his book about suicide *The Savage God* (1971). At Robert Lowell's memorial service in London in 1977 Hughes and Alvarez each read poems, shook hands and buried the hatchet, although they never met again.

Between 1973 and 1974 Hughes suffered from a general depression. He was anxious about the financial consequences of handling the copyright to the Plath estate. He came to realise that Gerald was never going to return from Australia and was not going to be tempted into running the farm at Moortown – nor the mink farming scheme, nor the antique dealing that Hughes had earlier proposed to his brother. Following his mother's death Hughes took responsibility for his father, who came to live close to him in North Tawton, but William gradually declined over the years until his death in Devon in February 1981. Frieda's early marriage and rapid divorce was obviously also a cause of concern. Hughes was always reticent about public appearances and the attacks of the feminists led him to give very few readings during this period. Ironically, the freedoms adopted by independent women in the 1970s also had consequences for men such as Hughes who were targeted by the more extreme feminists.

It should also be noted that during this period Hughes made a significant contribution to support new writing. For years Hughes had judged the WH Smith writing competition for children. In 1968 John Moat and John Fairfax established the Arvon Foundation in Devon to run week-long courses in writing during which a tutor and a small number of students live communally together, sharing the cooking, writing workshops and group readings of work-in-progress. They had tried out their idea on an initially sceptical Ted Hughes two years before. But when he visited the first experimental course as reader, Hughes was convinced not only that the apprenticeship format worked, but that the idea might offer support for anyone who wanted to write outside the formal education system. In 1970 Moat's wife, Antoinette, bought Totleigh Barton, a remote Devon farmhouse, and rented it to Arvon as a permanent base for courses. In 1975 Hughes leased Lumb Bank to the Arvon Foundation as a northern centre. In response to an Arvon debt crisis Hughes 'faced the problem by dreaming up and then engineering the first Arvon Foundation International Poetry Competition in 1980', attracting high profile sponsors and judges, big prize money and a huge number of entries to support the finances of the Arvon Foundation (Moat 2005: 26). The first winner was Andrew Motion, who eventually succeeded Hughes as Poet Laureate. But the contribution of Hughes as organiser and judge drained his energy: 'Ted said he wrote nothing for at least the next six months' (ibid.).

From the beginning John Moat recalls that:

> there were few Arvon matters he'd not be involved with: little com-
> mittees, ad hoc brainstorming sessions (he seemed to relish especially
> each new crisis), high and low level delegations. Endless times he and
> Carol, his wife, would open their house to meetings, or ask people in
> any way involved to meals ... Ted himself never ran a course, but was
> the visiting reader on many. Often he would simply drop by, or attend
> the readings of others. No ostentation, no suggestion he'd gone out of
> his way. But that energy of his, again it was something else – his pre-
> sence would have a magical effect, a contagion of imaginative excite-
> ment. Relate this to the entire field of his generosity and one can see
> how his association came to inform the operation.
>
> (Moat 2005: 26–27)

In Britain Hughes was recognised as a major post-war poet, who despite his
unusual and often challenging books, was adopted by the establishment at all
levels. He was awarded the Queen's Gold Medal in 1974 and the OBE in 1977.
Members of the royal family seemed to have a genuine interest in his poetry and
in the interests of his poetry. Later, 'he and the Queen Mother', in the words of
his sister Olwyn, 'became great pals with their shared love of fishing and Scotland' (letter to T.G., 26. 1. 2008). More than just a shared love of salmon and
trout fishing, the royal family may have had a sense that Hughes cared about
the British countryside in a way that combined both an ecological concern
about its management and a conservative notion of a nation underpinning it.
This most strongly expressed itself in Hughes's work in his writing about
rivers.

Memories of fishing in the canal behind his first home in Mytholmroyd provided some of the warmest poems in *Remains of Elmet* (1979) and then in
Devon Hughes came to know the owners of the fishing rights to local stretches
of salmon and trout rivers. Fishing trips to Ireland and to Scotland had been
taken whenever an occasion offered the opportunity. His son Nicholas shared
his enthusiasm to such an extent that he had decided to study Zoology at
Oxford and then to research aspects of fish biology. In 1979 father and son took
a fishing trip to Iceland and the following year to Alaska. By 1982 Nicholas had
organised a trip to Kenya to search for rare fish at the source of the Nile, which
Hughes joined for a short fishing trip. The next year Hughes produced a book,
in collaboration with the fishing photographer, Peter Keen, that had a single
focus, richly explored, with an international range of reference. *River* (1983)
seemed to many critics to be the celebration of a decade of stabilised and
adventurous work, hailing it as a profound and joyous book by a poet at the
height of his powers.

We now know that in the 1980s Hughes began to involve himself in a
growing local concern for the water quality of the rivers in Devon. The archival
evidence indicates the scientific background and environmental activism that lies
not only behind *River*, but behind a growing environmental concern in his
work, such as the poem 'If' which he later included in the *River* poems of *Three
Books* (1993). In 1983 Hughes contributed to the book *West Country Fly*

Fishing (Bark 1983) a chapter that began by celebrating the discipline and connectedness of fishing West Country rivers and then move towards an account of
the dramatic decline of the trout and salmon fishery in these rivers. An indication that the sub-text of this essay was really water quality is revealed in an
unpublished letter to his friend Keith Sagar:

> Did you see my piece in *West Country Fly Fishing*? ... The essay is an
> attempt to glorify the rivers while suppressing the knowledge that they
> are going down the drain. Even twenty years ago they produced 1/3
> of all salmon in the West Country. Last year only 43 salmon were
> caught on the Torridge. (It used to be a thousand to 1500.) It's become
> a farm sewer.
>
> (14. 12. 1983, BL ADD 78757, f. 139)

So in 1983 Hughes was instrumental in forming the Torridge Action Group to
call for a public inquiry about the implications for the estuary and rivers that
would follow from the particular form of new sewage works proposed for
Bideford. In this it was successful and Hughes was asked to represent the
Action Group by making a representation to the inquiry in September 1985.
Hughes summarised the concerns of the Torridge Action Group in a letter to
Keith Sagar in 1984:

> I've been involved in a local battle, of sorts, over Bideford Sewage system.
> The Water Authority, mightily leaned on by local building interests,
> are putting in a type of sewage system that merely screens the sewage
> takes out 20% 'solids' – mostly cardboard, plastic etc ... 1600 new
> houses go in immediately.
>
> (9. 3. 1984, BL ADD 78757, f. 143)

Hughes produced a brilliant statement at the inquiry that indicates as much a
concern for the health of local people and tourists from the current pollution of the
estuary as it does for the salmon population in the rivers, drawing on a range of
scientific evidence from both human and fish research into the consequences of
raw sewage being discharged into the Torridge estuary at Bideford.

The success of the Torridge Action Group in fighting this environmental
issue was to lead eventually to the formation of a national organisation. Those
who worked alongside him on these issues testify to the influence of his generous personality in leading them towards their goals (Douglas 2007). It was a
spirit Hughes would bring to the role of Poet Laureate.

The Laureate years (1984–98)

After his death many people remembered the force of personality of Ted Hughes
in his mature years. Craig Raine, for example, wrote:

> Ted had more charisma than anyone I've ever met, and a lot of that
> charisma came from the quiet intensity he projected outwards. He

wasn't self-absorbed, he was attentive. In this way, the poems were extensions of his natural personality.

(*Times Literary Supplement* 24. 11. 2006, p. 11)

Raine quotes Ben Sonneberg: 'I wrote in my notebook that meeting him was like Hazlitt meeting Coleridge for the first time: bowled over by his warmth and energy.'

Those who accept the role of Poet Laureate grasp a poisoned chalice for their reputation and their art. Expected to fail in the absurd task of producing major poetry for royal celebrations, the Poet Laureate is a high profile 'sitting target' for both the literary critics and the popular press. For such a guardedly private poet as Ted Hughes, whose work was far from personal or occasional, it was perhaps surprising that he would accept the invitation. But this would be to forget his training in anthropology, his belief in the healing power of poetry, his concern for the culture and the countryside of his country and his interest in the symbolic role of the monarchy. Seamus Heaney welcomed him in his new public role as the shaman of the tribe whose role had always been to put people 'in vital, imaginative contact with the geological, botanical, historical and legendary reality of England itself' (Scigaj 1992: 46). When the appointment was announced in December 1984, Al Alvarez wrote to congratulate him, suggesting that it was the first time since Tennyson that a major poet had held the post. There was, indeed, a public outpouring of congratulation, and a private one, too, in which many old friends, his former teachers, school friends and critics wrote with warm applause.

The first challenge came quickly with the christening of Prince Harry and for it Hughes produced what may have been his best Laureate poem, 'Rain-Charm for the Duchy' which had actually originally been intended for the *River* collection, as Hughes admitted in a letter to Keith Sagar (21. 1. 1985, BL ADD 78757, f. 150). The royal parents were delighted and Hughes was generally judged to have cleverly met the challenge with exactly the shamanic power expected of him. With this poem, Heaney said, Hughes had 'reaffirmed an ancient tradition and re-established, without sanctimoniousness, a sacerdotal function for the poet of the realm' (Scigaj 1992: 46). The Hughes scholar Neil Roberts expresses the ambivalence of sympathetic critics at the time when he points out that while Hughes had taken a role in a household that headed the Church of England, he:

> is not merely a non-believer but is positively committed to a rival religion which, in his opinion, Christianity has done its best to stamp out but which [Hughes believes] will triumph either with our co-operation or at our expense. This is, of course, Neumann's 'Great Mother' ... If he is able to sustain the poise and integrity of this first poem he might turn the Laureateship into an organ for creatively exploring the role of religion, ritual and mythology in our society.
>
> (Roberts 1985: 5)

For the next decade newspapers published Hughes's poems for royal birthdays, births and christenings, if with more than a little bemusement at their obscure symbolic structure. By 1992 Hughes was able to publish a collection of poems for royal occasions under the title of the first poem in the series.

Immediately following the Laureateship there continued a flourishing of works for children with the clear-eyed observations of *Flowers and Insects* (1986) and the first of a series of collections of stories in *Tales of the Early World* (1988). But the major book for children in this late focus on works for the young was the environmental sequel to Hughes's first hugely successful novel of a quarter of a century earlier, *The Iron Woman* (1993). This was just one example of Hughes's late attempts to gain recognition for the increasingly urgent environmental crisis through his art and role as Poet Laureate. In the Emory archive is a letter to his editor at Faber in which Hughes wrote, 'We could send John Major a gold-backed copy. Present all the chieftains with one, maybe … And all the cabinet' (26. 1. 1993, MSS 644, Box 54, FF1). In the British Library archive is a letter to Keith Sagar that reveals financial support for environmental campaigns as a result of the Laureateship: 'My Beatrice piece … I auctioned to the four main dailies. *Guardian* offered £750 … *Telegraph* offered £5000 – which was split between Greenpeace and Friends of the Earth' (2. 2. 1989, BL ADD 78757, f. 199).

Unknown to the wider public Hughes continued his political work to improve the rivers of England. He was pleased that his first Laureate poem had already had some localised effect: 'Surprising what effect the Poet Laureate label has', Hughes wrote to Keith Sagar. 'The line [in 'Rain-Charm for the Duchy'] about the pollution (quite mild and domestic) of the Okement caused great agitation in Okehampton (responsible for the refuse) – might even affect the Council's laissez faire. These are the perks' (21. 1. 1985, BL ADD 78757, f. 150). Ten years after the Bideford estuary inquiry, following Hughes's realisation that a wider remit was needed, a press release dated 2 June 1995 for the formation of the Westcountry Rivers Trust states its aims more generally as a 'concern about pressures on natural water resource' in the West of England. It intended to meet its aims through a broad range of activities, including education – 'the trust has already acquired an area of suitable river, allowing free access and fishing to children.' Ted Hughes was a founding trustee of the Westcountry Rivers Trust, the first of thirty Rivers Trusts that now form the large organisation that is the national watchdog for water quality in all the nation's rivers, the Association of Rivers Trusts. But the extent of Hughes's local environmental interventions is unrecognised, from his attempt to educate local farmers about silage pollution in the *Western Morning News* in 1984 (MSS 644, Box 168, FF7), to his letter to the Exeter *Express and Echo* in 1995 about saving the city's Stoke Woods from developers: 'England is losing old woodland faster than the notoriously plundered Amazonian rainforest' (MSS 644, Box 54, FF3).

At a dinner at Buckingham Palace the Duke of Edinburgh 'goaded a number of his guests to think up ways of getting environmental awareness – awareness of the issues – urgency of the issues – past the barrier that everybody now puts up against the incessant flood of chat about it' (*Letters* 576). Hughes came up with an idea that challenged the creativity of young people. Writing about 'the follies of the Sixties' in a letter to Keith Sagar, Hughes had added:

The Sixties also produced the whole idea of our ecological responsibility, fully formed – maybe the crucial awakening. And the idea of ecological interconnectedness, which is the fundamental assumption now of children under 18, is only the material aspect of the interconnectedness of everything in spirit.

(30. 8. 1979, BL ADD 78757, f. 27)

In 1990 Hughes founded the Sacred Earth Drama Trust in order to nurture an environmental awareness through creativity in the next generation. The idea was to establish a Sacred Earth Drama competition, inviting 'international eco-themed plays for the young to perform' (letter from Carol Hughes to T.G., 10. 9. 2005).

In order to promote the competition Hughes gave an interview to Vic Allen in 1990. Allen wrote in the *Sunday Telegraph* (18. 11. 1990):

Hughes talks so plainly about the danger of neglecting the environment that it seems remiss that poetry has played so little part in alerting people to it. Perhaps poetry was not up to such a painful job? 'There are plenty of painful things in Heathcote Williams's books,' says Hughes. 'That's probably why they work. Quite a lot of poetry is just that, isn't it? The voice of hurt. That's part of its truth.'

So the voicing of hurt was seen by Hughes to be potentially the beginning of a healing process between culture and nature on an international scale, but through encouraging the creativity of young writers, the next generation of conservationists and environmental activists.

When Hughes came to publish the farming poems of *Moortown* as a separate volume in *Moortown Diary* in 1989, he included notes at the end in which he made an attack on British agribusiness and its pollution of the national environment, subsidised by the EEC's Common Agricultural Policy and the multinational chemical industry. In 1990 Hughes wrote a political intervention for the *Guardian* and in 1992 a poem for *The Times*, both of which attempted to draw the attention of politicians and the public to the environmental problems that they were ignoring at their peril. His first adult collection following the Laureateship, and his first collection of individual poems since *Wodwo*, was *Wolfwatching* (1989). It was Hughes's most explicit collection of poems to address environmental issues to date and the last collection before the more personal backward-looking collections of his last years.

After *Wolfwatching* Hughes was prolific in the production of three kinds of work: major prose enquiries into some of the most significant literary enigmas of all time, translations of plays and poetry from the classical tradition that were pertinent to his situation and our own, and poetry that released his haunted years of silence about his relationships with Sylvia and with Assia. He came to regret the time demanded by the prose works, to delight in the relevance of the classical works and to wish that he had laid the old ghosts of relationships by publishing these collections earlier. In short, after *Wolfwatching*, the prose works and the reflective poetry seemed to choose him, while he chose the most significant of the translations.

But the responsibility for the Plath legacy continued to be problematic. After refusing many requests for the film rights to *The Bell Jar*, Hughes had allowed a film of the book to be made by a small film company. In order to heighten dramatic tension, the character based upon Jane Anderson, a school and university friend of Plath's, had been given a lesbian attraction for Plath, together with the suggestion of a suicide pact, which were not in Plath's novel. In spring 1982, Anderson, now a psychiatrist at Harvard, sued fourteen people connected to the film, including Hughes, who had simply sold the film rights. Hughes had to defend the case in America, which occupied him fully for almost a year, during which he was facing bankruptcy if he lost, until an out of court settlement dropped him from the case in 1987. The case had hung over him for five long years.

During this period Ann Stevenson began work as the 'authorised' biographer of Sylvia Plath. An American poet who had long lived in England, Stevenson had grown up with the same cultural tensions as Plath and had made the same transatlantic transition. She had previously written, not a literary biography as some had thought, but a critical study of Elizabeth Bishop. Hughes agreed to offer no more help than checking the facts, while Olwyn undertook the detailed support for the biographer's access to people and archives. This latter relationship became increasingly problematic as it became clear that Stevenson was coming to the bizarre view that Plath did not suffer from a mental illness. When Ann Stevenson eventually published *Bitter Fame* in 1989 with a note indicating that it was virtually a work of joint authorship with Olwyn Hughes, a controversy concerning the Hughes family's influence on the book was certain to follow, as, indeed, it did. If Hughes had been hesitating about publishing his version of his relationship with Plath in the poems that he had already begun to publish, the debacle of *Bitter Fame* must have been an influence on the continued writing and the need for the publication of *Birthday Letters*.

First Hughes cleared himself of the freight he was carrying from his relationship with Assia by publishing, in the most restricted way possible, poems looking back on that relationship. The production in 1990 of fifty copies of a beautifully crafted book with engravings by Leonard Baskin, to be sold at $4000 each, suggests that *Capriccio* was only intended for the keenest and richest collectors and libraries. It was as if Hughes were testing the water for *Birthday Letters* in the most tentative, and lucrative, way. A book of 110 copies at the same price, *Howls and Whispers* (1998), was issued with poems not included in *Birthday Letters* immediately after that publication. By then it was clear that Hughes was both putting poems on the record and securing finances for his family in choosing to release work in these expensive editions in his final years.

In one of the ironies of Hughes's life and art, that is perhaps not coincidental, at the time he was reflecting upon his relationships with two significant women from his past he was working on *Shakespeare and the Goddess of Complete Being* (1992). This huge prose project took five years to complete, although its framework had been established in 1971 when Hughes wrote an introduction to a selection of Shakespeare's verse. Then, having unlocked the key to the whole of Shakespeare's work, he turned to the enigmas in the three major works of Coleridge. When William Scammell collected the prose work of Hughes in the volume *Winter Pollen* (1994) it became clear that Hughes had been analysing in the works of others the themes that had preoccupied his own poetry. This accounts for the idiosyncratic nature of the prose work to which some critics responded negatively, especially in relation to the Shakespeare book. In the prose work Hughes was taking a Jungian anthropological approach to distinguish the myths that were healing from those that were not, together with the process by which the negative might be turned into positive effect. The real purpose of this for Hughes was to guide his poetry, which was his paramount form. Hence came his ultimate feeling that he had damaged his muse in giving so much time to prose work. Worse, he believed that work on the Shakespeare book had actually affected his immune system (*Letters* 719).

Hughes cannot have expected the impact he made with his translation of Ovid's *Metamorphosis* as *Tales from Ovid* (1997). It won the Whitbread Book of the Year Award in the year of his death. But Hughes had also been working on the translation of five plays during his final years, which, because they were put on at different theatres, were not recognised as the significant body of work they obviously represent when taken together. The commissioned plays by Wedekind from Germany (*Spring Awakening*, 1995), Lorca from Spain (*Blood Wedding*, 1996), Racine from France (*Phèdre*, 1998), the Greek classic *The Oresteia* of Aeschylus, (produced in 1999) and the play he chose himself, *Alcestis* by Euripides (produced in 1999), represent a selection from European dramatic literature that deal with a common theme – the passionate tensions in a man's decisions about his relationships with women. There is an obvious connection between this group of translated plays – especially the last two – and Hughes's final engagement with the ghost of Sylvia Plath.

The tragedy of *Birthday Letters* is that Hughes knew that it emerged too late for him to gain the benefit of this release for any further work. Just as he knew that this book gave him huge relief, he also knew that the poems should have been published decades earlier. Written over the previous twenty-five years, they had been ready for publication four years before they were delivered to Faber. As the book topped the bestseller list – unknown for a book of poetry – and won a succession of prizes, the WH Smith Award and the Forward Prize for Poetry among them, Hughes was suffering his final illness. He said to some people that the cancer of the colon that killed him had begun in 1990, although it was not diagnosed until April 1997. For years he had been pressing upon friends various forms of alternative medicine when illness had struck them. But, as his sister Olwyn puts it, 'He was pretty stoical about his health and probably put down any feeling of failing health as stress' (letter to T.G., 26. 1. 2008). Such was the strength of his intense privacy about illness that he declined to ask advice of his friend and leading American collector of his work, Fred Rue Jacobs, who had been successfully treated for this cancer for over a decade. Hughes's visit to Buckingham Place to receive the Queen's Order of Merit was his last public appearance, made only twelve days before he died on 28 October 1998 with his family at his bedside. His funeral took place in the church beside his home in North Tawton and in May 1999 a memorial service took place at Westminster Abbey attended by the Prince of Wales and the Queen Mother and his many friends and admirers from both sides of the Atlantic. The last interview he had given was to the US magazine *Wild Steelhead and Salmon* (5(2), Winter 1999).

In the last weeks of his life Hughes wrote many letters to friends and to critics with whom he had disagreed in the past. During the later years of his life his letters to those who addressed questions to him were so fulsome as to obviously constitute a record for the future, many of them now published in the *Letters* (2007). But they also came from a generosity of spirit that typified all his correspondence. In 1997 Hughes sold the bulk of his archive to the Robert W. Woodruff Library of Emory University in Atlanta, Georgia, which continues to acquire Hughes material, making it the most important centre for future studies of the work of Ted Hughes. In 2001 the British Library acquired the 145 letters Hughes wrote to Keith Sagar, which, together with the papers of Al Alvarez and Leonard Baskin, form a substantial and growing Hughes archive in the United Kingdom. Because the Sagar archive contains the letters of both correspondents, something of the seriousness and frankness of their dialogue can be witnessed, as in the following exchange:

> I have read you[r] piece on hunting [in the *Guardian*] with great interest ... You ask if it persuades me. Well, yes and no. You may be right that if hunting were banned, and if no effective protection could be enforced, the deer and foxes would suffer, perhaps literally, certainly numerically. I am all for pragmatic approaches to such issues. But your argument takes a great deal for granted and leaves a great deal (including the whole moral and spiritual dimension which characterizes your poems about animals) out of account. Even within the narrow terms of your argument I have some reservations.
> (from Sagar to T.H., 15. 7. 1997, BL ADD 78760, f. 190)

In a long, now published, reply Hughes wrote,

> I've known for some years what a hunted deer goes through physically. And a hunted fox. And a fish being caught for that matter.
>   For years I've kept having an idea that I daren't quite formulate: why aren't wild animals simply given the legal status of 'fellow citizens'.
> (*Letters* 691)

The publication of the *Collected Poems* in 2003 and the *Selected Translations* in 2006 was followed by the major posthumous work, the *Letters of Ted Hughes* in 2007. By 2008 the works of Ted Hughes were available in translation in the following countries: Albania, Belgium, France, Italy, Germany, Korea, Catalonia, Wales, Spain, Mexico, Poland, Greece, Brazil, Norway, Finland, Czech Republic, Slovenia, Sweden, the Netherlands.

At Hughes's funeral his friend Seamus Heaney said, 'No death outside my family has left me more bereft.' Nearly ten years later Heaney was still feeling a huge absence, as he said in an interview:

> Ted Hughes was like a gable, a psychic gable that you could put your back to. He had a brotherly status in that way. He was important to me to begin with, to start the writing, and then that he commended the work was very important, and then I got to know him and felt – as so many people did – that there was an element of care for you.
> (McCartney 2007)

In 2005, John Moat, who in 1966 had tried out on Hughes the idea for what were to become the Arvon Foundation courses, reflected upon the way a constant curiosity and unstinting generosity combined to give the Arvon Foundation, and the nation, a unique champion for the culture's imaginative writing:

> As his own identity evolved, became 'ennobled' by the Laureateship, this identification [of Hughes with Arvon] remarked in high places and remote fishing lodges, did Arvon no harm at all. But to Ted life was all of a piece, a continuum of constantly awakening curiosity to be taken moment by moment. Each instance that took his interest became the object of an intense engagement. For Arvon this meant, as if by appointment, engagement with what some of us imagine was one of the overseeing mage intelligences and protectors of this nation's Writ.
>
> (Moat 2005: 27)

The joys and tragedies, the loves and loss in the life of Ted Hughes could be viewed as the passions of a poet whose personal inclination was towards the private, but whose muse and reputation drew him into a public role. The work, in turn, offers a different perspective on the life so that its personal tensions might be understood against larger dynamics in nature – the attraction to two charismatic but suicidal women, the concern for privacy yet also for the culture of English poetry and new writing by children and adults, the tension between the life of the individual and a deep commitment to family and his children. These tensions in the life actually represent the nature of what it is to be human. This is the equivalent of the struggle of the hawk in the rain, the October salmon and the ebbs and flows of the seasons. Indeed, whether sought or not, Hughes lived the marriage of heaven and hell and the flayed coming into full being of the protagonist of *Cave Birds*. All of the work suggests that he knew this about the complexities of his own life.

2

Works

The Hawk in the Rain **and** *Lupercal*

With his first volume Ted Hughes announced his major themes in a voice that, while being strikingly individual, also betrayed rather too conspicuously its influences. What was remarkable at the time was that neither themes nor voice were recognisable as the then fashionable mode of Movement poetry. Rather, this first volume seemed to deliberately challenge the urbane attitudes and tentative voices of Movement poets such as Robert Conquest, John Wain and Philip Larkin. *The Hawk in the Rain* (1957) evoked powerful forces in external nature and in human nature. It seemed to suggest not just that each could be understood by reference to the other, but that there was a kind of natural continuity between the raw energy of the hawk and the first passion of a lover, or between the spent energy of a caged lion and that of a now 'wrecked' famous poet, or between the self-delusive energy of the caged jaguar and that of the human 'egghead', or between the mysterious, distinctive vitality of a fox and that creative force which produces a poem with a life of its own.

If non-human and human natural forces were Hughes's major subject in this collection, it was his attitude towards them that divided his first readers. Was he celebrating life forces, or was he dangerously attracted to violence and destructive forces? Worse, was he sneering at timid women and uncritically admiring of courageous men? And was the intensity of the language actually controlled by the variety of verse forms? It is now clear that Hughes was writing a deliberately anti-pastoral poetry that attacked emotional and intellectual complacency about inner and outer nature in order to be able to seek more positive explorations of the inner life that humans might have among the creative and destructive forces of their home environment. West Yorkshire Methodism, South Yorkshire industrialism, Cambridge class and gender elitism, had each informed Hughes's awareness of the emotional repression and confident complacency of the English post-war reconstruction of the 1950s in which these poems were written. Drawing from his observations of nature, leading a full inner life in a society that had recently witnessed the capacity for both Hiroshima and Auschwitz was going to require more poetic courage and boldness than could be mustered by the Movement poets' diffident parochialism.

Destructive forces had to be confronted as they are in the poem 'Wind', even if they inevitably led to a humbling of the human presence in confronting these powerful forces. The poem 'The Horses' suggests that humans might need to learn something from the patient integration with their environment of frost-still horses at dawn to remind them, in their busy materialistic project, that they are part of a larger elemental world. In one of Hughes's most enduring poems, 'The Thought-Fox', the text that is apparently conjured up before the reader's eyes seems to suggest that poetry itself can draw its life from the kind of sensory alertness of a fox, if only it can allow such quality of attention to enter 'the dark hole of the head'.

At what ought to be the frontiers of human thought, Hughes suggests in 'Egg-Head', that vital imaginative space is filled with forms of knowledge that keep such forces at a comfortable distance while pretending to let them in. The image of the egg-shell head is taken literally in order to make this point in what might be regarded as a flawed manifesto poem for this first collection. The satirical tone of the poem is established by the assertion that the egg-head has 'dared to be struck dead / Peeping through his fingers at the world's ends'. This childish image of the scientist or philosopher is rendered bathetic by the next line: 'or at an ant's head'. The sense that the forces at work in a leaf, or at the ends of the earth, might, in fact, create threatening energies that we don't understand is created by the use of nouns as verbs in 'whaled, monstered sea-bottom' and 'eagled peaks'. The brain's protection 'resists receiving the flash / Of the sun, the bolt of the earth'. Its own constructions, that appear to be engaging with these elemental forces, are actually the self-deception that produces the arrogance of 'a staturing "I am"'. So the birth from this eggshell is the 'braggart-browed complacency' of the intellectual who can only 'trumpet his own ear dead' because he has not really been listening to the 'otherness' of the material world that he thinks he can 'spurn' like 'muck under / His foot-clutch'. Most of Hughes's subsequent poetry has been a search for an alternative way for humans to be at home with these elemental forces outside and within themselves.

But this is a flawed poem and its weakness is shared by many in the first collection. Its poetic influences are too conspicuous and too unassimilated. 'Egg-Head' has the alliteration and frequent hyphenation of words into a double-punched rhythm characteristic of the poetry of Gerard Manley Hopkins. Like Hopkins, Hughes's dense language is developed in complex sentences, but in the case of 'Egg-Head' the traditional rhyme scheme is outrun by the length of its sentences. That the last five stanzas are all one sentence does produce the breathless absurdity of the egg-head's self-absorption that stumbles towards the final dactyl of 'trumpet his own ear dead'. But the effect is overdone to the point where the poem becomes almost unreadable. Ironically, this is also an indication of what was to be one of the strengths of Hughes's early poetry. His poems often had an enquiring structure of extended thought that characteristically produced the long, much qualified, sentence. This is thinking poetry about powerful energies.

Elsewhere in the collection other transparent influences are equally distracting: Dylan Thomas's grammar in 'The Hawk in the Rain' ('the hawk / Effortlessly at height hangs his still eye'), D.H. Lawrence's free-verse narrative reflectiveness on observations in 'The Horses', the Metaphysical poets in 'Song', Wilfred

Owen in 'Griefs For Dead Soldiers', and throughout the volume a use of archaic expressions that derive from Shakespeare ('holiday ran prodigal' in 'Two Phases', 'I come to you enforcedly' in 'Billet-Doux'). But actually it was the distinctive Anglo-Saxon power of Hughes's language ('Till, with a sudden sharp hot stink of fox') that made an immediate impact on readers. This was usually qualified by the ambivalence (not always seen by early critics) of his attitude towards hawk, jaguar, fox and horses. The will of the hawk and the intensity of the jaguar were each presented as to some extent self-delusions as much as they were admired for their sheer vitality, surviving against the odds of weather and cage respectively. Some of the finest poems in the second collection were to focus on lives and processes in which a strength is actually at the same time a weakness.

Lupercal (1960), the second collection, might be said to have declared its theme in its opening line: 'All things being done and undone'. The second line appears to suggest that the poet is aware of his interest in his own ambivalence: 'As my hands adore or abandon'. Frequently the medium of the poet's enquiry in this collection is the underworld, or the realm of dreams. Lupercalia was the festival of the Roman wolf-god at which barren women, running through the streets, were believed to have their fertility restored by the whips of the priests. Thus, in this book's title, violence and creativity are brought together in the icon of the wolf, now, of course, a creature of the realm of dream and myth for an English poet. The last line of the collection, in the poem titled 'Lupercalia', might be a cry to the wolf-god for the function of the collection itself in a barren consumer society in the shadow of the Cold War: 'Touch this frozen one'.

While 'Russia and America circle each other' in the opening line of 'A Woman Unconscious', the only available images of wolves conjured in 'February' are all either stuffed, 'caged, storied, or pictured'. Only dreams, like this poem itself, can attempt to make 'wolf-masks, mouths clamped well onto the world' that are adequate to the barren times. So, the best poems in *Lupercal* might be characterised as the masks of 'Hawk Roosting', 'The Bull Moses', 'Pike', 'An Otter', 'Thrushes' and 'View of a Pig'. Each poem is so well 'clamped onto the world' that it is aware that strengths can also be weaknesses: that as model masks for humans, the instinctive life can be self-destructive ('Pike'), or self-deluding ('Hawk Roosting'), or just instinctively automatic and allowing no room for reflective moral choice ('Thrushes'). But in 'Thrushes' the commonly admired human modes of living are presented as equally thoughtless and ultimately repressive of instinctive emotional life. The result is the distorting, distracting, dangerous forms these energies take in the subconscious underworld where they either 'orgy and hosannah', or 'under what wilderness / Of black silent waters weep'.

The search for a mask/poem that might be able to provide an image capable of holding these natural tensions in balance leads Hughes to 'An Otter' that 'belongs / In double robbery and concealment– / From water that nourishes and drowns, and from land'. The otter 'keeps fat in the limpid integument / Reflections live on', that is, by finding a life in the continuity between the dualities of surface/underworld, land/water, robbery/concealment, nourishing/drowning. Yet, for all that mysterious achievement, the otter cannot outflank human predators.

A mask that is 'clamped well onto the world' has to finally show that the otter can also become no more than a human consumer item: 'this long pelt over the back of a chair'.

In the attempt to take a hard look at the material evidence of the world (a process celebrated in 'Wilfred Owen's Photographs') Hughes ran the risk of seeing only clamped jaws, as he does in 'Relic', rather than the vitality they sustain. Just as later he was to write in *River* 'Only birth matters' (see Works, **p. 59**), in 'Relic' he sees only that jaws eat and are eaten in the sea where 'Nothing touches but, clutching, devours'. His statement that 'None grow rich / In the sea' is to deny, for example, the rich life of salmon in the sea that Hughes was later to celebrate in *River*. Similarly, when Hughes attempted to celebrate the force for survival against the odds in the icon of 'Snowdrop', he characterised the plant as a brutal, metallic, single-minded kind of feminine force running counter to the hibernation of much around her. This is one of the dangers of an anti-pastoral poetry that can become programmatic, as in 'To Paint a Water Lily', where leaves that are both 'roofs' and paving stones to upper and lower worlds are barely allowed any aesthetic beauty because the presentation of both worlds is concerned to focus on their containing carnivorous 'horrors'.

It is perhaps characteristic of this temptation to distortion that when Hughes tries to present weaknesses as strengths the results are unconvincing. 'The Retired Colonel' will hardly do as a head to mount 'beside the head of the last English / Wolf' simply for his 'kept rage' and 'his habits like a last stand'. The tramp asleep in the ditch of the poem 'November' is surely deluding himself in simply relying on the 'strong trust' that 'slept in him' like the patience and pride of creatures on a gibbet in the rain that the writer appears to be admiring at the end of the poem. 'Dick Straightup' presents the opposite problem of an unqualified celebration of a deeply knowing character produced by an uncompromising landscape who ultimately 'goes lost in the heaved calm / Of the earth you have entered'.

One aspect of Hughes's anti-pastoral project in his first two collections is to find representations of a world that does not have superimposed upon it the human desire to find 'purposes'. The Humber estuary speaks in 'Mayday at Holderness' with a voice that accepts everything that comes to it from the hinterland of the North of England and says, 'Flowerlike, I loved nothing. / Dead and unborn are in God comfortable'. The estuary accepts both 'tributary graves' and 'birth-soils'. It sees 'couples at their pursuits in the lanes' in the landward direction, while beneath the North Sea 'smoulder the wars'. It is aware that '"Mother, Mother!" cries the pierced helmet', just as it is aware that the decomposition of leaves is 'the furnace door whirling with larvae'. This is not just the simplistic awareness that from death comes regeneration, but the more complex idea that life itself is being 'done' and 'undone' at the same time. 'Crow Hill', unlike 'Relic', catches the cyclic process that is continuously present in landscape and animal and human lives: 'What humbles these hills has raised / The arrogance of flesh and bone'. This poem is a rare example in this second collection of a rhyming poem. In *Lupercal* these more complex ideas are given the simpler voice and looser forms that achieve the more vivid and subtle effects of poems by which Hughes had now made his name.

Wodwo

There was a seven year gap before Hughes published his third collection, *Wodwo* in 1967. The contrast with the two earlier collections indicates a clear stage of development, although few poems from the collection have proved lasting. The five stories and a play that accompany the poems form the second of the three parts of the book and all 'are intended to be read together as part of a single work' (see Works, p. 71). For Hughes, narrative, drama and poetry were not just becoming complementary modes, but possibly all present in any one mode. The story 'Snow' is a poetic drama in which an airman who has apparently survived a crash in the Arctic keeps himself sane in a continuous whiteout by testing how far he can walk from the chair he carries on a harness. The radio play 'The Wound' is a dream narrative in the mind of a soldier with a horrific head injury. The poem 'Gog' is a narrative drama in three parts presenting the growth of an iron warrior familiar from various mythic forms.

Wodwo is considered to be the volume in which Hughes found his mythic voice and began developing a sense of a structure that could explore a mythic drama within the scope of a volume of poetry. It is tempting to assume that it is because of the death of Sylvia Plath in 1963 (see Life and contexts, p. 15) that many of these poems and stories constitute an attempt to understand the death process. In fact, all but three of the poems in *Wodwo* were written before her death. Those later three poems are 'Song of a Rat', 'The Howling of Wolves' and 'Skylarks' (*Letters* 721). But the careful structure of the volume might be understood as an amelioration of that dominant theme. Indeed, some of the most lasting poems are to be found in the opening and closing of the volume where life forces seem to briefly engage with the terrible images of destruction or ennui.

The first part of the collection contains poems that might be seen as having grown out of the earlier collections. They are the most accessible descriptive poems in the volume, although the language is both more anecdotal and more portentous or enigmatic ('This will be serious for the hill. / It suspects nothing.'). In fact, this is the language of a traditional storyteller and the final poems in this first section do move into the realm of myth that characterises the poems in the third section.

Although persistent regeneration is celebrated in the opening poem 'Thistles', it is a Viking blood-lust of revenge that is evoked to characterise it. The gentle humour of 'the rubber tongues of cows' in the opening line and of the final image of sons 'stiff with weapons, fighting back over the same ground', contributes to the delicate balance of the aggressive and regenerational forces the poem is celebrating. But the second poem, 'Still Life', makes a brilliant counter to a simple admiration for dogged survival and is a more complex achievement. In an existential world without purposes, a West Yorkshire or Devon stone outcrop 'pretends to be dead of lack'. 'It thinks it pays no rent.' It gleams black with rain 'as if receiving interest'. In fact, such an attitude becomes a kind of purpose: 'it expects to be in at the finish'. But such complacent self-satisfaction ignores the 'sleeping', 'recovering' creative process contained in the fragile 'otherness' of the harebell. For in the force that made its trembling blue veins, which 'any known name of blue would bruise / Out of existence', is also that of 'the maker of the sea'. But is 'the maker of the sea' a mysterious natural evolutionary process, or a god? This poem offers no answer and does not raise the question, content to have raised the creation myth to counterbalance the stone's closed focus on 'the finish'.

Another approach to the same theme is made by the poem 'Pibroch' which is followed by four important poems that close the book. This closing sequence seems to represent a careful balance of the full range of tensions in the drama of the volume. 'Pibroch' begins at a further stage of thinking than that of 'Still Life'. Its title derives from a bagpipe lament and the poem is a formal lament for a lack of purpose or meaning in an existential universe in five stanzas of five lines each. Unlike sedimentary outcrop stone, the sea, an earlier element in evolution, is 'without purpose, without self-deception'. So it is 'probably bored with the appearance of heaven'. This cleverly suggests both the literal appearance of the heavens and the evolutionary 'appearance of heaven', a notion created by human culture. A pebble is also tempted to invent a religious meaning for itself by 'dreaming it is the foetus of God'. This is one of its 'fantasies of directions' that might be represented in human culture by images of heaven as a place 'where the staring angels go through', or 'where all the stars bow down'. But these concluding images have been rendered ironically suspect by the preceding statement that 'aeon after aeon / Nothing lets up or develops'. Sea, stars, stone, wind, tree have been presented in this poem as merely existing, rather than 'developing' towards a 'purpose'. Yet the poem recognises the temptation to invent 'a fantasy of directions' – 'heaven', 'angels', symbolic 'stars' – that is hard to suppress.

It seems that Hughes's grief and remorse following the death of Sylvia Plath found expression in 'The Howling of Wolves', the next poem at the end of *Wodwo*. 'It howls you cannot say whether out of agony or joy.' Uncomprehending of its fate that it must 'feed its fur', 'the wolf is living for the earth', 'innocence crept into minerals'. But following this poem Hughes has placed 'Gnat-Psalm' in which the short life-dance of gnats is both a joyous dance of death ('Riding your bodies to death') and a humbling image of absorbed suffering that is almost beyond the understanding of the poet: 'Your dancing / Rolls my staring skull slowly away into outer space'. To return to earth – to home, in fact – and a different kind of innocence from the wolf's, Hughes has next chosen to juxtapose the poem 'Full Moon and Little Frieda'.

Here free verse is used to dramatic effect in a small narrative that leads to a potentially healing enigma. Frieda is the child of Plath and Hughes, and the poem recounts a magical moment in which she connects for the first time a word with its subject. The tension of the evening's delicacy, caught between long and short lines, is focused on the listening small child so that cows can represent both threat and sustenance to her: the 'dark river of blood' of their red backs above the hedge become 'many boulders / Balancing unspilled milk'. The dissipation of this tension by the child's cry of 'Moon!' is a revelatory moment concerning not just language, but the physical universe of which the child is now a part. Once again, as in the evocation of 'the maker of the sea', Hughes uses a creation myth to catch the way the moon has given the child life at the moment the child has discovered the life of the moon: 'The moon has stepped back amazed at a work / That points at him amazed'. That both are 'amazed' at their 'creation' of each other emphasises the essential reciprocity that Hughes's poetry has been seeking while exploring the continuity between dualities in his earlier work. An earlier version of this poem was twice as long. The decision that the poem was complete at this moment suggests that the writer, too, did not immediately see his own revelation.

The volume does not end with revelation, however, but with more questions, more observations and the need for new poetic modes. 'Wodwo' was one of the highlights of Hughes's poetic career thus far, if not of his complete achievement since questions do, after all, need answers, however tentative. The epigraph of the collection identifies the wodwo as a mythical creature of the woods met by the hero of the Medieval narrative poem *Sir Gawain and the Green Knight*. In the poem the question 'What am I?' can only be answered by the way the creature relates to its natural environment guided by an instinct that can be observed by the creature itself: 'me and doing that have coincided very queerly'. (This poem was written before gay culture had added to the meaning of 'queer'.) The absence of conventional punctuation not only creates the effect of an emergent language, but of a continuous process of questions and observations leading to more questions. In the wood everything seems rooted, but the creature is aware that it is not. Its only motivation seems to be to continue to search for answers to its questions. It seems appropriate that this most exploratory of books is concluded with the words, 'very queer but I'll go on looking'.

It is not only the poems that evoke very queer threats in *Wodwo*. The stories may begin in the everyday world of a walk through rain returning to a familiar landscape, a Sunday lunchtime at a pub, or a harvesting, but something strange emerges from these settings as each story discovers something unexpectedly threatening within a familiar place. Two poems take the familiar Christian creation story and begin by imagining alternative developments in which it is the serpent who is the controlling force. They appear to have taken the same opening formulation. 'Reveille' begins: 'No, the serpent was not / One of God's ordinary creatures'. 'Theology' begins: 'No, the serpent did not / Seduce Eve to the apple'. At a time when Hughes was developing his own creation stories for his children, his imagination and his language were moving towards what would become the major vehicle of the *Crow* project.

Crow and *Cave Birds*

In May 1958 Hughes and Plath met the artist Leonard Baskin in America while Plath was teaching at Smith College. But it was not until 1967, the year of the publication of *Wodwo*, that Baskin invited Hughes to write poems to accompany Baskin's engravings of crows. The result was a project for an epic narrative cycle of poems that was never completed. The first two-thirds of the project was published as *Crow, From the Life and Songs of the Crow* in 1970, having been cut short by the suicide of Hughes's partner Assia (see Life and contexts, **p. 16**). The project was revived in the form of *Cave Birds* and published in 1975. But the poem sequence *Prometheus on his Crag* that was published within the collection *Moortown* in 1979, together with the shorter sequence 'Adam and the Sacred Nine' in that book, can both be seen as further attempts to reach the conclusion of the original *Crow* project.

It is ironic that the book by which Hughes was probably best known until *Birthday Letters* was always the most misunderstood because Hughes never published the narrative context for the poems. In the 1970s Hughes always introduced readings from the poems with the same story. The following is a compilation from private recordings made at readings during the 1970s (Keith Sagar has reconstructed a much longer version of this story in *The Laughter of Foxes* (2006: 172–80)):

> After having created the world, God has a nightmare that ridicules his creation, particularly God's masterpiece, Man. The ensuing argument is interrupted by a message that Man is at the gates asking God to take life back. God challenges the nightmare to do better and the result is Crow. God shows Crow around the universe and sets him various tasks and ordeals, in the course of which Crow becomes more intelligent and resourceful. Since all history is happening simultaneously, Crow can move freely from the beginning of the world to its end, observing and getting implicated in various aspects of creation. Crow begins to wonder who his creator is and he encounters female figures whom he never recognises as avatars of his own creator so that he always bungles the encounters. Finally he comes to a river he must cross where an ogress insists that he carries her across on his shoulders. Her weight strangely increases until the water is at his mouth at which moment she asks him a riddle which he must answer for her weight to decrease until she starts to get heavier again. This happens seven times. When they do eventually reach the opposite bank the ogress turns into a beautiful young woman who runs off into the woods. Crow follows.

While it is clear that this creation narrative derives from Hughes's readings in folklore, the character of Crow originates in the specific folktale figure known in Native American culture as the Trickster, and in English folklore as the Guiser, a playful, over-sexed, pre-moral character whose cultural function in folktales, says the anthropologist Paul Radin of the Native American Trickster, is ultimately to demonstrate the need for moral values: 'He possesses no values, moral or social, is at the mercy of his passions and appetites, yet through his actions all values come into being' (Radin 1956: ix). So through the naive survival figure of Crow, Hughes can ask fundamental questions about a range of human assumptions, concepts and narratives that are commonly found in twentieth-century Western civilisation, since all history is happening simultaneously. In the process the need for essential, if putative, human values arises out of what would otherwise be a bleak nihilistic existence.

This project was also conceived as a poetic challenge: 'The first idea of *Crow* was really an idea of a style ... the songs that a Crow would sing. In other words, songs with no music whatsoever, in a super-simple and a super-ugly language' (Faas 1980: 208). Of course, this is unachievable, but it does indicate the reductive attempt of the style and the anti-romantic conception of the project. Indeed, there is a case for saying that despite the fact that the project was unachievable for its author, the sequence as it stands is a powerful text that has already had a huge cultural impact. One could argue that if *Crow* is read together with *Cave Birds* the completeness of the project, in so far as it can be complete, is not only inescapable, but stands as perhaps Hughes's most profound work.

The first *Crow* poem to be published demonstrates the deft poetics at work behind an apparently simple style and idea. 'A Disaster' begins with an image of Crow as the indifferent observer who must eat whatever carrion he finds to survive: 'There came news of a word. / Crow saw it killing men. He ate well.' Here, instead of men having created the word, they are being killed by an idea that apparently has taken on a reified life of its own as the Word. But, of course, it is dependent on people for its existence, so when 'the word trie[s] its great lips / On the earth's bulge, like a giant lamprey', it has to die. Simile, alliteration and dramatic imagery are part of the music of the poetics that serve as a huge joke against human self-delusion. Tested against material reality this ideology, social movement or religion cannot sustain itself – 'Its era was over'. Crow is left to 'muse' on what he has observed, as are readers, who are left with some searching questions to answer about which 'Words' they live by.

In *Crow* Hughes systematically questions a wide range of 'Words' that are at the height of their era in the latter half of the twentieth century. 'Lineage' parodies the Old Testament form of a birth line, beginning with the primeval birth scream (or Big Bang), leading to some telling causal links ('Granite begat Violet … Guitar begat Sweat'), to reveal that Adam begat Mary who begat God. Since God is of woman born (or 'man-made') in this poem, he can produce nothing except the idea of nothingness, the mystical 'never never' out of which any fabulous beast might be begat to satisfy another psychic need (a Black Beast, for example). Instead, a real crow comes 'trembling featherless' in a filthy nest to test other 'Words' in his down-to-earth way in the rest of the sequence.

Thus are tested the contemporary myths of the Oedipus complex ('Revenge Fable'), scientific determinism ('Crow's Account of the Battle'), Romantic self-projection ('Owl's Song'), pastoralism ('Crow and the Birds'), the reification of evil ('The Black Beast'), the suppression of evil with force ('Crow's Account of St George'), the Christian God ('Crow Communes'), sexuality as the dominant force ('A Childish Prank') and LOVE ('Crow's First Lesson'). The horror and anguish that have been produced by some of these 'Words' in the twentieth century are not shirked by the poetry, even perhaps to the point of over-correction for a readership that has not experienced war. Indeed, the persistence of a comforting false consciousness is illustrated by the poem 'Glimpse', in which Crow himself wants to Romanticise the leaves. Again material reality dramatically shows how false this is by cutting off his head with a leaf's edge. Instantly he substitutes what is even more false – a god's head through which he now sees everything. The creation of various forms of transcendent false consciousness – heavens, purposes, Words, gods – is hard to stop, even when they prove self-destructive.

At the same time as Crow is destroying false conceptions, there are a number of poems, tentatively scattered throughout the sequence, in which he creatively discovers the emergence of a conscience. Fundamental to this is his learning a diminished sense of himself (by getting rid of his desire to see with a 'god's head') in the face of the awesome mystery of the material world. 'Crow and the Sea' and 'Crow on the Beach' signal this incipient process.

Typically, Crow tries to form a relationship with the sea in his own terms: ignoring it, talking to it, sympathising with it and hating it. 'He tried just being in the same world as the sea / But his lungs were not big enough.' Of course, he is in the same world as the sea, but because he cannot attune to the dimensions of its nature, he is unable to feel that he is. Finally he is 'crucified' by his realisation of his relative insignificance, since he cannot even walk away from the sea. (He will always be approaching another one.) The pain of this to his ego is as inevitable as the pain of death. But it is an ironic moment of growth. In 'Crow on the Beach' he goes a stage further and, in response to what he perceives as the sea's pain – its 'ogreish outcry and convulsion' – he senses that help is needed, but that he is unable to give it, partly because he is unable to understand. The poem ends with his struggling 'to wonder, about the sea / What could be hurting so much'. Crow seems to have discovered that empathy can only emerge out of humility.

Similarly, guilt for culpability in acts of violence can only arise once the consequences of violence have been registered. In the poem 'That Moment' Crow seems to register with a quiet awe the finality of a single violent death. The tone of the poem is subtle, catching the casualness of a pistol lifted away 'like a cigarette lifted from an ashtray', the unique individuality of 'the only face left in the world' that now 'lay broken', the dignity of a body that nevertheless is abandoned in a world that it has abandoned, the finality of the repeated word 'forever' and the honest guilt behind the imperative to go on living despite having let in the above complex of emotions: 'Crow had to start searching for something to eat'. The respect implicit in searching elsewhere for carrion indicates a shift in Crow's consciousness that surfaces again more explicitly in 'Crow Tyrannosaurus'.

In a universe sustained by the food chain, every creature is a tyrannosaurus and none has the option of stopping eating to 'try to become the light' – another false consciousness. Crow is 'trapsprung' to eat a grub when he sees one. Only human beings fool themselves with some pretentious forms of 'the light'. In a clever example of his use of form, Hughes uses pairs of words to associate weeping with the grubs being stabbed by Crow. But in the following line the weeping is now that of Crow himself as 'Weeping he walked and stabbed'. Crow seems to be weeping for the inability to act from the choices a conscience brings with it. Through an awareness of his own limitations in instinctive violence Crow has poignantly created a value for human choices directed by conscience. The most that Crow can feel is the guilt driven by empathy demonstrated in 'Crow's Nerve Fails'. Then he is the prisoner of all that he has eaten. 'His prison is the earth.' Given this existential trap it is hard to tell whether the reader is invited to laugh or sympathise in response to the last line: 'Heavily he flies'.

Perhaps the answer is in the last group of poems in the collection as it was arranged and abandoned in 1970. 'Two Eskimo Songs', the penultimate poems, are fables about accepting the self, with all its contradictions and apparent weaknesses, including the need to search for a better self. The quest of water to find what life would mean for itself leads only to painful insights. 'It came weeping back it wanted to die.' At this moment of despair, 'utterly worn out,' it is ironically also 'utterly clear' – 'It lay at the bottom of all things'. The word 'bottom' indicates a nadir that is also a discovery of its own nature. 'Littleblood' is not Crow's simple song celebrating the life-blood, but an earned insight into the creative/destructive universe gained by 'sucking death's mouldy tits'. Every one of those last three words dramatically qualifies the previous one in ways that can only be understood fully by having read the whole sequence. Respect for the interrelated life and death processes in the material world has led Crow to begin to appreciate the complexity of his own creative/destructive nature. From the challenging, questioning, playful narrative of Crow has emerged the need for a humanity that is capable of humility, empathy, outrage, horror, guilt and responsibility in order to survive.

It now seems that the riddle questions (see Works p. 40) in *Crow* about the relationships between 'he' and 'she' would have been the link poems into the final third of the book in which, after all his mismanagement of his encounters with the disguised figure of his female creator, Crow would have achieved a symbolic marriage with her. The poem 'Crow's Undersong' is Crow's attempt to envision the goddess of nature who is his mother/creator, if only glimpsed in the riddles of an 'undersong' from under his consciousness. This is a celebration of all that remains of a raw force that is now 'under' the trappings of civilisation and conscious, rational life, indicating how far back she has now retreated. Crow's plainness of speech is apparent, yet, almost despite himself, there is also a lyrical beauty in images of animal eloquence: 'She brings her favourite furs and these are her speeches'. She is still needed since she represents hope for a human reconciliation with nature. She reminds humans that the city is a symbol of both their alienation and their capacity for creativity. 'She cannot come all the way' until humans have accepted the lessons of the *Crow* project.

So, just as *Crow* was an opportunity to start a new poetic project following the death of Plath, Hughes had to start again from a different place after a second personal tragedy, the deaths of Assia and Shura curtailed that poetic project (see Life and contexts, p. 19). The climactic, pivotal poem of *Cave Birds* had already been written as part of the *Crow* sequence; 'Bride and Groom Lie Hidden for Three Days' was the answer to the riddle question 'Who gave most, him or her?'. But now a new sequence based on a series of characters in an 'alchemical cave drama' emerged from a closer collaboration with Leonard Baskin, who produced an image for each poem in the sequence. A complacently arrogant cockerel is put on trial for the neglect of his inner spirit. Witnesses appear to confront him with the evidence of his own material vulnerability and mortality which he has ignored in the past. He is alchemically transformed to a 'flayed crow in the hall of judgement', confronted with his own death and offered a series of illusory heavens. Because he has rejected these, in a new state of enlightened humility, he is symbolically married to a female figure who is both his own inner spirit and the goddess of nature. He is reborn or 'risen' as a falcon, although a brief Finale poem undermines any sense of complacent finality by warning that a goblin might pop up to disturb the ritual's apparent 'end'. *Crow* had asked the questions in its pyrotechnic poetry, but *Cave Birds* was its harrowing and hopeful reflective answer, destined to live in its shadow.

The poem 'Bride and Groom Lie Hidden for Three Days' remains one of Hughes's most important poems, both for its profound poetic insights and its symbolically empowering position in the *Crow/Cave Birds* project.

The sequence of twenty-one poems about *Prometheus on his Crag* was written in 1971 when Hughes was working with Peter Brook on the *Orghast* project (see Works, p. 93). As a meditation on the mysterious pain and resilience of the human condition, the sequence is clearly another way of coming at the *Crow* project. Chained to his crag for stealing fire and giving it (and therefore life) to humans, Prometheus is visited each day by a vulture that eats his liver, which grows again each night. In a voice that Hughes described as 'numb' (Gifford and Roberts 1981: 57), Prometheus tries to understand the paradox of his predicament. In Poem 18, 'Even as the vulture buried his head', a lizard says to Prometheus, 'Lucky, you are so lucky to be human!' The final lines of the sequence reach for a suggestion of the reintegrated relationship with the world achieved in 'The Risen': 'He treads / On the dusty peacock film where the world floats'.

Less airy is the reworking of this final image at the conclusion to the sequence of twelve poems titled 'Adam and the Sacred Nine', also published in the collection *Moortown* in 1979. Newly created, Adam lies listless, uncertain as to how to be fully himself as a human being, and is visited by nine birds that are fully alive, like the Phoenix, 'in the blaze' of themselves. In a predicament that is the opposite of that of Prometheus, Adam knows that he is 'made of joy', but does not know its source or how to live it, since the examples of fully realised lives that visit him cannot provide him with models of what it is to be distinctively human. When Adam stands, in the final poem, he discovers that the sole of his foot perfectly fits the 'world-rock', that it is no wing, but that, as the foot says in the last words of the sequence, 'I was made / For you'. Adam's apparently simple yet crucial discovery is the human equivalent of water's discovery in 'How Water Began to Play'. This little lyrical sequence cannot carry the weight of concluding the interrupted *Crow* project as *Cave Birds* clearly does. But it is an example of how Hughes continued to return, in different mythic sequences, to that project's fundamental challenge: how to understand human nature in the context of the world's nature.

Gaudete

Gaudete (1977) is the most unconventional and critically contested of all the major works of Ted Hughes. It is an episodic narrative told mainly in a long-lined free verse form. Since it began life as a film script, it is not surprising that it retains a gradual revelation of narrative through a sequence of highly visualised scenes usually focusing on one of the characters. It opens with two epigraphs, a brief Argument and a Prologue. It concludes with an Epilogue in which a prose narrative introduces a series of forty-five lyrics which some critics have praised as not just the finest achievement of the book, but of Hughes's whole work. Indeed, *Gaudete* has been described as containing both Hughes's greatest religious poetry and rural stereotypes typical of the BBC radio rural soap *The Archers*. Following *Wodwo* and then *Crow/Cave Birds*, *Gaudete* was another bold and innovative book drawing upon mythic modes and folkloric tropes to further explore the connections between inner and outer natural energies. That the result is generally agreed to be flawed in various ways should not deflect the reader from finding in this book poetry of powerful psychological insight and moving metaphysical vision.

The Argument summarises the narrative of the book. The Reverend Nicholas Lumb has been carried away into the spirit world to perform an unspecified task and in his place is a changeling made from an oak log, who, taking a rather 'wooden' approach to his ministry of the Gospel of love, turns the Women's Institute (an English rural women's social organisation) into a coven to be impregnated in the hope of producing a Messiah. The men of his parish discover what is going on, hunt Lumb down and kill him at the very moment, the Argument tells us, that the spirits have decided to cancel him. The original vicar turns up in the West of Ireland, whistles up an otter and goes off, leaving behind a notebook of 'hymns and psalms to a nameless female deity'.

Three important aspects of this book are thus identified for the reader at the outset. First is the dominating presence under the narrative of the elusive female goddess whom Crow came closest to evoking in 'Crow's Undersong'. Second is the anticipation of a narrative of sexual farce that is perhaps a foil to the worship of the goddess. The experiences of the two Lumbs which we are being invited to observe, invite a contrast between two forms of worship, one of which is distorted into a dangerous joke while the other is represented only by a series of psalms. Third, however much this narrative might seem, at times, to be rooted in rural reality, it is in the mode of a folktale and therefore is a sort of riddle, or at least not to be fully comprehended by the rational interpretation of symbols, since the narrative is controlled by the world of spirits.

The two epigraphs from Heraclitus and Parzival emphasise a unity of opposites, reminding the reader of the final insights of *Crow* symbolised by the image of 'Littleblood' 'sucking death's mouldy tits'. If 'Hades and Dionysos are one' (Heraclitus), in the cycles of regeneration for example, then attempts to oppose them result in 'one flesh, one blood, doing itself much harm' (Parzival), as if two brothers are fighting each other. Indeed, the book's title is a praising of the paradox of virgin birth and a reminder of the Christian religion's difficulty with sexuality. (The title is taken from a Latin hymn and the word means 'rejoice': 'Gaudete, gaudete, Christus est natus / Ex Maria virgine, gaudete'. Hughes first came across this as he heard his daughter Frieda play the recording by Steeleye Span in 1973.)

The Prologue begins as the Reverend Lumb finds himself in a Northern English town that has literally gone dead. 'The whole town is a maze of mass graves.' An Irish tinker leads him to a beautiful, half-dead animal woman who is lying in wolf skins. Sensing that he is being asked to do something for her, he reveals his belief in the separation of body from spirit, saying that since he is not a doctor, he can only pray. Instantly he feels a blow. A group of men tie him to an oak tree and whip him into unconsciousness. He comes to without the scars, in a different body, and is ritually reborn by being drowned in the blood and guts of a white bull strung above him. He emerges from a basement into the street of a busy town.

Then begins a series of male views, through binoculars and telescopes, of Lumb's liaisons. The reader is forced to share the characters' uncertainty about what exactly is being seen. As in the preceding Prologue, no interpretation is offered. But quickly the stereotypes of immediate characterisation give way to moving inner states. Major Hagen's face has 'paradeground gravel in the folded of gnarl of his jowls'. Commander Estridge's 'small tight ferocious hawk's face / Evolved in Naval Command'. The latter is disturbed by his dream of beautiful daughters having become a reality, 'Like leopard cubs suddenly full-grown, come into their adult power and burdened with it'. From his share of this burden he retreats to watch the village from his telescope while his elder daughter is hanging herself in her bedroom because she is pregnant by Lumb. Suddenly Dionysos and Hades have become one with a momentum that disturbs even the wooden Lumb himself. Through his telescope Estridge had been watching Lumb on another assignation.

Lumb knows that his fate is to precipitate a social explosion: 'the blood in his veins / Is like heated petrol'. In one of a series of engagements with the land, Lumb wishes for freedoms of choice that are beyond him, that is, the other possible lives he knows everyone else has. He leans his head against a tree and prays that he is able to escape his fate by leaving before nightfall, 'and the tree stands as his prayer'. The reverberation of this passage, since Lumb actually is a tree, yet cannot have human moral choice, has a pathos beyond the humour, a metaphysical subtlety and emotional charge that is carried by the physical detail and waves of thought expressed by the rhythms of the free verse. In *Gaudete* the land often provides the grounded connection between the characters and their sense of their own natures when under stress. Always that sense is one of flux and change in nature, rather than a static beauty: 'giant wheels of light ride into the chestnuts', 'the sweating gasping life of division and multiplication', 'the hair-fine umbilicus of life in the stalk of grass'. Apart from Lumb, it is usually the women in the narrative who most easily draw strength from their connection with external processes of nature in their environment. Sometimes this can produce bathos, however potent and archaic the image, as when Mrs Holroyd, sensuously sunbathing 'like a plant', watches her bull rubbing against a tree and bringing down blossoms 'settling along his shoulders and loins and buttocks, like a confetti'.

It is from the flux of mud that Lumb has two encounters with spirits. The first is with his double, who emerges from a lake to chase after Felicity, Lumb's companion on this fishing trip. Lumb fights the double and as a thunderstorm bursts the two men 'wallow pummelling, / Plastered with peat-mud, under the downpour', facing each other, 'One grinning and the other appalled'. Lumb tears off the hand of the double that has been gripping his and throws it into the lake to which the other has retreated, wailing. Lumb embraces the sobbing Felicity. Again, no interpretation is offered and the episode is sustained by its own dramatic life, like a mysterious narrative branch of a folktale.

The second encounter opens with a hand (the same hand?) wrenching the steering wheel from Lumb's grip as he drives his van so that he is thrown out. The blackness he thinks is the river turns out to be a cattleyard where he is beaten and herded like the other cattle in pouring rain by men in oilskins. A piece of paper is handed to him 'as if it were some explanation', but it disintegrates in the downpour (thus teasing the critics). He is stampeded with the cattle, falls under their hooves and comes to consciousness buried in mud on a hoof-ploughed plain where the men of his parish lie dead and the women are buried up to their necks, screaming. Squirming in mud and watching him is 'one creature that he can free'. As he draws the mud-being up into his arms, he sees the face of a woman that recalls the half-animal woman of the Prologue who also needed Lumb's help. The men in oilskins reappear, hold him down, and he watches himself enact her birth from between his legs. Her half-animal face is now undeformed and perfect. Lumb scrambles away and climbs out of a river to find his van in a meadow with the doors open, 'as if parked for a picnic'.

Clearly, these dreams from Hades are not unconnected to the life of Dionysos in which Lumb is engaged. The world of spirit seems to be just under the surface, or rather within the physical world of mud and rain. It is in such elemental dream episodes that the human and the animal become one. Indeed, it is in such mythic tales that we reach an understanding of how the knowledge of the doctor and the priest, the rational and the intuitive, the body and the spirit, must be one. Explanations on paper disintegrate before the material reality of our rainy world.

The encroaching ritual climax for the coven, that Lumb had wanted to escape, turns out to be a disaster for both the characters and the writer. Mystic Maud is one of the dark disasters of the book's characterisation. Down in the church basement, where the Women's Institute gather, occult props go missing, magic mushrooms are slipped into triangular sandwiches, Lumb carries a stag's head, smoke clouds from 'herbs in ashtrays', Felicity realises that she is a hind to be sacrificed, her head held between Maud's thighs, and Maud realises that Lumb is about to desert them, denounces him, and, in the words of a *Crow* poem, 'everything goes to Hell'. Lumb escapes the chasing women only to be shot dead in the lake by one of the posse of men. In the lake Lumb suddenly understands at last 'Why he has been abandoned to these crying beings' who are chasing him 'In order to convert him to mud from which plants grow and which cattle tread'. Growth and decay, the fertility and putrescence of mud, are mere mechanical facts in this rural world. The mumbo-jumbo of the occult rituals of a distorted religion has been able to take hold here because the material world is regarded as without spirit. Lumb sees that, here, the lake water is 'a spiritless by-product / Of the fact that things exist at all'. The land and all its complex powers and processes, is, here, 'an ignorance, waiting in darkness – He knows at last why it has become so'.

What 'has become' of material nature through the separations of the culture inhabited by the wooden Lumb, is countered by the poems praising the spirit of nature attributed to the returned original Lumb. Hughes has written, 'They started being vacanas – as in that *Speaking of Shiva* book [trans. A.K. Ramanujan, Penguin Classics, 1973] – but then took off on their own' (Weissbort 2006: ix). In these poems, a humility, awe, compassion, puzzlement, acceptance and ultimate celebration of both growth and decay come from a voice of centred connectedness. This is a difficult voice to sustain and some of these poems are abstract constructions of horror and joy ('The sea grieves all night long') that verge on self-parody. At its best ('Churches topple') it is the voice of an ordinary man who rejoices in the 'miracle' of a cutting, creating river, or of being able to whistle up and observe an otter, a spirit helper towards comprehending the sacred in the animal, in the human self and in their relationship.

Remains of Elmet and *Elmet*

For a writer who had been careful to keep his personal life as much out of the public gaze as was possible, the publication of a book about the landscape and life of his childhood in the Calder Valley of West Yorkshire must have seemed to Hughes to be still holding the personal safely at a distance. In fact it was a project he could not resist when the photographer Fay Godwin sent him pictures of the area around Heptonstall to which he had sent her, promising her some interesting material. He sent her poems in return, prompted by the photographs, and she took more photographs. Together they sequenced the poems and photographs on the table at a friend's house and *Remains of Elmet* (1979) came into being, another collaborative project in which Hughes had engaged (see Gifford 2001). When this book had long been out of print, they revisited the project with more photographs and more poems to produce the book simply titled *Elmet* (1994). Most of the poems in the former book were included in the second, but in addition to more personal family poems in the second, Hughes included a few poems from earlier collections that were about this landscape.

Two of the best poems from the first book were omitted from the second, probably because Hughes felt they were too obviously responses to the photographs. The first of these is titled 'Remains of Elmet' which describes 'the long gullet of Calder' as eating, in an extended metaphor, the road, railway and canal in the fullness of its own geological timescale. This respect for the landscape's accommodation is one of the themes of the project. In his Introductions to both books (the second much more elaborated than the first) Hughes observes the temporary nature of the waves of human uses of the landscape. When he grew up here in the slump of the 1930s, he had a sense 'that you were living among the survivors, in the remains' of what had always been a marginal 'badlands' where the lawless lived. 'The mills began to close, the chapels to empty, and the high farms under the moor-edge ... were one by one abandoned' (*Elmet* 11). The gullet of Calder now 'admits tourists / To pick among crumbling, loose molars'. All that remains is 'a wind-parched ache' in the diminished human population of this valley that links Yorkshire and Lancashire.

Always the poems celebrate the landscape and its elemental process as the dominant force to which human culture must adjust and thus be shaped by. The poem 'Moors' elaborates the idea of a stage on which epics of Shakespearean proportions are enacted by the elements in 'the performance of heaven' ('Any audience is incidental'). The poem's imaginative flight is finally brought down to earth with a simple image as the actors 'escape from a world / Where snipe work late'. The real world of hard work for survival here is represented by the snipe's 'drumming' to establish its territory at dusk. In these conditions, 'heather only toughens', and provides nectar for bees from what is 'a mica sterility' ('Heather'). In the poem about 'Heptonstall', the hill-top village to which Hughes's parents moved after all their children had left home from Mexborough, the famously large cemetery produces the image of a 'hill's collapsed skull'. But this skull might also be that of a sheep or of a bird that, in a wider context, has also had to struggle against the elements. The poem concludes with a subtle twist after showing that while Life, Death and Stone each 'tries' in this place, 'Only the rain never tires'.

The second important poem omitted from the second book, 'Lumb Chimneys', provides an organic image for industrial decay after noticing that in Fay Godwin's photograph (*Elmet* 43) this structure seems to have grown like the ferns and trees that now surround it. The poem concludes that 'Before these chimneys can flower again / They must fall into the only future, into earth'. This sense that the failed human projects in this landscape can be understood as an organic part of the processes at work in this land is caught in the brilliant opening line of the brief poem 'Shackleton Hill': 'Dead Farms, Dead Leaves'. (This line is also the poem's title in *Remains of Elmet*.) The dead farms of this landscape are the dead leaves of a human culture that is also part of 'the long / Branch of the world'. When cattle farming has become too marginal an existence, cattle disappear like migrating birds that are 'the cattle of heaven'. The roofless arches of Heptonstall Old Church, in the poem of that title, suggest the carcass of a great bird that landed there and died as 'The crystal in men's heads / Blackened and fell to pieces'.

This sense that the 'crystal' of the human enterprise was 'blackened' at some point does not prevent Hughes from celebrating the exhilaration of the adventures launched by successive waves of habitation. 'Walls at Alcomden' imagines the farming adventure as a ship setting out. 'The stone rigging was strong' and the men themselves 'grew stronger riding the first winters'. The walls that Fay Godwin has photographed (*Elmet* 66) are now all that remain of 'the hulk, every rib shattered'. 'When Men Got to the Summit' evokes the dogged resilience caught from the landscape itself that readied this population for the bracing austerity of Methodism: 'They filled with heavy silence'. The houses and streets that 'came to support them' on their hill-top settlements will inevitably fracture like the belief in the 'foursquare scriptures', just as 'soft rheumatism' will apparently weaken both people and houses. In Fay Godwin's photograph in the first book there is a television aerial on the chimney of the abandoned houses which the poet has noticed, since he concludes the poem with the heavy irony of a television blinking out of what was once a wolf's den, 'for some giddy moments'. But the key image of the poem might represent the process celebrated by the whole book: 'The hills went on gently / Shaking their sieve'.

When Hughes writes about the resilience of the people of this place, he draws attention to the way their language and accent seem to have emerged from their engagement with the elements of wind, water and stone. The 'Crown Point Pensioners' have vowels that 'furl downwind, on air like silk', the 'r' in 'furl' requiring the long silky curl in its pronunciation that is characteristic of the Lancashire/Yorkshire border. 'Attuned to each other, like the strings of a harp, / They make mesmerising music.' If the shared speech community is celebrated in this poem, the historical inheritance of an individual is celebrated in 'For Billy Holt', in whose nose and chin the longships of the Vikings are 'anchored'. Out of poverty they 'cut rock lumps for words', emphasising the local preference for plain single-vowelled words in the spondees of this line. This Viking inheritance, the poem suggests, has produced an acceptance of death that has no problems in finding that its homeland is a graveyard like the village of Heptonstall. Yet there are also poems in the collection that celebrate the unlikely absurdity of cricket, played in the narrow valley bottom, and football, played on the open ridge-top.

'Sunstruck' contrasts a hot Sunday game of cricket with the Monday world ever present in the high windows of 'the wage-mirage sparkle of mills'. The spin-bowler's angle seems to be narrowed by the 'shaggy valley parapets'. But there are no such inhibitions for those playing 'Football at Slack'. Although the weather conditions render the game rather absurd, this poem is about a resilience that does not take itself too seriously. Wind, rain and mud can only make the 'bobbing' shouts of these players seem 'fine and thin, washed and happy / While the humped world sank foundering'. Indeed, their performances take on the quality of the mock-epic tales that will be retold after the game. They are really only bouncing about, like their ball, but by the end of the poem, when the wingers leapt, 'they bicycled in air' and 'The goalie flew horizontal'. Even the elements themselves look on in admiration of the human spirit in evidence here, so that the sky's most impressive display appears to watch the players. The poem ends with a touch that is both witty and profound: 'And once again a golden holocaust / Lifted the cloud's edge, to watch them.'

Here is the spirit that has survived the failures of farming, industry, Methodism and the still remembered 'cataclysm' of the First World War 'where', Hughes writes in his second Introduction, 'a single bad ten minutes in no man's land would wipe out a street or even a village'. Among the poems from his early collections that Hughes included in the second book, *Elmet*, wanting them to be read as originating in this place, is 'Six Young Men' from his first book, *The Hawk in the Rain*. The poem contemplates a photograph of six smiling men on a 'Sunday jaunt' who were all to be killed six months later in the horror of the trenches. The depth of this war in the communal memory accounts for its presence in so many of the poems about family members introduced into *Elmet*. The book's cover-photograph shows, in the distance to the left, one of the many war memorials that stand in high places in this region. The word 'cenotaph' has a personal resonance in the poetry of Ted Hughes (see 'Out' in *Wodwo*).

Elmet opens with a poem in which the author sees his mother in the face of his eighty-year-old uncle and ends with a poem that borrows its title from Wilfred Owen, 'Anthem for Doomed Youth', which is partly a lament for the author's own youth, shared with his older brother, and partly a lament for the region's youth, evoked by the final word 'poppies'. In 'For the Duration' the poet regrets not asking his father to break his silence about the First World War, knowing that the war is relived in his father's nightmares: 'No man's land still crying and burning / Inside our house'. Perhaps the most moving of these poems is 'Walt', in which the poet's Uncle Walt spends a whole day crouching from the range of a sniper in a shell-hole in no man's land sustained by remembering walks in the local landscape of home. The poet standing with him as he recalls this story is the same age as his uncle was then and they both know those walks, so the litany of names in the landscape becomes a gift of sustaining power. But the uncle had been cursed earlier that same day by a German prisoner and the poet hints that this curse has 'brought down' Walt's wife and children in some way. So when Walt says to the poet, 'Somewhere just about here. / This is where he stopped me. I got this far', there is a suggestion of a whole life curtailed in some essential aspect by the curse that counters the power of the locale.

One of the new poems introduced to *Elmet*, 'Chinese History of Colden Water', acts as a summary of the whole project, but also leaves an enigma that reverberates beyond the closure of many of the poems in the book. If *Remains of Elmet* presented a social history as a natural history, *Elmet* presented a personal history as a social history. Once each volume's agenda has been perceived in this way, many of the poems seem to be illustrations of it. Indeed, this is partly true of the poem 'Chinese History of Colden Water'. But its framing device adds a dimension of mystery beyond the social history embedded in the land's processes. In this poem one of the Chinese immortals has fallen into the valley and been lulled to sleep by the whispering of the wind in the hills and the rain in the valley. He dreams images of the valley's history – hammers, head-scarves, clog-irons, looms, biblical texts – and then wakes at the horror of it all. Only the hills, the waves of light and the whispers remain before him. His eyes are washed clear by the light that also, finally, 'washed from his ear / All but the laughter of foxes'. Ultimately Elmet is the kingdom of foxes and their laughter appears to be mocking the human presumption that it could be a home for industry, farming or religion.

Moortown

When Hughes produced the collection titled *Moortown* in 1979, he took the opportunity to publish, in a section titled 'Earth-Numb', a number of individual poems and short sequences that dated, in the case of 'Heatwave', to as far back as 1963. Two of those sequences have already been discussed as extensions of the *Crow* project (see Works, p. 44), but several strong individual poems, such as 'The stone', 'Tiger-Psalm' and 'Nightwind, a freedom', can now be read under the title 'Earth-Numb' in the *Collected Poems*. This is in order to distinguish the two parts of *Moortown*, since the title sequence of this collection was subsequently published separately ten years later (with extensive end-notes) as the book *Moortown Diary*. The latter is a remarkable work of personal responsibility for livestock and land that is infused with a deep understanding of living with birth and death, with weather and landscape, with the forces of the seasons in poetry that has a deceptive ease of expression.

Hughes explains in his Introduction to *Moortown Diary* that these poems, which are individually dated between 1973 and 1976, are diary entries in the form of 'improvised verses', set down on the day of their origination. In an endnote to the poem 'Birth of Rainbow' he writes, 'thinking about it that night I pushed myself out of bed to make the note, knowing that by the next day I would for sure have lost the authentic fingerprints of the day itself'. 'The note' Hughes refers to is the poem, unchanged for publication, he tells us in the Introduction, for fear of introducing 'fake' elements. It should not be assumed from this that these poems might be columns from the *Farmer's Weekly*. 'As I came to a close,' Hughes goes on to say of 'Birth of Rainbow', 'Frost's line "Something has to be left to God" strayed into my head.' Apart from intertexuality, the poetics in these 'note' poems achieve some startling effects and moving insights into a life lived close to the management of animals in the particular landscape of North Devon.

In 1973 Hughes and his wife bought ninety-five acres of farmland five miles from his home for his father-in-law, Jack Orchard, to manage for the rearing of beef cattle and sheep (see Life and contexts, **p. 19**). Since these 'notes' record 'interesting things happening' (*Moortown Diary*, p. x), Hughes makes no apology that many of the poems 'concern the nursing if not the emergency hospital side of animal husbandry. All sheep, lambs and calves are patients: something in them is making a steady effort to die. That is the farmer's impression' (BBC Radio 3, 10. 5. 1980). Indeed, some of the best-known poems in this collection are the most graphic for an urban audience. But usually there is much more at work in the poem than horrific detail. Whenever Hughes read from this collection in public he always included 'February 17th', by the end of which some members of the audience were left feeling distinctly uncomfortable (some actually fainted). The poem, on these occasions, had an anti-pastoral force against the common cuddly associations that lambs have in an urban culture. In it a dead lamb cannot be forced out by the mother giving birth and the poet cannot get a helping hand past the dead head that has emerged. So, to save the life of the mother, he runs two miles for the injection and the razor, cuts off the head and manages first to push against the birth push of the mother to get a hand in and then to hook a knee in order to pull with the birth push until there is movement: 'In a smoking slither of oils and soups and syrups– / And the body lay born, beside the hacked-off head'. The alliteration of these final two lines creates two quite opposite effects. The long run of the 's' sounds is onomatopoeic in enacting a flow, while the two beats of the 'b' and of the 'h' are a staccato enactment of body and head, birth and death, confronting each other. This echoes the earlier image of a living mother facing the dead head of its offspring in the mud, 'with all earth for a body'. Here is a forceful and primeval image that links these processes back into the cycles of the earth itself.

What should not be overlooked in this poem is the trial being undertaken by the poet himself, not at the distance of a myth, as in *Cave Birds*, but in taking personal responsibility for an actual life and death struggle in a North Devon field. The Introduction indicates that the same responsibility is undertaken on behalf of the land against the pressures of what Hughes calls 'the EEC Agricultural Policy War' that heavily subsidised the use of chemicals to pump into the cattle, onto the land and inevitably into the rivers. Hughes admits that this pressure, like 'the technological revolutions and international market madness that have devastated farmers, farms and farming', is under the surface of what these poems record. But they are an indication of the sense of responsibility that lies behind such linguistic effects as 'the disc harrow – / An intelligence test for perverse / Animal suicides – presented its puzzle'. If the poet has left the harrow in the way of a curious and already sick calf, he is implicated in its suicide attempt, he implies in 'Little Red Twin'. This calf lives, but the poet has produced some moving responses to her attempts to defeat him: 'Her eyes are just plumb softness, they thought / She'd come to be a cow.' Has domestication bred out some survival mechanisms? 'We leave her / To her ancestors, who should have prepared her / For worse than this.'

In 'Ravens' it is a three-year-old child confronting a dead lamb that has already been opened up by ravens, asking the poet, 'Did it cry?', who shares in the anti-pastoral learning curve of the North Devon shepherd who cannot be other than honest in reply: '"Oh yes" I say "it cried."' But the context is some kind of counterbalance: 'its first day of death was blue and warm'; magpies, skylarks and budding blackthorn are at ease; 'And the skyline of hills, after millions of hard years, / Sitting soft'. At the core of this poem is the integrity of the relationship between the enquiring child and the unflinching poet who confirms what the child already guesses.

In fact, most of these poems are acts of celebration of the farmer's responsibility. This is achieved as much through their ease of form as their linguistic care. There is a sure hand behind these 'note' poems that carries both knowledge and compassion in the georgic quality of the detail. Knowing how to do things right in this landscape, its weather conditions, its particular problems – like its ravens – and its culture of farmers who are 'the labourers at earth's furnace', is the continuing trial underlying these poems. Such an accommodated life is celebrated in the final six poems reflecting on the life of Jack Orchard, whose death in 1976 brought the hands-on Moortown experience to a close for the poet and to whom the collection is dedicated.

'A Monument' recalls Jack Orchard struggling in mud and rain to align and properly fix a fence, 'Precise to the tenth of an inch', through a thicket where it will only be seen by the odd straying cow. The poem's title is matched by the respect of the final phrase, 'using your life up'. The poem 'Hands' finds images of accommodation to the work by the body with moving personal detail that catches either strength or delicacy, as the work requires it. Hands that were typically huge for a farmer in the opening of the poem are, in death, the elegant hands of the farmer's mother at the end of the poem. In this collection such poems are more than a poet's elegies to his wife's father. They are icons of value in Hughes's larger project of asking how our species might live at home on its home planet. In *Moortown Diaries* the earlier myths that explored this question have come home to roost, finding one kind of answer in the engagement that is farming. When that iconic figure dies the responsibility seems to be reversed, such was the depth of the relationship: 'From now on the land / Will have to manage without him'.

Season Songs and *Flowers and Insects*

It is typical of Ted Hughes to say of *Season Songs* (1976, second edition 1985) that they 'began as children's poems, but they grew up'. He was aware that many poems that might have begun in a book project for children had a power for adults that should not be underestimated. Indeed, some critics have given close attention to the linguistic invention and healing function of the best of these poems. While Hughes's contribution to children's literature will be considered in a separate section below, it seems appropriate here to describe the qualities of two collections that contain what must be regarded as the serious work of a poet not only at the height of his powers, but pursuing his poetic project as an ever-curious mediator of our relationship with nature. *Season Songs* and *Flowers and Insects* (1986) should not, in other words, be regarded as anything other than an extension that has grown quite naturally out of the poet's core preoccupations.

Season Songs had its origin in 'Five Autumn Songs for Children' written for the Little Missenden Harvest Festival in 1968. It then became *Spring, Summer,*

Autumn, Winter in a 1974 Rainbow Press limited edition before expanding into the beautifully illustrated American (Viking) edition of 1975 that preceded the 1976 Faber edition. Fuller still is the second Faber edition of 1985.

While some of the poems in *Season Songs* are in the form of songs obviously written for children, their agendas are far from sentimental. 'Leaves', which is based on 'Who Killed Cock Robin?', uses a simple rhymed four-line stanza to deal with the death process at work in the leaves of autumn. The question 'Who'll make their shroud?' is answered by the swallow, saying, 'there's just time enough / Before I must pack my spools and be off'. The movement of swallows is seen as sewing in the air after the reader has been made to think for a moment on the word 'spools'. Thus the leaving of swallows is integrated into the emotional sense of loss in autumn that is focused upon the death of leaves.

The experience of people, and children in particular, is also integrated into the sense of a season's qualities in a poem such as 'Work and Play' in which the natural images of summer are contrasted with the polluting serpent of cars heading to and from the beach. One of the simplest texts, 'The Warm and the Cold', finds striking similes for the way creatures can be warmly at home in a winter in which, in the opening lines, 'Freezing dusk is closing / Like a slow trap of steel'. After three long stanzas of similes such as 'the badger in its bedding / Like a loaf in the oven', the final three lines introduce humans for the first time in a surprisingly ambiguous way: 'The sweating farmers / Turn in their sleep / Like oxen on spits'. It seems that the heat found by the farmers to counter this deep frost is as disturbing to them as is the frost itself to 'the flimsy moon' that the rhyme offers as comparison: she has 'lost her wits'. Even farmers who are closest to nature are in danger of losing their wits in trying to adapt to the winter's deep night frost. The spits the farmers turn on, then, are both their dreams and their heat, neither of which can quite find as satisfactory a balance in these conditions as nature's other creatures.

Elsewhere in this book, Hughes draws upon his familiarity with creation myths to create a breathtaking image of the rightness of a single part of nature. In 'Autumn Nature Notes', for example, as the chestnut's conker 'opens an African eye', Hughes turns back to the source in a perfect image of the creator as master-craftsman: 'A cabinet-maker, an old master, / In the root of things, has done it again'. But the poem then rejects the human for the mythical, giving dignity to 'a royal tree / That does not know about conkers / Or the war-games of boys'. Unknowing of our constructs, or our uses of its seeds, and seemingly independent of our gardens, this tree will reign over them for two hundred years.

This sense of the annual reappearance of signs of the seasons is given the significance of reassurance in 'Swifts', where the simple excitement of the date of their reappearance, as they 'materialise at the tip of a long scream', gives way to the reflection, 'They've made it again, / Which means the globe's still working'. There is a poetic shift here that is linguistically exhilarating – from the brilliant detail of the earlier phrase that encapsulates the swifts' sudden appearance out of nowhere into our lives that apprehend them as a speed that is a sound, to the larger perspective in which 'global' is both size and time. This can come in the briefest of phrases, such as 'Spring bulges the hills' in 'Spring Nature Notes', or in the huge sweep in two lines about 'Swallows': 'So she exchanged the starry chart of Columbus / For a beggar's bowl of mud.' Again, there is a delayed effect in realising what the mud bowl, that might still be associated with the African images from a few lines earlier, actually is and how, exactly, it is exchanged. So the exhilaration for the reader of becoming aware of the range of the poet's grasp is, in effect, an uncompromising demand that the reader make an effort of comprehension that produces an almost spiritual enlargement of the reader's sensibility.

What, for example, is a 'December River'? 'This vein from the sky is the sea-spirit's pathway.' That is more than a whole water-cycle in a single line of poetry. It is an enlarging sense of the spirit of water as it mutates from sky to river to sea in one 'vein' of life. That this is a 'vein' inhabited by the salmon that make an appearance half-way through the poem is almost an unexpected addition. But once again, a depth of understanding drives the language of the poetry. Coming up fifty miles of river to spawn, the salmon have negotiated the force of water against them 'With love-madness for strength, / Weightlifting through all its chimneys of tonnage'. This language has been earned by observation, but is infused with an almost religious awe for the vitality in the fish that achieves heroic feats through its reproductive force. That this is also a journey towards death is suddenly seen in the grimace of a dead salmon that seems to express the satisfaction 'Of getting right through to the end and beyond it'. That last phrase is not a nod towards religious transcendence, but the material evidence of this salmon now taking part in 'earth's already beginning mastication'. The intervention of the poet in burying the salmon, in a trench in the pool it is being swirled in, is less satisfactory. Earlier he has admitted daily fishing through the summer for salmon from this pool: 'I offered all I had for a touch of their wealth– / I found only endlessly empty water'. 'But I go now, in near-darkness, / Frost, and close to Christmas, and am admitted' to the presence of this dead salmon. The humbled stance that is associated with being admitted to the Christ child (who is to be crucified) hardly mitigates the leisure pursuit of the fisherman who now wants 'to get it / Wedged properly mine'. The line break is, perhaps, the giveaway to the poet's possessiveness.

This is an issue more properly addressed in relation to the many fishing poems in *River* (see Criticism, **p. 146**). The humbled observer is the stance most commonly adopted by the poet in both *Season Songs* and *Flowers and Insects*. 'Eclipse', for example, from the latter book, has the poet looking through a magnifying glass at two spiders mating in a mode that is 'horribly happy'. This long poem describes an observation of more than half an hour. The detail of the minute operation is probably unique in poetry as it hovers between precise description and uncertainty about what is actually happening. It is therefore nature poetry at the very edge of the comprehension of the poet, outflanking even his most attentive efforts. This poem is another form of poetic trial, a test of the poet's integrity, out beyond any sense of easy descriptive poetry for children. The poet's expectations and assumptions are continuously challenged by the minute activity in front of him. He is expecting to witness 'the famous murder' of the male by the female once mating has taken place. But just when he thinks it is over another series of elaborate operations take place. The poet's huge humble human patience is exhausted, and out of his sight either murder, or 'still some days of bliss to come', are being enacted beyond his awareness.

Of course, this trial is essentially a test of the poet's formal resources. He has to repeatedly ask questions to admit that 'something / Difficult to understand, difficult / To observe was going on'. The line that has the word 'difficult' at each end makes a formal emphasis that inextricably links the disciplines of understanding and observation. But what is remarkable is the way Hughes uses the mechanical images (as in 'the globe's still working' from 'Swifts') to convey the detailed organic workings of natural processes. What appears to be grotesque in the female spider's 'hideously dexterous' use of 'her boxing-glove nippers' is described as being 'like the mechanical hands / That manipulate radio-active matter'. The delicate sensitivity of the spider's actions is as crucial to her reproductive success as if she were handling fissile material because she is actually squeezing in her 'crab-nippers' the 'nipple cock' of the male to take from it 'a bubble of glistening clear glue'. Far from being reductively mechanical, the similes taken from scientific manipulations add to the sense of the marvellous being revealed by the poetry. Here is a creature 'Making no error after millions of years / Perfecting this art'. Again the line break delivers two slightly different statements that are unified in their workings. She cannot afford to make an error at this precise moment after so long leading up to it. On the other hand, this is not the art of a particular spider, not 'her art', but 'this art' that has taken so long to evolve towards perfection.

This long, complex act of procreation has taken place among a 'whole rubbish tip of carcases' of insects eaten by the female spider. The poet leaves the two spiders as they have left him, out of sight somewhere beyond the window-frame that also frames rain. He imagines them sharing with him a sense of 'rejoicing / As the sun's edge, behind the clouds, / Comes clear of our shadow'. The dualities at work in the poetry here are left to stand for the dualities of procreation and death that have been balanced by the poem's absorbing drama for what seems to have been an age. Not all of the poems in these two volumes are charged with this level of intensity and thematic reach, although usually they are aware of being a part of those larger processes. That these descriptive nature poems may have 'begun as children's poems and they grew up', now seems unimportant to their impact as dramas of the largest and most vital tensions in the cycles of nature.

River

With the publication of *River* in 1983, some followers of the work of Ted Hughes felt that his poetic career had reached its apex (see Criticism, **p. 141**). Indeed, only two further major collections of poetry were to be published before his death in 1998. *Wolfwatching* (1989) was an apparently ad hoc collection of recent work of the kind with which he had begun in *The Hawk in the Rain*, and *Birthday Letters* (1998) was, of course, a quite different kind of work that some have argued to be slightly aside from the poetic project of Hughes's life's work. So, following *Remains of Elmet* and *Moortown Diary*, *River* was the last themed collection of his own work to engage directly with humans' relationship with the forces of the natural world. The iconic figure of that relationship in *River* is the most primitive – the fisherman hunter, but in his most self-conscious mode as the twentieth-century poet himself.

Just as fishing had always been a part of Hughes's life, so too had a river. Although the two rivers of his childhood – first the River Calder in West Yorkshire, then the River Don in South Yorkshire – were so polluted that they contained few fish, Hughes fished in the canal alongside the first and in an oxbow lake beside the second, as he points out in a Note on the *River* poems when they were revised and reordered in *Three Books* (1993). In Devon, Hughes's village, North Tawton, takes its name from the River Taw, one of the rivers flowing from Dartmoor that appear in this book. Of course, the symbolic value of a river as a 'vein' in the life of the 'sea-spirit' that regulates our globe, has already been noted in the poem 'December River' in *Season Songs*. So this collection is, for Hughes, about more than just his most intimately known part of our environment. It is also about a key indicator of the state of our relationship with our home. By adding his Notes Hughes made this clear in his later, more radical version of *River* in *Three Books* where, in addition to the Notes, thirteen poems were added and nine poems omitted from the original version now reproduced in *Collected Poems*.

As might be expected from the writer of *Season Songs* and *Flowers and Insects*, Hughes celebrates the carefully observed lives of the inhabitants of rivers in his freshly minted metaphors and similes that reach for an appreciation of the essential qualities of these creatures. The kingfisher is 'a sudden electric wire, jarred rigid'; the legs of the moorhen 'are still primeval– / Toy-grotesque'; 'out of his glowing exhaustion' the mayfly 'heals a giddy mote'. The otter that is its subject is not even mentioned in the poem titled 'Visitation'. It is the river's playful 'twists' at night that leave only 'these pad-clusters on mud-margins / One dawn in a year, her eeriest flower'. In this brief selection of conceits there is much more than visual description evoked. Uniqueness, the primeval, healing and mystery each deepen the reader's attention.

Although most of the rivers in this collection are those of Devon, rivers in Alaska, Canada, Ireland, Scotland and elsewhere in England indicate the range of the poet's experience as a fisherman. In particular there are poems concerned with different states of rivers, most obviously from 'High Water' to 'Low Water', but also there are poems in which the state of the river is expressed as a relationship with the land, as in 'Fairy Flood'. In this poem a fairy daughter is eloping from 'the fatherly landscape', 'Bleeding him empty remorselessly'. In 'Last Night', on the other hand, 'the drought river of slimes' suggests 'something evil about the sunken river / In its sick bed darkness'. But there is also the frisson of standing in a river that is vibrating with the fullness of its life, as in the poet's experience of a river in British Columbia after heavy rains in 'The Bear': 'all the giddy orgasm of the river / Quaking under our feet'. At this heightened moment the vision of a dead bear is carried past the poet in the river like a 'sea-going … scapegoat, an offering', presumably for the experience of the river's orgasm.

In his Notes to *Three Books*, Hughes recalls something strange happening to his oxbow lake in South Yorkshire and tracing the source of the new stench that killed fish to a stone shed containing 'sodden, dark-stained grass – reeking the new smell. It was the first silage'. This was in the 'early 1940s'. In a poem titled '1984 on "The Tarka Trail"', the first part describes following the tourist 'trail' of the river made famous by Henry Williamson's book *Tarka the Otter* which had fascinated Hughes as a child. Hughes had first met Williamson twenty years earlier and spoke at his memorial service (published in Sewell 1980). By 1984 pure chemicals were draining from the farmland into the rivers of North Devon: 'surfactants, ammonia, phosphates – the whole banquet / Flushed in by sporadic thunderbursts'. Here is a sewer that cannot be scoured out 'enough to resurrect a river'. Hughes makes the point in this poem that 'you cannot leave this hospital' because the corn farmer, with the support of 'The Min. of Ag. And Fish', 'heaps the poisons into you too'. The increased herds of milking cows upstream have also increased the problems of slurry and silage: ninety cows produce 'oozing effluent "equal to the untreated / Sewage of a city the size of Gloucester"'.

The hard facts of this poem do not neglect the facts about the corn farmer himself – he is named Peter. He is a 'nature protector', keeping 'lush hedge-banks', 'carefully nursed / Neglected nettles', and is a keen birdwatcher. Yet he pours chemicals – 'pesticides, herbicides, fungicides' – over his corn 'thirteen times / Between the drill and the reaper', to pay for private schools for his children, the poet reports.

The second part of this poem is titled 'Nymet' and it begins and ends with the etymology of names for this river. What might at first appear to be a more literary poem, quickly indicts 'the radioactive Irish Sea', the South West Water Authority and the Express Dairy Cheese Factory, each of which 'uses' this river that might also be named 'Sewer / (More truly: The Washer at the Ford. / As in the old story. / The death-rags she washes and washes are ours.)'. As the poem 'If' puts it, 'If you have infected the sky and the earth / Caught its disease off you – you are the virus'. If the 'five rivers of Paradise' are now the running sores of the earth's sickness, there is no longer any healing 'pure drink' available: 'Already you are your ditch, and there you drink'. ('If' was included in the *River* sequence only in *Three Books*.)

These two hard-hitting poems, however, do not dominate the collection. That claim must go to a few poems about the ecology and mythology of salmon, most notably two poems that should be seen as a pair. Hughes opened the selection of the *River* poems in *Three Books* with 'Salmon Eggs' and placed near the end the poem about death, 'October Salmon'. 'Salmon Eggs' uses religious imagery at its climax to suggest the sacred in the long birth process at the end of the salmon's epic journey from birth-pool to sea to its own birth-pool again. Again, the Note about the ecology of Atlantic salmon in *Three Books* is helpful to a full appreciation of this process. On the 'time-riven altar' of the river's bedrock, eggs are laid where there are also 'the sunk foundations / Of dislocated crypts' since the female salmon will also die here. 'And this is the liturgy / Of Earth's coming – harrowing, crowned – a travail / Of raptures and rendings.' The balances, delicately held in juxtaposition here, are part of an elemental momentum that the poetry catches deftly with its two lines beginning with 'Of'. This momentum is a crucial sign of the essential process of 'Earth's coming', our environment in a healthy state of regeneration. It is not surprising that this should be regarded as sacred, another statement of what our Christian culture mythologises in stories that might be evoked by the two words, 'harrowing, crowned'. The pain of the cost within the celebration of the 'crowning' of the cycle is perceived by the poet as experienced by the river itself when he writes that it is 'undergoing itself / In its wheel', just as 'the sun rolls' and 'the earth rolls'. This is all so hard to fully comprehend that the poet turns his attention aside and ends with the line, 'And mind condenses on old haws'.

While the river's whorls in 'Salmon Eggs' say, '*Only birth matters*', the male salmon in 'October Salmon' is worn out in earth's 'insatiable quest' that was 'inscribed in his egg'. Now he rides the river to his death, already dressed in the decay he is living, 'his whole body / A fungoid anemone of canker'. Now there is no glorious religious imagery since he's with 'bicycle wheels, car-tyres, bottles' in the river where people walking dogs 'trail their evening shadows across him'. But in the final stanza Hughes produces another memorable image of the marvellous balance at work in the earth's energies here, 'the torn richness' that includes the presence of human rubbish. This, writes Hughes, is 'The epic poise / That holds him so steady in his wounds, so loyal to his doom, so patient / In the machinery of heaven'. The verbs catch that poise before the long gap testing patience at the line break tumbles into the unlikely but completely right combination of 'machinery' and 'heaven'. So this, too, is sacred as the complementary other – October, male, sub-urban, death-orientated – half of the cycle initiated by 'Salmon Eggs'.

In *Three Books* placed next to the poem 'If' about human neglect of responsibility for the planet's health is its antidote, the poem titled 'Go Fishing'. The imperative of the title is to undergo a transformation in the river, to 'be assumed' as if by creation itself, 'a wound' in this poem, for which 'this flow were all plasm healing'. In this poem there is no suggestion of actually doing any fishing. That experience is described in several others. In Alaska, beside 'the furnace boom of the Gulkana', the alien river produces a fear in the poet of something he decides is in himself, the fool he always hated who, for three days, can do no more than 'scratch the windows of the express torrent'. On the plane home, the voice of the river 'moved in me', 'a deeper / Waking in my body'. In England, 'a routing flood-storm' in the poem 'Salmon-Taking Times' modulates into the river's having 'a wedding delicacy' that is 'like a religious moment, slightly dazing'. For the hunter of salmon in the poem 'Earth-Numb', 'the lure is a prayer', but this poem is one in which the hunter is most disturbed by a sense of being hunted. The poem itself has disturbed some readers who are critical of the death of the fish that is described with some empathy by the fisherman (Moody 1987; see Criticism, **p. 146**).

At readings Hughes introduced this poem as having been written on the eve of the fishing season as a way of conjuring a good encounter with a fish the following day. It is therefore a hunter's way of tuning in to the right way to approach the hunt and, as such, it might stand as one representation of a right relationship with a particular environment and its potential food. The humility of the hunter who might also be hunted is thus an essential recognition of the ecology of food-chains. The tension of the dawn created by the grammar of the lines of the first stanza, each of which is broken by a parenthesis, engenders a first alertness. 'The river's black canyons' are imagined as a necessary precaution against stepping into them. When the fish bites, the poet imagines 'A mouth-flash, an electrocuting malice / Like a trap, trying to rip life off me'. So the terror is reciprocated: it 'Gleam-surges to and fro through me' between the sky and the river. But, although the odds are not in the fisherman's favour entirely, when 'the fright flows all one way down the line', the fish is already the 'ghost' that 'grows solid', hovering and slithering between water and land.

Hughes puts himself in the position of the fish in the final lines of the poem in a manner that seems intended as a mode of respect and reality, an honouring of the death-process. The phrase, 'trying to think on shallows', for example, while it will provoke outrage in some readers, is perhaps intended as the instinctive honest empathy of the hunter for his prey. 'The eyes of incredulity' are what is perceived in the salmon by this attentive fisherman, who is partly satisfied that the 'fix' of 'their death-exposure' is on 'the celandine and the cloud'. To end the poem with this line is to return the whole encounter to its larger environment and its creative/destructive networks of relationships, of which the fisherman poet is inevitably a fully conscious and alert part.

Wolfwatching

Wolfwatching (1989) is the last unthemed collection of poetry that Hughes was to produce as he became absorbed by translation and the preparation of *Birthday Letters* in the final decade of his life. But carefully structured as ever, beginning with the predator, 'A Sparrow Hawk', and ending with that 'love-whip', 'A Dove', *Wolfwatching* pivots about 'The Black Rhino', written in support of the environmental campaign to save the species from extinction researched by an old friend, Martin Booth – the Rhino Rescue scheme in Kenya. But these three poems are hardly representative since more than half the poems in *Wolfwatching* are actually about family memories and family members. Even Sitting Bull appears to be 'on the reservations' of the defunct South Yorkshire coalfield and astrological conundrums seem to start in the trees, ferns and wet mossy rocks that might be West Yorkshire's Hardcastle Crags, recalled from the poet's childhood. What is remarkable about this volume is that there is no division between poems about wild creatures and celebrations of family members, about animal spirits and family spirits, about the vivid present and the past that is embedded in it, about concern for the loss of wild species and the loss of family spectres. In the ecology of Ted Hughes, human life and its culture is an aspect of nature whether the poetic mode in use in *Wolfwatching* is personal, mythic or parodic.

'Compassionate wisdom, unforced gentle strength, a new humility and deeper humanity' – these are the qualities that Keith Sagar finds in *Wolfwatching* (2000: 31). This may well be a positive representation of what Olwyn Hughes has referred to as 'that saddest of all the books' saying, 'I read it again after the funeral. I didn't realise how sad it was' (letter to T.G., 11. 10. 2003). One could argue that what Sagar sees as the 'compassion, new humility and deeper humanity' derives in large part from that very sadness, from the depth of explicit grief in *Wolfwatching*. It is possible to see grief, or absences of different kinds, expressed in every one of the poems in the collection. Certainly it is explicit in every poem of the first half of the book and the poet is himself aware of and slightly bemused by this. 'Where did all those tears come from?' asks the first line of 'Source', a poem that conducts a search for an answer. Olwyn Hughes confirms that it is about the poet's mother, Edith. It is a profoundly moving poem asking what the function of unbidden weeping ('Your tears didn't care. / They'd come looking for you') can be in the life of a woman who is happy. The answer to this conundrum lies, the poet senses, in 'connecting yourself / To something beyond life, a mourning / That repaired you / And was necessary.' Late in his life, the poet is returning in this poem to a sadness he found in his mother 'before my schooldays' that 'Could dissolve yourself, me, everything / Into this relief of your strange music'. Suddenly one somehow understands why the previous poem, 'Telegraph Wires' ends with the strange conclusion that is almost called forth by the rhyme, something that: 'Draws out of the telegraph wires the tones / That empty human bones'. Apparently 'The ear hears, and withers!' because what it hears are 'Such unearthly airs'. An apprehension of the 'beyond life' in Wolfwatching leads to weeping, but that may also be healing, a necessary 'mourning / That repaired you'.

The sparrowhawk that opens the collection is a return to very old ground in the image of the mythic hunched warrior, although he is evoked in a very modern discourse with his 'sun's cooled carbon wing' and his 'laser' eyes, 'Still wired direct / To the nuclear core'. These are actually modern words for our conceptions of nature's working mysteries. And it is the elusive mystery of the sparrowhawk, its 'overtaking thought' as a being beyond words, that dominates the poem. On the one hand, the alert sharpness of the predator is still how most things live in a post-Darwinian world. On the other, this is not simply the 'selfish gene' at work (Dawkins 1978). It is a creature with a way of both slipping away from your eye-corner and 'materialising by twilight and dew' as its mode of being. Which is how we get to 'the oaks of the harp'. Here is not the thunder of the falcon 'filling the doorway / In the shell of earth', but the gentler, more elusive music of mythic truth-telling in the bardic harp of the sparrowhawk's oak wood. Hughes deviates from conventional ornithological spelling (sparrowhawk) in his title, reminding us that this is really the 'Sparrow Hawk', smallest and most modestly ambitious of its genus Accipitridae (which includes the eagles and vultures). The collection's tone of absence and lament has been set in a poem that apparently sets out to celebrate, with modern rhetoric, a 'wired' predator.

Questions about predation are answered by 'The Fool's Evil Dream', the first of 'Two Astrological Conundrums' that follow 'A Sparrow Hawk'. Actually, in these poems there is no pastoral green cycle of birth and decay, despite the rhetoric of 'rocks sticking through their moss jerseys' and the 'fish-still-alive-from-their-weed-river smells'. At a personal, spirit level, the poet suggests, there can only ever be weeping at the fact that it is the infant that the tiger takes. There is only the giving of everything because the impulse to escape death by procreation can only ultimately lead to the deaths of first parent, then infant. But that is part one of two cosmic conundrums. In the second dream, the modern technology of the steel bow is the frame of the bardic harp. Sometimes, this poem suggests, hesitation with that bow takes all your strength as you begin to see that really the star in the Raven's eye at which you've taken aim is the whole universe – with you in it, wondering what voice is reminding you that you are in it. These are conundrums that can perhaps only be understood at certain astrological moments of conjuncture, at rare moments by rare seers. But the mysterious source and force of the weeping should cause at the least some strenuous hesitation in loosing the technological arrows of desire.

If the source of the deep grief in this collection originates for the poet 'before my schooldays', the poem 'Slump Sundays' makes it clear that the absence of the souls left behind at the Somme has produced a sense of defeat in those returning, like his father: 'Inhaling it, I came to / Under a rainy ridge'. Even more knowingly, the poem 'Dust As We Are' explains why the poet's soul was fed with the silent, suppressed grief of his father's generation. So we understand why the following poem, 'Wolfwatching', demonstrates what is happening to the poet in this collection. Wolfwatching is what Hughes does well, enjoys doing, at length, and returns to, like the old wolf of the poem. His writing directly in front of the caged creature becomes an observational meditation characterised by a single new word (letter to Sagar, 21. 4. 1977, BL ADD 78756, f. 69). But in this poem the young wolf's hopefulness turns to hopelessness before our eyes. An incredibly rich genetic inheritance is erased by the boredom engendered from our contemporary way of treating wild nature. He is in a zoo as an icon left 'between nothing and nothing'. One cannot help recognising a knowingness in the lines, 'The day won't pass. / The night will be worse.' Deeply felt tired grief clearly underlies this, suggesting a continuity between the poet's personal experience of grief, the family grief, the generational grief, the community grief, the grief of industrial work and world wars in the Calder Valley (see Works, p. 48) and the grief of the caged wolf, symbol of the treatment of so many species on the earth and in the rivers, as of the planet itself.

So it seems that before we arrive at the poem 'The Black Rhino', the poet wants us to understand the accommodation to grief of his original community and his own sensibility. The 'seed-corn' of tales brought back from the killing fields, past and present, serves as a common mother-tongue that is, of course, located in the lived landscape of the victims and the survivors, and their guilt. Only the poet's depth of understanding and respect lift these poems from their anguish. Yet it is from this grief and anguish that the impulse for an environmental responsibility towards the future lies. Anguish for the future potential absences drives conservation and the pain of environmental degradation should be reflected in poetry, as Hughes made clear in his interview with Vic Allen in 1990. Allen wrote in the *Sunday Telegraph* (18. 11. 1990):

> Hughes talks so plainly about the danger of neglecting the environment that it seems remiss that poetry has played so little part in alerting people to it. Perhaps poetry was not up to such a painful job? 'There are plenty of painful things in Heathcote Williams's books,' says Hughes. 'That's probably why they work. Quite a lot of poetry is just that, isn't it? The voice of hurt. That's part of its truth.'

So the voicing of hurt is presented in *Wolfwatching* as potentially the beginning of a healing process, a necessary 'mourning that repaired you'.

'The Black Rhino' is another 'wolfwatching' poem (although it is likely that this time it is the poet who is caged, in a car). Yet the weight of knowledge about its ancient history and its recent exploitation turns the opening part of the poem into a parody of observation through the lens of a video camera. The second part is a cooler, shorter-lined dream dialogue in which, although the

'man'/narrator's analysis of the ironies of the sacrifice of the rhino for its sup-
posed healing properties is sympathetic to the rhino, the rhino's reply overrides
ethical/cultural analysis with the simple statement 'You are the crime'. The
third part of the poem is an intense wheeling about in anguish, a fast filmic
sweep of atrocities, in the long lines that some reviewers such as John Lucas felt
'not to be poem enough' (*Times Literary Supplement* 20. 10. 1989, p. 1148)
despite its imagistic, vivid language. But the poem slows to an almost casual
conclusion: 'The Black Rhino / Is vanishing // Into a soft / Human laugh'. The
'soft' laugh of the unknowing is the opposite of the knowing laughter of foxes
in the *Elmet* poem 'Chinese History of Colden Water' (see Works, p. 51). It is
perhaps not even as knowing as the laughter that covers anxiety and guilt at the
end of 'Dust As We Are' where the poet is speaking of his own growing soul
fed by an awareness of 'the massacre of innocents': 'A strange thing, with
rickets – a hyena. / No singing – that kind of laughter'.

At the end of Hughes's note on *Wolfwatching* for *The Poetry Book Society
Bulletin* he enigmatically left a question hanging in the air: 'The only question
(insofar as there is a question at all), why consult just these familiars at just this
time?' (142, Autumn 1989, p. 3). By 'these familiars' Hughes obviously refers to
what he has just been discussing in the previous paragraphs: tributes to family
members, rhino, whale and 'my old schoolfriends in the South Yorks coal belt'
in 'On the Reservations'. By following 'Anthem for Doomed Youth' with an
anthem for the doomed Black Rhino, Hughes has explicitly demonstrated the
continuity between hunting and war, people and planet, family memories and
the dodo, the 'portly birds' of his adolescent dream that 'broke' in the doomed
future of his environmental grief and anguish. (On 13 July 2006 the *Guardian*
reported that the West African black rhino appeared to have become extinct.)

Wolfwatching seems to be asking the question, 'For what was all this long
personal suffering in families following the First World War if we cannot now
engage the "environmental war" (Hughes's own phrase: Gifford 1995: 130)
necessary for the survival of ourselves, our culture and our fellow creatures?'
The doomed youth of the poet's father's generation paid the price that enabled the
poet, brought up by the anguished survivors, to confront the doomed planet.
Interventions such as writing 'The Black Rhino' in support of a conservation
campaign indicate the way grief can begin the repairing process through creativity. Conservation recognises that the elements of the power circuit are out of
balance and takes responsibility for loss. It is propelled by grief in the face of an
increasing absence that it seeks to heal, or at least ameliorate.

The poems that follow 'The Black Rhino' in *Wolfwatching* each take on a
resonance beyond their apparent specific focus. It is tempting to see certain lines
and phrases in each of the remaining poems as now relating back to the kind of
concerns lying behind 'The Black Rhino'. 'She grieved for her girlhood and the
fallen. / You mourned for Paradise and its fable' ('Leaf Mould'); 'We stand,
nervous. Metaphors / Fail the field of force' ('Manchester Skytrain'); 'Nothing
will connect. / He peers down past his shoes / Into a tangle of horizons – //
Black, tilted bedrock struggling up, / Mouthing disintegration' ('Walt'); 'Take
What You Want But Pay For It'; the despair of the extinct fossil and the soon
to be extinct whale; the bitter satire of communities left like American Indian
lives 'On the Reservations' in the aftermath of the collapse of the Yorkshire

coal industry (his second childhood home); the final convulsions of 'A Dove' that lead to the last line of a collection that began with absence in the presence of the sparrowhawk and ends with a realisation that demands repairing interventions.

For the final conundrum is that grief for the loss of the honourable spirits of elders and the vital spirits of sparrowhawk, black rhino, iconic whale and disintegrating earth, is driven by the roller coaster of 'the love-whip', a force that we must realise cannot be invested only in each individual because it leads 'Into one and many'. These final words of the collection lead back to the notion of ecology and its complex but unavoidable challenges. In the conundrum of 'Into one and many' lies the potential for healing, 'a mourning / That repaired you / And was necessary'. By suggesting that readers of *Wolfwatching* ask, 'why consult just these familiars at just this time?' Hughes was hinting that perhaps this collection throws down a challenge for our times.

Rain-Charm for the Duchy and other Laureate Poems

In 1984 Ted Hughes was made Poet Laureate in what was generally agreed, especially by fellow poets, to be an appropriate appointment. Hughes had a sense of the symbolic role of royalty and of the symbolism of nationhood that was embedded in the natural life of the land that had always been his subject. In 1977, in commemoration of the Queen's Silver Jubilee, Hughes had written, along with Larkin, four lines to be set in the pavement outside the offices of Faber and Faber in Queen's Square, London, in which he had celebrated the role of the crown at the hub of the nation's soul 'to keep it whole'. Hughes responded fulsomely to the symbolism embedded in the poetic opportunities offered by the royal occasions for which he might write – births, marriages and deaths – that, again, had been the most important symbols in his poetic work to date. In 1992 Hughes published a collection of Laureate poems under the title of the first he had written, *Rain-Charm for the Duchy and other Laureate Poems* and with a series of Notes attempted to explain the notions behind some of these difficult poems. The Queen's Square quatrain forms the epigraph under the title 'Solomon's Dream'. A dream of national wholeness is one thing, but whether it is wise to base it upon the symbolic role of the Crown in the Britain of 1992 is a question that hangs behind this collection as it reveals such unswerving poetic enthusiasm for its function.

When the appointment was made in early December 1984 there was an immediate opportunity – an implicit challenge to the new Laureate – for a poem to celebrate the christening of Prince Harry on 21 December. The poem Hughes produced for the occasion, 'A Rain-Charm for the Duchy, A Blessed Devout Drench for the Christening of His Royal Highness Prince Harry', is quite unlike any others he subsequently wrote, probably because it was actually a clever adaptation of something which had originally been intended for the *River* collection. A long drought is broken by a thunderstorm in Exeter as the poet sitting in his car watches a girl run through the torrential rain, watches dark tors 'dragged over the city' and thinks, not of the barley, but of the larvae, the mosses, the dried rivers of the region being brought back to their full lives. In a litany of names each is evoked in a thumbnail sketch that includes images ranging from cherubs to detergent bottles and sounds ranging from the rumbling of wagons to the trundling of Pepsi-Cola cans. In a Note Hughes explains that these are the rivers of the Duchy. The climax of the poem seems to become explicit about its role for a christening as the two moors, Dartmoor and Exmoor, that are the source of these rivers, hold up their 'stone-age hands' full of water as an offering. But the poet's mind is not on Westminster Abbey: 'I thought of those other, different lightnings, the patient, thirsting ones' that turn out to be the salmon waiting to be able to come up these rivers to spawn. In the last phrase of the poem they are 'beginning to move'.

This was a bold first poem that offered the momentum of the cycle of salmon rejuvenation to the 'promise' inherent in a christening, linking the two through both a symbolic drenching and a realistic drenching. All the Laureate's subsequent attempts to put the realistic at the service of the symbolic never quite achieved such a grounded sense of a reality that was actually experienced by the Royal Family's ordinary subjects. The symbolic came to dominate and with it the elaboration of arcane modes drawing upon astrology, mythology, British history, Shakespeare's imagery, Sioux and Sufi stories and heraldic iconography. The detailed Notes for *Rain-Charm for the Duchy* show Hughes utilising all his accumulated knowledge as a trained anthropologist in his role as national mythmaker. Hughes resurrected the notion of the royal masque in poems that were a series of tableaux of images. He made rhyming songs for royal children in a variety of forms. In these poems the members of the Royal Family are reified as unquestionably wise and exercising an unvaryingly happy and harmonious rule over their people. 'The tabloid howl that tops the charts' can be dismissed, apparently, because 'Britain', in the fortieth year of her reign, 'Laughs with the Queen and keeps her wise'. This is the message of the poem 'Falstaff' that is the second part of 'The Unicorn', written for the fortieth anniversary of the Queen's accession. In the simple assertions of symbolic equivalence that is typical of these poems, Falstaff simply is Britain. He is the 'Licensed Clown', as Hughes puts it, therefore it is presumably guaranteed by whoever granted this license that he, the 'Britain' of this poem, laughs with the Queen and not at her. Even in 1992 most ardent monarchists would not think the world was that simple.

In the third poem of this sequence, the Queen's sleeping lion is her people who will only awake to defend her in wartime. But 'to be near' (which is rhymed with 'war'), 'His colour runs / Into her corgis'. To heap bathos upon bathos, the Queen's corgis are the 'imps' of the sleeping lion. In the final line of the fifth and final poem of this sequence, some of her people see in 'the Crown ... their life'. This is actually the last line of the collection and therefore has the force of suggesting that the Queen's subjects owe their lives to the monarch. This is more than saying that royalty is 'one sacred certainty that all can share'. It is more than suggesting that the Queen Mother had borne 'the events of such a century / Some ask if the earth herself can bear it'. The conclusion of this collection ignores the calls for attention to the inner life of the individual of *Cave Birds*, for a critical examination of our culture's assumptions in *Crow*, for an awareness of our culture's integration with nature in *Remains of Elmet*, for our culture to take responsibility for its relationship with nature in *Moortown Diary* and in *River*. In this collection 'villains, disasters in the sun' cannot 'trouble one / Who has done what she has done'. The people, it seems, should simply, fatalistically, invest the integrity of their lives in the Crown.

Birthday Letters, Howls and Whispers and Capriccio

Hughes spoke about writing his own version of the events in his life with Sylvia Plath in an interview in 1989, when he said that this version would be published anonymously (Wright 1999: 9). Ten years before, in 1979, the first of the *Birthday Letters* poems, 'You Hated Spain', had been published. In 1995 he published eight of these poems about Plath in *New Selected Poems 1957–1994*, but remained indecisive about whether to publish the whole collection, which was ready at that time. Although the Faber edition dust-jacket indicates that 'they were written over a period of more than twenty-five years, the first a few years after her suicide in 1963', Paul Muldoon, among others, believes, quite erroneously, that the 'tonal consistency' suggests that they were written 'within one time frame ... perhaps even at one sitting' (2006: 34). Against this Hughes wrote to Joanny Moulin that 'They were written in all kinds of ways, different times, different approaches. (I never thought of them as a sequence.)' (Moulin 1999a: 142). Actually they were revised right up to final publication. What sadly seems clear is that following the publication of *Birthday Letters* in 1998, nine months before his death, he finally regretted not having published the book earlier, since he believed that the delay had been 'blocking' his imaginative life. Certainly he felt a huge release when the book was published, finding that 'I suddenly had free energy I hadn't known since *Crow*' (*Letters* 720). The book's popular reception brought Hughes a new generation of readers who might have been surprised to find that this volume is not typical of his output. But its importance to both the poet and his reputation cannot be ignored. It is a remarkably brave and moving collection displaying a confident ease with tone and form.

This book is a return to the fundamental notion at the heart of *Cave Birds*: that individuals must take responsibility for their inner life, even though they may be observing, in a *Crow*-like way, whatever bizarre events the fates have drawn them into. The belief in fate is established early in *Birthday Letters* as Hughes describes his first encounters with Plath. Almost immediately they 'went in a barrel together / Over some Niagara', clearly not knowing, as in any marriage, quite what they were getting into. The scar on Plath's cheek gave the clue to her previous suicide attempt, but although Hughes heard the warning of a 'sober star' to 'stay clear', his fascination is so strong that he echoes John Donne in finding in his lover's body 'my new world' (24). For Hughes, the American Fulbright scholar was, in Donne's pun, 'my new found land'. But the passion of Plath's love is given a more ambiguous quality from the beginning. Triggered by the death of Plath's father when she was eight years old, her relationship with a male lover is characterised as 'a shot' in the poem of that title, giving the cliché a sinister edge. In this poem Hughes suggests that for a long time he did not realise that Plath's bullet of love had actually gone through him to the real target – her father – who was the invisible presence behind Hughes. Precisely this same image is repeated in the poem 'Black Coat', which is set on San Francisco's North Shore beach. The poem ends: 'I did not feel / How, as your lenses tightened, / He slid into me'. *Birthday Letters* assumes a familiarity with the details of Plath's biography, the story of her marriage to Hughes, their separation and her suicide, together with her poems (see Life and contexts, p. 12). One can only recommend Erica Wagner's book *Ariel's Gift* (2000) for the background to each of the poems in *Birthday Letters*.

Most of the poems in the first half of the book remember, with real affection, their first years together. At first, only occasionally does a shadow fall across those memories, as when Hughes mistakes Plath's obvious ambition for a desire for fame, in the poem 'Ouija'. He asks the ouija board whether they will be famous and Plath suddenly becomes disturbed, saying, 'Don't you see – fame will ruin everything'. Maybe, Hughes conjectures, Plath had heard a voice that he had not, suggesting that fame could, indeed, not be avoided and that when it came it would 'have to be paid for with your happiness, / Your husband and your life'. This poem suggests that he has had to pay the price of Plath's fame, just as she has. The obsession that the memories of this book attempt to exorcise through poetry is a movingly sad testimony to one aspect of that price.

Plath's mood swings and neuroses begin to accumulate as the book progresses. 'You Hated Spain' is one of four poems about their honeymoon in the little fishing village of Benidorm in 1956, each of which is about Hughes's adjustment to a different aspect of Plath's unease with the place and with herself. Their life together in America is described as a series of relocations that could satisfy neither of them so that neither of them was able to write satisfactorily there. 'What a waste!' Hughes now exclaims about their living as full-time writers in an apartment in Boston, near Boston Common and with views of the Charles River. In '9 Willow Street', Hughes writes that 'Happiness / Appeared – momentarily', as though it was a wild American bird, blown off course, 'and gone / Before we could identify it'. It is significant that Hughes writes that this bird 'Peered in at your window', as though the crucial thing was only the happiness of Plath. But what he was dealing with, and learning to minister to in poem after poem, is characterised in 'The Bird' as Plath's 'Panic Bird', not knowing what it was looking for, he says, but under a glass dome – Plath's Bell Jar – to which he was stuck looking in like 'a zoo gecko'. At the end of this poem, the glass only shattered with Plath's death and left the gecko falling into 'empty light'.

There is more of a shared reluctance to cross the thresholds of 'glittering offers' in America in the poem 'Fishing Bridge'. But again, the shared preoccupation with searching for their souls as new writers, which the poem says led only to 'dead-ends' and 'reversals', led Plath into a maze that the poem suggests could only end in her death. The following poem, 'The 59th Bear', reflects upon Plath's use of a partly comic experience with a bear to focus on death as she wrote about it in a short story. The poem takes some trouble to establish the absurdity of both the context and the incident, together, finally, with the distance at which they came to hear of a death. So in the final reflection Hughes distances himself from Plath's obsession with death by saying with honesty, guilt, culpability and excuse, 'At that time / I had not understood'. It is a statement repeated more than once in *Birthday Letters*. As late as their last summer together in Devon, Hughes writes, in 'Setebos', that he 'hadn't a clue' about the drama being played out with Plath's mother present playing Prospero to Plath's Miranda and his Ferdinand, as though they were in *The Tempest*. When Plath reverts to Caliban, crying 'Who has dismembered us?', Hughes hides like Ferdinand: 'I crawled / Under the gabardine'.

There is a series of poems beginning with 'Stubbing Wharfe' in which Hughes is more explicitly unequivocal about some of his mistakes in this relationship. Having failed to find the equanimity for writing in places offered in America, the problem of where to live in England is presented as the problem of satisfying Plath in this: 'A house of our own / Answering all your problems was the answer / To all my problems.' The tension in the line breaks, resulting in a line that has an answer at each opposite end of it, indicates the deft way the apparently conversational free verse often makes the emphasis in *Birthday Letters*. Sitting in the same pub in Mytholmroyd – Stubbing Wharfe – in which, forty years before he was born, his grandfather had sat singing wrapped in a sheet after having been dragged, drunk, out of the canal, Hughes reveals how rooted he is in this part of West Yorkshire. His idea of an old house up a side valley that they might renovate, Plath saw as 'only blackness'. Hughes ends this poem with a wonderfully resonant easing of the tension that had them both smiling. Five men come into the pub after playing bowls, laughing unstoppably at the fact that since their star player had a raging ulcer, the ulcer must have actually been the star of the match. The black Yorkshire humour has its own unspoken resonance for *Birthday Letters* here.

In the following poem, 'Remission', pregnancy and birth bring out 'the you / You loved and wanted to live with'. The poem ends with an ambiguous statement. In helping with the birth Hughes writes, 'I helped you / Escape incognito / The death who had already donned your features'. That such a disguise can only be temporary is emphasised by the poem following 'Remission', titled 'Isis', that focuses more on the Plath giving birth as an Isis figure now connecting moon and earth through fertility. Yet the bulk of the poem is about the figure of Death in the background, even as Hughes describes the new mother on the phone announcing to the world 'What Life had made of you'. In the last line of the poem it is as though Hughes were trying to point out, too late, that the new baby made the mother exultant precisely because it was 'what had never died, never known Death'.

It is at the end of the poem 'Epiphany', after Hughes has decided not to take home the fox cub offered for sale – that might have been 'what tests a marriage and proves a marriage' – that he concludes with two poignant lines: 'I would not have failed the test. Would you have failed it? / But I failed. Our marriage had failed.' The verb 'had' suggests that it had failed at that moment when he decided not to take home the fox cub, that Plath's anticipated reaction had repressed some intrinsic part of himself (knowing that the reader would associate his identity with the famous poem 'The Thought-Fox'). Yet he has earlier enumerated the good reasons why the fox could not have lived with his new family in their 'crate of space'. So one is left with the conclusion that this is a wider admission of guilt.

Certainly, in the poem titled 'Error', Hughes takes responsibility for taking Plath to Devon: 'I sleepwalked you / Into my land of totems'. Yet both of them 'lay listening / To our vicarage rotting like a coffin', which prompts the question 'What wrong fork / Had we taken?' It is unclear whether this is a question that was asked at the time, or is being asked in the present. The poem's title suggests the latter. But the poem 'Daffodils' is poised between exuberance and regret as Hughes remembers them gathering their garden windfall to reluctantly sell, 'a custom of the house' they are told. Although they thought of the daffodils as a windfall, Hughes writes, the couple 'never guessed they were a last blessing' of their last spring together. This undercutting is established early on when Hughes, addressing Plath in this poem, says that he is the only one who remembers that spring's daffodil harvest and although 'your daughter came with her armfuls', she cannot remember: 'She cannot even remember you. And we sold them'. Hughes has clearly lived with this fact for so long that it does not even have a line to itself. So the final dramatic image of the scissors lost that spring, 'Sinking deeper / Through the sod – an anchor, a cross of rust', becomes a token of a lost memory that isolates Hughes, as it isolates daughter from mother, in an unsentimental way.

It is following this series of poems in which Hughes accepts responsibility for some 'wrong forks taken' in the marriage (none of them concerning another woman) that a narrative crux is reached in the poem 'The Rag Rug'. Hughes thought that Plath was happy in making it, but her diaries reveal 'what furies you bled into that rug'. She was braiding and coiling a serpent, in Hughes's image, that was to lie coiled between them. 'It survived our Eden', the poem concludes. At the centre of the poem Hughes asks whether he was 'the child or the mother' of what she wrote in her diary as dragging out of her own navel. The question of whether he was victim or cause he puts more explicitly by asking if Plath was making something 'To free yourself from my contraction or was it / Pushing me out and away?' These questions remain unanswered in the poem. The serpent, it is suggested, remains between them.

The last quarter of the book deals with the aftermath of Plath's death and the final poems are the most controversial in their intertextual assumption of the reader's knowledge of poems by Plath that have the same titles, or are based on the same incidents as those Hughes now refers to in *Birthday Letters*. Several poems, but most notably 'Suttee', refer to the force of the later poems of Plath and the joint effort ('I was midwife') of giving birth to these powerful works which were shocking to both of them as they appeared: 'dark flames and screams / That sucked the oxygen out of both of us'. In 'Apprehensions' Hughes implies that Plath had a terror that something in her writing would 'Suddenly burst out and take from you / Your husband, your children, your body, your life'. This suggests both Plath's paranoia and her awareness of its possible outcome. It is not to suggest that the poetry itself is to blame for the ultimate losses, but that the inner forces that drive the poetry were fearful to Plath herself. This kind of fury, Hughes suggests in a poem that takes its title from one of her most bitter attacks on him, 'The Rabbit Catcher', could arise out of his misunderstanding of her ('What had I done?') and her misunderstanding of him (his 'country gods').

There is no misunderstanding in the poem 'Dreamers'. Hughes knows at the first meeting with Assia Wevill that the dreamer in him has fallen in love with the dreamer in her (see Life and contexts, **p. 16**). The poem is addressed to Plath, the significant partner of Hughes's life, from the first line: 'We didn't find her – she found us'. The 'us' is the subject of *Birthday Letters*. Hughes says that all three of them were to become the puppets in a terrible Fable. The final lines of 'Fairy Tale', the only poem addressed to Assia in the book, make it clear that falling in love with her was a ghastly mistake for Hughes. He trips over her corpse into the abyss after opening the forty-ninth door of her palace with the skeleton key of a grass blade she had given him. (Assia actually sent Hughes a single grass blade in an envelope to call him to her in London.) On the other hand, the poem 'The Inscription' clearly expresses a regret that Hughes was not able to find the right words towards reconciliation when Plath visited him in his London flat after their separation. 'He reeled', he says of himself, 'when he should have grabbed'. The depth of the wound she had given herself by hitting at him was what she hid from him, although the final line, in reference to her real words, or her poems, or her yet unseen journals, describes 'the shock of her words' that had 'Fatally gone through her and hit him'. This was a blow (the reading, and later the editing, of her journals) that was to last the rest of Hughes's life.

The final poems in the book are sometimes howls of incomprehension, sometimes a metaphor searching for meaning, sometimes a complaint against Plath's father, or her 'supporters' who removed the word 'Hughes' from her gravestone in Heptonstall. Two things stand out from these poems. First is the way Hughes sees Plath alive in the features of her children and realises, in 'The Hands', that the fingerprints inside what they both did are the same. Second is the continuing force of the grief, even after thirty-five years. In the poem 'A Short Film', Hughes, watching a home-movie of a ten-year-old Plath, can think only of the hurt of her memory and the explosion of her death. Each time her death is remembered it is 'a bracing of nerves / For what had already happened'. Perhaps this is the most telling expression of the aliveness of grief in the book.

A further eleven poems from the *Birthday Letters* project, which Hughes felt to be different in tone, were published in the same year with the title *Howls and Whispers* in an edition of only 150 copies at a price of $4000. They really add nothing that is not in *Birthday Letters*. More significant is the collection of the same price, but in an edition of only 50 copies, that contains twenty poems remembering Assia (see Life and contexts, **p. 16**). *Capriccio* was published in 1990 and, with *Howls and Whispers*, is now in *Collected Poems*. Its first poem is the same as the last in *Howls and Whispers*, but with a different title, suggesting the overlap in relationships. The charisma of Assia is what drives the poems in *Capriccio*: her beauty ('a folktale wager'), her European Jewishness that linked Russia, Germany and Israel, her power as Lilith, her thirst for his spirit, her earth goddess aura as Inanna, her offering up of herself to Aphrodite's temple, 'the brimming power of your gaze' ('The Pit and the Stones'). But the dominating tone is one of bitter regret. Their relationship is characterised in 'Folktale' as a futile mutual searching of each other: 'they ransacked each other for everything / That could not be found'. At times, 'Words seemed war. They / Melted in our mouths / Whatever was trying to cling' ('Snow'). As in some moments in *Birthday Letters*, Hughes has a 'bridegroom's wretched expression / Which understands nothing' ('The Mythographers'). But there is a devastating analysis in 'Rules of the Game' of the way in which Assia was taking something from Plath to fill the vacuum that Plath made her feel in herself. The fullness Plath had 'won' and the emptiness of Assia is unquestioned in this poem.

In 'Possession', the shame of Hughes's infatuation he describes as like having his children, whom he had thrown to the dogs, watch him 'copulating with the dust of the highway'. The thirteenth poem is the most comprehensive review of the relationship. In 'The Pit and the Stones' Hughes sees himself as 'one for your collection', a goat who saw 'Absolutely no sense in his tether / But his own weakness'. Beneath him is the pit where she is to be impaled. When she takes him with her onto those spikes the jubilation of the crowd watching is incomprehensible to him. But, as he wrote in the third poem, this is to be his dubious 'fame' for the rest of his life.

Stories

Difficulties of a Bridegroom is the title Hughes gave to the book that he wanted to publish in 1995 as his *Collected Short Stories*. As burgeoning writers, both Plath and Hughes wrote short stories and plays. It was common on both sides of the Atlantic at the time for young writers who wanted to earn a living from writing to sell stories and plays which might subsidise their writing of poetry. Hughes made a firm decision sometime following the publication of *Wodwo* to concentrate on poetry and write no more prose narratives, although two later requests for stories provided the opening and closing pieces for 'the sequence' of *Difficulties of a Bridegroom*. So, late in his life, Ted Hughes assembled this book of eight stories and a play that represents how he wished to be remembered as a writer of prose narratives. Most of the works date from between 1954 and 1962 and are the stories and the play from *Wodwo*. The title derives, Hughes tells us in a Foreword, from a phrase Hughes used from 'some time around 1962 … as the working title for almost everything I wrote for the next few years'. He names *Crow*, *Cave Birds* and *Gaudete* as growing from the same preoccupation. So to give this title to this book is to suggest that these are somehow preparatory to the full exploration of the idea of 'Difficulties of a Bridegroom'. 'These nine pieces hang together in my mind as an accompaniment to my poems,' Hughes writes to open the Foreword. But, crucially, the final story, published after *Crow* and *Gaudete*, in the same year as *Cave Birds*, is described as 'one form of the closing chapter, a metaphor for the successful final event, of my alchemical title'.

If this book has an 'alchemical title', in what way do these narratives reflect that? In fact, in each case a central character's sense of reality is challenged so that they undergo a trial during which they are transformed in some way. Mr Grooby, in 'The Harvesting', actually wonders if his disorientation isn't his 'simply growing old, beginning to fail in the trials'. The parallel with the three major poetic works is obvious and Hughes's idea that these stories might be understood as 'metaphors' for stages of the larger, and more important, poetic project gives them a significance that has been critically neglected until recently.

The most common form of narrative involving alchemical change might be the ghost story. So, as Hughes puts it in his Foreword, the 'natural overture to the sequence of which "The Head" is the finale' is a ghost story written in 1993. This story begins by asserting that the ability to see ghosts is a fact. This is given authenticity by the apparent autobiographical opening: 'My mother saw ghosts now and again'. The normality of occasional experiences of the abnormal – not other worlds, but other aspects of our world – is established by the opening story 'The Deadfall'. The use of real places around Mytholm-royd and what we know to be autobiographical facts, also suggest that the narrator of this story is the author and that this is a true story (see Life and contexts, p. 9).

Hughes and his older brother go camping locally to shoot rabbits. They find a gamekeeper's deadfall, a heavy slab of rock propped up with sticks and baited with a fresh pigeon, probably set to trap a fox. In the night an old woman calls Hughes by name out of the tent and leads him by moonlight to the deadfall to release a fox cub trapped by a leg at a corner of the stone. In the morning his brother lifts the slab back completely to reveal a large dead fox which he takes back to their camp and buries. In the process of smoothing soil out Hughes finds a little ivory fox. His brother suggests that the old woman was the ghost of the dead fox and that Hughes has seen his first ghost.

Three of the *Wodwo* stories are also autobiographical from his childhood in Yorkshire, Hughes says in the Foreword. 'Sunday' is about a boy going to a pub to watch Billy Red, the rat catcher, catch in his teeth a rat released for this purpose in the pub yard. The story ends: 'He found himself unable to speak. With all his strength he began to run.' The effect on the narrator is a little more explicit in 'The Rain Horse'. Returning to revisit a familiar hill near a farm after years away, this narrator shelters from rain under trees, his city suit soaked and his shoes covered with mud. He is watched by a horse that seems to run at him, then stalk and attack him as he tries to escape across fields. Reaching the farm, he shelters in a barn and the story leaves him, after his taking off and wringing out his clothes, sitting 'staring at the ground, as if some important part had been cut out of his brain'.

But the clearest transformation takes place in 'The Harvesting' when Grooby is affected by both the heat and the competition as he waits to shoot a hare in the diminishing last stands of corn being cut by a combine, knowing that the watching colliers' whippets might beat him to it. After becoming disorientated and then knocked out by his gun's recoil, he narrowly escapes being run down by the combine. Finally he is chasing the hare, but is reluctant to shoot it when he realises that it wants to give in and surrender. This moment of empathy seems to somehow result in his becoming the hare. As the dogs overtake him he feels he has been picked up and flung. Then he feels 'vague, pummelling sensa-tions far off in the blankness and silence of his body'.

In each of these stories the central characters are challenged by the elements and an encounter with an animal. Their trial transforms them because they have difficulty comprehending a reality they can barely recognise, although that reality is nature. Finding an accommodation with the mystery, power and spirit in nature seems to require an ego-diminishing experience of shock. When the ego is so complacent in its ability to make sense of everything that is thrown at it, the absurdity that results can be shocking to the reader. Such is the function of the subtle and disturbing story 'Snow'.

This story from *Wodwo* anticipates the humour of *Crow* and the cockerel arrogance of the hero of *Cave Birds*. It deploys the false logic of the poems 'Hawk Roosting' and 'Egg-head'. The narrator tells us that he has survived a plane crash and is walking in a blizzard. He is maintaining his sanity by proving to himself certain 'facts' about his situation, although he is aware that his mind could be his enemy too. These 'facts' become increasingly hard for the reader to believe, apparently establishing that for five months he has been walking in this unchanging whiteout covering 'something equivalent to the breadth of the Atlantic'. By heading constantly into the wind he thinks he is not trusting to luck or instinct: 'The facts are overwhelmingly on my side.' He is carrying 'a farmhouse sort of chair' on his back in a special harness, proof of a well-designed universe beyond the blizzard. His game keeps him sane, he says. The game is to walk the exact distance away from the chair into the blizzard from which he is able to find his way back to the chair – fourteen paces. This is his way of proving to himself that he is keeping control, his mind firm. The only 'harmless madness' he allows himself is giving names to individual snowflakes. The last words are: 'All the facts are on my side. I have nothing to do but endure.'

So here is a comic form of enduring by rationalisation – the very kind of rationalisation that would deny the experiences represented by the other stories from *Wodwo*. On the other hand, Hughes displays little respect for organised religion in his satire on competing religions in Northern Ireland in 'O'Kelly's Angel'. When he wrote this story in 1954 the Troubles were dormant, Hughes writes in the Foreword, although he says that 'history overtook it'. When O'Kelly captures and cages an angel, the major religious groups lay claim to it in increasingly violent terms until, in the battle that ensues, the angel's cage comes crashing down on the rival leaders and the angel is released, to return to the heavens. For Hughes, organised religion always misses the point in a self-destructive way. It is perhaps in dreams that Hughes feels that a non-rationalistic apprehension of reality and of alchemical transformation can take place. The radio play 'The Wound' that is collected in this book from *Wodwo* is an example of an exploration of this mode that was actually first written from the author's dream, as he explains in the Foreword.

Private Ripley and his Sergeant are walking towards a chateau. Ripley is confused about what has gone wrong, but knows that he is in a bad way after escaping from horrific trench warfare. The chateau turns out to be the house of the dead occupied by women who chorally give details of their post-mortems, including the 'enthusiasm of the journalists under the windows'. Having expected these visitors they have prepared a banquet before the dance. Ripley resists these temptations, describing the place as a 'lousy old brothel, all tarted up'. The Sergeant recalls their last fight and that Ripley also ate their dead comrades to survive, before Ripley witnesses the dismemberment of the Sergeant by the women. When his dead comrades appear to urge Ripley to join the dance, Ripley again resists in disgust and thus is not dragged under the ballroom floor by the women as his comrades are. Ripley's clinging to life throughout the play is dramatically focused, finally, in his relationship with the Girl. At first repulsed by his sense of the used whore in her youthful face, when he trusts her, he finds that she saves him. It is his words, 'Will you marry me?', that attract the attention of the stretcher-bearers and save him from the stages of the death process he has clearly been journeying through.

It is the Girl who convinces Ripley that he is suffering from a massive head wound, and his acceptance of his wound, as of his guilt about the cannibalism, together with his integrity in the face of a series of tests, enables him to survive the play of life and death forces working at the hole in his head. Offering marriage to the old hag who turns out to be a young girl is final proof of his integrity and she convinces him that he can walk – over nine miles, out on his feet, straight towards the Soldiers who realise that he's the sole survivor of Massey's platoon. They notice that he is 'grinning away as if he'd been crowned'.

Hughes confirms that this play is his 'Gothic/Celtic version of the *Bardo Thödol* – the journey of the soul in the forty-nine days after death, ending in rebirth' (see Life and contexts, **p. 14**). The redemptive stage of the 'Difficulties of a Bridegroom' project is the hero's marriage to the female goddess, providing she can be recognised in the testing forms she takes. This happens in *Cave Birds*, and the epigraph poems of *Gaudete* are the hymns to that marriage, as are, in different forms, the poems of *Moortown Diary* and *River*. *Difficulties of a Bridegroom* provides a narrative guide to the understanding of the link between Hughes's major poetic works.

But this book's 'metaphor for the successful final event' of this larger project is the story titled 'The Head'. Its parallels with the opening story of the book are obvious, although it is also in a fantasy mode that is the opposite of auto-biographical. The whole story is set up as an explanation of the first sentence: 'My wife is strange, I know.' The narrator and his brother are hunters who sell skins and heads to tourists. Hearing that large quantities of game are gathered at a certain place, they go there and try to hire a local Slott Indian as a guide. They are told that this is a rare sacred gathering of the animals to be counted by their Lord and that they cannot have a guide because there should be no hunting during that particular week. If they do, the Lord of the animals will kill the hunter, cut his head off, skin it and leave it, doing the same to his spirit, but sending his spirit head home 'like that, absolutely mad and in anguish'. Perhaps the gift of an Egyptian dagger to the chief by the brother changes his attitude, but the chief says that, since they are set upon going anyway, he will give them a guide as mad as they are.

The guide is scared into inaction as they take him along, but, finding the right place, they set about days of killing everything, skinning the animals and leaving the bodies in a pile at their camp they call the Cemetery. Their guide disappears and his flayed head is found on a stake in the river. Realising that he is killing without pleasure, the narrator declares that he will kill no more. In the night the narrator sees a shawled old woman grieving at the Cemetery. She approaches the camp, takes the narrator's gun, looks at him with her deathly face and, with 'unnatural gliding speed', disappears into the river.

Telling his brother that he has killed the last creature he will ever kill and that he has thrown his gun in the river, the narrator finds that his brother laughs and threatens to kill him. So he plans to run away in the morning. Next day he finds that the Cemetery is empty and in the middle of the ground is his brother's flayed head, asking to be taken along. The narrator begins a journey in which he tries to leave the head behind several times and each time the head bites him and has to be carried. As the head appears to be asleep, the narrator buries it in a foxhole and returns to the Indian village. Multiple screams suddenly bring everyone to where a man has been killed by a 'squat bird, the size of a big owl'. It is the head, now with wings and talons, and it has mistaken its victim for the narrator. The villagers frighten the bird off with their spears, but decide that the narrator must fight and kill the bird with the Egyptian dagger. At dusk the narrator stabs and stabs at the bird whose screams diminish and turn into 'soft feminine moans'. On the ground the narrator finds the 'naked slender body of a woman', whom he carries back to the village, finding that she is completely unharmed. The story ends: 'I married her and never hunted again. And this is the strange wife I now have.'

The girl whom the narrator brings home and marries is like the female figure of 'Crow's Undersong' who 'cannot come all the way'. She is described as 'strong, quick and intelligent', but she cannot speak or write. By killing his own brother who is a slaughterer of wild life, the narrator has been able to marry the wild spirit of nature. Since the brother was a destructive part of himself that he managed to overcome with courage and a strong survival impulse, he has found his feminine partner and a wholeness in his relationship with inner and outer nature. This is 'one form of the closing chapter' of the *Crow* project that was revisited in *Cave Birds* and *Gaudete*. This has been the ultimate trial to which the other stories and the play in this book have been preparatory in their testing encounters with animals and land and weather. The possibility of the alchemically changed state of the narrator of 'The Head' has been hinted at in the strangely altered perceptions of the central characters of the other stories. Hughes points out that what he calls 'the centre of gravity' of these narratives – the charge that brings about those altered apprehensions of reality – are powerful and challenging images. He suggests that this charge 'passes from the caged angel to the other-life other-world of snow, to the caged and helpless rat, to the domineering horse, to the hare that the protagonist becomes at the moment of its death'. The 'successful final event' that this 'centre of gravity' is moving towards is the metaphor of marriage. By bringing these stories and the play together in this way late in his life Hughes was providing in *Difficulties of a Bridegroom* a key motif and an exemplary process that can be used to understand the rest of his work.

Children's works

Rarely has there been a major poet who has produced so much work for children. The range of that work includes not only twelve volumes of poetry, but a brilliant and still much used book about how to write poetry, *Poetry in the Making* (1967), a collection of plays, *The Tiger's Bones* (1974) and several collections of creation stories, at least one of which has become a classic, *How the Whale Became* (1963). Two short novels for children have the potential to become major influences on our culture. Over thirty-five years the first of them, *The Iron Man* (1968), has become one of the most popular texts in primary education in the United Kingdom. The famous educationalist Margaret Meek nominated it as the book that changed her life, saying, 'If I had only one text to teach children to read, this would be it' (*Guardian Higher* 17. 6. 1997). In 2008 *The Iron Man* was available in translation in six countries. The sequel novel, *The Iron Woman* (1993), might also be expected to have a wide influence on young readers.

What is remarkable about this body of work for young readers is that none of these books is anything other than a part of the author's central creative project. Indeed, some of them have to be regarded as major contributions to that project. There are two reasons why this is so. First, Ted Hughes can adopt a strategy of overlap in his sense of his audience. In introducing a reading from *Season Songs* (1976) on the radio Hughes spoke of writing 'within hearing of children' (BBC Radio 3, 6. 9. 1977). But he has also written about producing writing 'which adults can overhear' (*Letters* 482). In an important letter to Lissa Paul in 1984 Hughes wrote that his writing for children 'reaches adults – maybe – because assuming this is not for them, they suspend their defences and listen – in a way secretly – as children' (*Letters* 482). Claas Kazzer has pointed out that the narrative underpinning *Crow* is a children's creation story (1999: 193). The two collections clearly written 'within hearing of children', *Season Songs* and *Flowers and Insects* (1986), have been discussed above as also important works for adults (see Works, p. 53). So as Hughes is pursuing his major themes and preoccupations he adopts a shifting degree of audience overlap for different books.

Second, Hughes's writing about the way he thinks of his work for children clearly indicates that his sense of his role as poet and storyteller for adults is not only informed by his seriously considered role as a writer for children, but is identical with it. When Hughes wrote about the narrative function of *The Iron Man* in his first essay titled 'Myth and Education' (1970), he was elaborating a function that also fitted his work for adults. When Hughes told Lissa Paul that when writing for children he could pursue his themes without having to get through the defences put up by adults, the assumption was that he was developing the same interests as in his writing for adults, but with an audience that was 'still open'.

It is an indication of its importance for Hughes that he continued to write for children throughout his career, long after his early work had emerged from entertaining his own children, as was the case with *The Iron Man*, for example. Indeed, after the death of Sylvia Plath writing for children was his main form of writing and included commissioned talks and plays from BBC Schools' Broadcasting. During the seven year gap between *Lupercal* (1960) and *Wodwo* (1967) Hughes published his first four books for children. The three collections of poetry are influenced by the humour and popular rhyming style of Dr Suess (whom he had reviewed in 1962), but they are each based upon a curiosity for the otherness of, first, family members in *Meet My Folks* (1961), then imaginary creatures in *The Earth-Owl and Other Moon People* (1963) and then the Loch Ness monster in *Nessie the Mannerless Monster* (1964). In 1963 the stories in *How the Whale Became* gave Hughes his first narratives about a very human God who can make mistakes in crafting his particular kind of Creation.

The poet Simon Armitage believes that Hughes' life-long concern with producing books for children was strategic and that in return, 'it was in the

classrooms of Britain where Hughes's poetry found much of its loyal audience'
(2000: xii). Armitage goes further, claiming that:

> poems like 'Wind', 'The Bull Moses', 'The Horses' and of course
> 'Hawk Roosting' are not only fastened in the imagination of a whole
> generation, but for some, like myself, were a kind of Rosetta Stone –
> the means by which the surrounding world could suddenly be translated,
> understood, and experienced.
>
> (ibid.)

The reason for the appeal and value of the poetry in particular, Armitage puts
down to the rare sense for the reader 'that clarity and complexity can exist
simultaneously, like clear, still water, into which a person can see to a ponder-
ous depth'. Praising the continuing value of *Poetry in the Making*, Hughes's
talks for BBC Schools' Broadcasting, and drawing attention to the proportion
of his output written for children, Armitage says, 'I find it impossible not to see
this as strategic ... and part of Hughes's ambition to enter the world of intuition,
innocence, and possibility' (2000: xiii). One should not forget that remarkable
sentence in Hughes's second 'Myth and Education' essay: 'Every new child is
nature's chance to correct culture's error' (*Winter Pollen*: 149).

During five successive nights Ted Hughes composed instalments of a story
for his own children which became *The Iron Man*. The story possesses some
key features that will appeal to all young readers: a fascination with machines,
with space, with the direct challenge to a trial of strength. But it also functions
as a counter to many common solutions to narrative problems in children's
literature, typified by the St George and the Dragon story in which the Dragon
must be defeated by physical force, and perceived evil must be repressed, as
Hughes makes clear in his first 'Myth and Education' essay (1970).

Despite his name, the Iron Man comes out of the sea and returns to the sea
after his first appearance. He is an image of evolution, coming out of the source
of life on earth, but made like a machine that eats only metal. He is an ingenious machine that can re-assemble himself, once, in a vivid and surreal image,
his hand has found his eyeball. He peers over hilltops in a way that establishes
a real landscape; his hand and eye are brought together by scavenging gulls; he
appears first to a farmer's son and he provides a problem for a community of
farmers. So, in the opening of this story, the machine age and the natural are
brought into a conflict that is personified in the Iron Man and the farmer's
son, Hogarth.

Trapping and burying the Iron Man will only lead to a horrifically disturbed
rural picnic, the story suggests. The Iron Man represents a problem that cannot
be buried. The most satisfactory solution is a recycling of the by-products of
the machine age. He can feed on the scrap-yards that defile the edge of every
English town. Enter the Space-Being. Growing in outer space, the Space-Being is
a problem that will come to threaten the earth. It is the 'space-bat-angel-
dragon' that has grown from a spot on a tiny star and eventually comes to land
on Australia and covers the continent. Unlike the Iron Man, it eats living things and
it demands to be fed. Characteristically, the people of the world declare war on
it. But having used all their weapons they have not begun to damage it.

Hogarth asks the Iron Man for help and the Iron Man challenges the Space-Being to a trial of strength – literally a trial by fire – but the Iron Man can stand heat better and consequently wins.

Asked what it can now do for the earth, the Space-Being says it can only fly and sing. So it is found a place in the universe by singing the music of the spheres which has the effect of calming the people of the earth. They stop making weapons and think about how to live peacefully together 'to enjoy this strange, wild, blissful music from the giant singer in space'. Each of the words Hughes uses to describe this music suggests an accommodated relationship of the machine age with nature that does not challenge, or seek to diminish, its wild strangeness. In his earliest children's work such as this story from 1968, Hughes was able to bring his narrative to a redemptive stage, a feat which eluded him in his adult work until *Cave Birds* ten years later.

The sequel to *The Iron Man* was written a quarter of a century later and might be thought of as an update of the earlier book, where the agenda is not so much peace on earth as the very survival of the earth. The gender bias of the first book is also counterbalanced in the second. The final message of *The Iron Woman* (1993) is not about weapons but about waste, and it is made explicit only in the final pages. The environmental agenda is raised from the start of the book. Indeed, birdwatchers are now common enough to replace farmers as the representative inhabitants of the countryside in the opening of the narrative.

But Hughes's Jungian function for this narrative is much the same as that outlined for *The Iron Man*: a child is the first to identify a huge problem of the age and negotiates with what is fearfully Other to bring about a resolution. In addition, this text is able to include the previous one by assuming that readers know it – and know also that a narrative of an ultimately redemptive structure has been shown to be possible. More practically, Lucy, the female protagonist of the second book, is able to write to Hogarth to draw on his knowledge of dealing with the Iron Man.

Because Hughes has decided to write 'within hearing' of older readers in the second book, its language and imagery are more sophisticated. The brilliant opening of *The Iron Woman* creates a mysterious sense that all is not well in the river and marsh that is Lucy's playground. The first subtle sign is that Lucy hears a lark singing in the night. When the Iron Woman appears to Lucy, as though in her nightmare, she tells Lucy that she has risen out of the marsh on behalf of all its creatures who are suffering agonies from the poison of the Waste Factory. She has come to destroy the Waste Factory and 'the ignorant ones', 'the poisoners' who work there. With the sharply telling detail possible in this second book, Hughes has Lucy reflect that her father, who works at the Waste Factory, has just received an increase in pay because the factory is now importing waste to process, having recently doubled in size.

So when Lucy writes to Hogarth for help, she, too, is now hoping to solve a problem for her own family that is also a problem for the world. That the girl and the boy work together on this can now be seen to be a part of Hughes's larger use of gender in his symbolic narrative structures (see Works, p. 43). Further, this is not about destroying a factory, but changing its workers' attitudes. Lucy and Hogarth are able to do this because they have access to the terrible noise that was the Iron Woman's original cry – the sound of the pain of the suffering of all the poisoned creatures out there in the marsh. When Lucy touches the manager of the factory she sets off a chain reaction throughout the factory that turns everyone into 'high-voltage scream batteries' for whoever they touch. This is not an ordinary protest, the factory senior managers realise. The experience of that scream has a profound effect upon whoever hears it, producing a genuine horror at the pain it expresses.

When the Iron Man calls upon the space-bat-angel-dragon to invest all its power in the Iron Woman – an 'unearthly power' – she uses it to turn all the men in the country into fish that have to be taken to water by women as quickly as possible. There they experience the pain of the poisoned water. This is shown on television around the world. Any male who lands at a UK airport becomes a fish. But the Iron Woman is not convinced that this is enough to effect lasting change. 'Only their words change', she had said earlier. Meanwhile the bubbles of the fish seem to produce a fog of webs that covers the country. Out of these webs comes the cloud-spider-god of Wealth and of Gain, who finally admits to being the spider of Mess. Iron Woman gets the spider to repeat that the person who will clean her up is Mother. This seems to refer to the Iron Woman, who has climbed into the spider's mouth and is sucked back up with the spider when the Space-Being spins back into space. The Iron Woman returns burnt, as if from a furnace.

At this point, the mess having apparently been cleaned up, the men emerge from water asking for towels to dry themselves. Their hair has turned white. The scream is a faint ringing in their ears that becomes louder when they look at anything with the potential to pollute rivers. So from the Prime Minister down they all listen more carefully and think more deeply. Strange yellow webs grow overnight over any rubbish of any size, from the Waste Factory to domestic bins, gradually dissolving the waste. Mixed with water it provides a fuel that is non-toxic in rivers. Importing waste now has a new economic function for the Waste Factory. But where do the webs come from? '"Deep, big, fright"' and '"deep, big, change"', says the Iron Woman. The novel's final image suggests that the music from far up, that now rings in their ears, is again the ability to hear the music of the spheres.

This children's story is as far as Hughes comes to directly addressing the environmental crisis that overtook his writing career. Neil Roberts refers to it as an 'urgent, and didactic, ecological intervention' (2006: 177). In the 1950s Hughes instinctively focused on tuning his poetry in to the other world of nature and quickly exposed contemporary examples of the hubris of human constructions of it. In 1993, in a story for children, he still sees the need for 'deep, big, change' in our relationship with the forces and resources of our planet. The god of Wealth and Gain has produced Mess. Mother can clean it up, but it will need a new form of energy that is sustainable for our environment. All a story can do is to demonstrate the power of the human imagination to represent the urgency and nature of the problem and the potential to find a solution. 'They had all learned a frightening lesson. But what could they do about it?' These are not the last words of the book. The yellow webs come out of the capacity to turn fright into change in a radical way. It is a capacity of the human imagination, the same capacity that has produced *The Iron Woman*, this remarkable story for children. Neil Roberts says of *The Iron Woman*, 'In no other work that he wrote for children is his conception of this audience as "nature's chance to correct culture's error" (*Winter Pollen*: 149) so literally pertinent' (2006: 178).

In the year of his death Hughes lobbied the Palace as Poet Laureate for the recognition of the seriousness and importance of writing for children by the creation of a Children's Laureate. Six months after Hughes's death Quentin Blake was appointed the first one.

Following the early work of Keith Cushman (1983), critical writing on Hughes's works for children has been offered by Lissa Paul (1999), Claas Kazzer (1999) and Neil Roberts (2006: 167–78).

Criticism and letters

Winter Pollen (1994) is a selection of the prose essays, criticism, introductions and reviews by Hughes that provides the best platform for a discussion of the poet's achievements in prose essays. Hughes's literary criticism of other writers inevitably reflects his preoccupations as a poet, but his thoughtful and detailed focus on the work of others should not be neglected. It is totally serious and committed in its own terms as a contribution to debates about the work of those other writers. Nevertheless, since the poetry of Ted Hughes is ultimately of greater cultural significance, the opportunity offered by a reading of *Winter Pollen* to gain insights into the poetic project should also not be overlooked, especially since the prose selection was published just four years before the poet died. At the time of its publication Hughes wrote to a correspondent:

> [The] problem with my prose generally, I think, is that my ideas exist in some other medium. So my prose is a translation – almost as if I were formulating the idea from its primeval (that other medium is primeval) nature for the first time. So the ideas never get beyond a sort of centaur-like existence – harnessed to my essay's prose gig.
> (T.H. to Dr Iris Gillespie, 22. 2. 1994, MSS 644, Box 54, FF2)

There is a case for arguing that *Winter Pollen* is best read backwards. It is arranged roughly chronologically, but the final essay in the collection is, in effect, a summary of the dynamics of Hughes's life's poetic journey with all its themes, motifs and thinking articulated in an essay on Coleridge's struggle with his muse. The form of Coleridge's struggle is not that of Hughes, who has been more successful in his negotiations with his muse. But that an analysis of Coleridge's insights, nightmares and resistances represents Hughes's view of his own poetic mission, or cultural positioning, is indicated by the suggestion that 'the biological reality of a mythos' in Coleridge's psyche 'can be read as a large-scale, brilliantly concise, diagnostic, luminous vision of England's spiritual/ intellectual predicament' (439. All references in this section are to *Winter Pollen*). The story of Hughes's most sustained prose diagnosis of this continuing predicament begins with his discussion of Shakespeare's Complete Works and reaches its most comprehensive statement in the final essay on Coleridge. All of the remaining prose essays and reviews can be seen to have been contributory to this final culmination in which Diane Middlebrook suggests that 'Hughes rose to new levels of ingenious rhetorical charm, even for him' (2004: 268).

Hughes's first copy of Shakespeare's Complete Works was one of his most prized possessions. His thorough knowledge of the plays derived from the time of his national service at a remote radar station on the Yorkshire moors which he described to Keith Sagar as a period when he 'read and re-read Shakespeare and watched the grass grow' (1972: 3). So Hughes was the obvious poet to contribute to a new series launched by Faber, which today includes Simon Armitage's selection of *Ted Hughes* (2000). In *A Choice of Shakespeare's Verse* (1971) Hughes wrote an essay that was to be expanded twenty years later into the magnum opus of his mature years, *Shakespeare and the Goddess of Complete Being* (1992). Two months before he died, Hughes wrote to Keith Sagar about the latter book: 'main problems of the book: it is too long, it deals with every play and leaves nothing to the reader; it needs the reader to know Shakespeare better than a very few do; style too complicated; I added too much arcane material' (10. 8. 1998, BL ADD 78761, f. 63). For those seeking a summary of the argument of the 1992 book on Shakespeare, the 1971 essay concisely explains the Hughes thesis. (It is included in *Winter Pollen* under the title 'The Great Theme: Notes on Shakespeare' and the later book is represented by an extract titled 'Shakespeare and Occult Neoplatonism'.) In this essay historical, religious and political tensions of the period are used to introduce what is essentially an erotic narrative explored throughout the Complete Works that Hughes calls 'Shakespeare's fable'. In 1979 this essay was regarded by at least one critic as 'the central document in Hughes's thoughts about poetry' (Uroff 1979: 29).

In the essay Hughes argues that, for Shakespeare, Elizabeth, the virgin queen, has replaced the Pope as earthly representative of divinity and is a substitute for the Marian, Queen of Heaven worship, aspect of Catholicism. But she has not only become the symbol of the divinity of royalty and church, as Queen of England she also stands for the Celtic pre-Christian goddess of nature in both its creative and destructive aspects that by Shakespeare's time had separated out into Venus and Hecate. Against these values Hughes points to the rise of Puritanism and the anticipation of democratic government that was to result in the Civil War. Hughes identifies behind the theological and political debate an archaic mythological battle that gives the plays their energy and poetic depth. This is why, he argues, apparently political plots are actually enacted through the sexual drama of drives and morality, emotional and sensual forces evaluated against notions of right behaviour in a poetically charged drama that can be formulated as a single fable, engaged at different levels and to differing degrees throughout the plays.

At the centre of this fable, Hughes suggests, is the pattern of tensions and transformations in the narrative of *Measure for Measure*. The inhumanly puritan Angelo cracks down severely on a city of sexual corruption. Isabella, who is about to enter a nunnery, pleads with him for her brother's life. Under Angelo's new regulations, her brother must die because a sexuality driven by love has resulted in pregnancy out of wedlock. Angelo rejects Isabella's pleas which nevertheless expose his moral severity as unsustainable and transform him into a sexually driven beast. His very repression exerts a force upon his nature that distorts his attraction to her and he becomes 'a lust-mad tyrant' as Hughes puts it. Isabella's humane puritanism is also transformed into a callous destructive force when she is prepared to let her brother die rather than give in to Angelo's desires. Hughes suggests that Angelo's Calvinist perception of nature, 'and especially love, the creative force of nature', as divided into 'abstract good and physical evil' produces a counter force for wholeness. 'Nature's attempts to recombine, first in love, then in whatever rebuffed love turns into, and the puritan determination that she shall not combine under any circumstances, are the power-house and torture-chamber of the Complete Works' (192).

In *Shakespeare and the Goddess of Complete Being* Hughes calls this 'fable' the 'Tragic Equation' of the plays and analyses it as a myth in which Nature's drive for wholeness produces the image of the Goddess of Complete Being. Whereas in the earlier essay Hughes had regarded the last romance plays as 'cheating' by their use of magic to halt the full development of the equation that is played out in the tragedies, in his book Hughes describes the final plays as revelations of the need for a recognition of the Goddess. In his presentation copy of this book for Leonard and Lisa Baskin Hughes wrote, half-jokingly, a list of eight 'Directions for use'. The final direction is: 'Read the book as a Court Case between the rational puritan (the criminal in the dock, the tragic hero) and everything he rejects (the plaintiff, the howling woman)' (BL Rare Books, Hughes 76). Following a judgement on the tragic hero and his acknowledgement of the distortion of his passionate impulses, Hughes argues that rebirth is a qualified possibility. His chapter on *The Tempest* argues that the frenzies produced by repression can be transformed by their receptive and controlled full experience into a rebirth to a sense of wholeness, but that this remains only a hopeful possibility.

In the last two essays in *Winter Pollen*, which are published there for the first time, Hughes undertakes a journey through English poetry which leads to revelations that are more than possibilities. What this journey really amounts to is a reflection on his own poetic project and its position within the historical dynamics of English poetry, including Shakespeare's.

The first of these long essays is titled 'Myths, Metres, Rhythms' and it takes its starting point in reflections on two failures by other poets to understand particular poems by Hughes. In the first an American urban poet, who apparently appreciates other poems by Hughes, is completely mystified by one about a wren. Hughes realises that this unnamed poet has never seen a wren, watched its behaviour or known about its rich role in English folklore – what Hughes calls the 'mythos' of the wren. The mythic meanings associated with the wren are not just part of the cultural inheritance of a group or sub-group, Hughes argues, but are based upon the observed characteristics of the wren. Its 'singing frenzy', for example, cannot successfully be described as a kind of 'ecstatic convulsion' if it has not been seen. Mythic qualities are thus based upon an experienced reality and the writer can only communicate, 'can only grope along, transmitting what are intended to be meaningful signals', to the extent that a resonance is stirred in the reader's personal mythos. Of course, a decline in biodiversity restricts the mythos of the writer and of the reader as far as signals from the natural world are concerned. Hughes gives an example from his typically generous response to a correspondent who asked about the meaning of a poem from *Flowers and Insects* titled 'In The Likeness of a Grasshopper'. Hughes goes to some length to explain his metaphors in this poem and the elaborated narrative of the grasshopper as a strange mechanical trap set by the Summer to catch a Song before setting the trap again a yard away. He realises that the grasshopper is no longer a common association with an English summer and that a mythology has been closed for his readers, especially children, who used to catch them and for whom this poem is partly intended.

This essay then turns towards a more extensive, but equally lucid, explanation of 'the rhythms that give musical expression' to mythologies of meaning in language. Again the springboard is an interesting case of failure to be able to engage with the author's intention. Hughes reveals that in a review of his first collection, the poet Roy Fuller found that the final line of 'The Horses' – 'Hearing the horizons endure' – was for him 'unsayable'. In 1958, the year after his first collection was published, Hughes wrote to his brother Gerald in Australia, 'If you read them [my poems] as if you were speaking with great emphasis to a person on the other side of a large room – then they come right' (MSS 845, Box 1, FF7). As himself a singer of ballads and a memoriser of poems for recitation, Hughes knew that reading aloud was the key to fully understanding a poem (see the Introduction to *By Heart* (1997)). But he also realised from hearing poetry readings that his musical mode was different from that of Roy Fuller and some other poets. So he begins to unpack the history and range of metre and rhythm in English poetry to find out how this has arisen. What might be described as an explanation, because it is so clearly expressed, carefully organised, historically informed and detailed in its analysis of effects, is really an enquiry of characteristic depth and clarity.

There are, Hughes suggests, two 'musical traditions' in English poetry. The first is that of a regular metre, often associated with rhyming poetry, and his example from Addison combines both. But he then goes on to show how what he calls 'the natural qualities' of words used in ordinary speech can give free verse a conventional rhythm that enables it to be 'sight-read straight-off'. In his example from Robert Graves there is a pentameter at work in his free verse, as there is in a translation he quotes from Miroslav Holub by George Theiner. Although there is no metre, the rhythm can only be read in one way. Hughes then gives most attention to forms of 'unorthodox metres', demonstrating that Hopkins's 'sprung rhythm' actually has antecedents in the poetry of Christopher Smart, William Blake and Samuel Taylor Coleridge. Here there are alternative ways to accent the verse and the patterning of stresses obviously gives different effects to the meaning of the words. All this is available in textbooks of poetic technique, but Hughes's language conveys the excitement of a poet feeling the pulse of the subtle sense of the poetic line, as in his metaphor of the 'brilliant kinaesthetic dance' that the reader is forced to enact in experiencing the content of a quatrain from Hopkins's 'Inversnaid': 'Every phrase is a different, vivacious rhythm, a spontaneous-seeming, surprising, fresh response to one thing after another' (333). This is the critical language of living discovery, of poetic technique making embodied meaning. Here is Hughes at the climax of a detailed discussion of metre in Hopkins's 'The Windhover': 'This same, slightly off-balance, brilliantly constantly-corrected balance produces those flickering, stabbing touches of the wings, trimming the ailerons, that carry the bird across and up off the page like a hallucination' (340).

In his discussion of Hopkins's 'reversed rhythm' Hughes begins by saying, 'as everywhere in this business, defining terms seem inadequate'. It is in his detailed consideration of the options for musical interpretation of particular lines that he reconstructs the intended effects of Hopkins, Milton, Keats, Coleridge and most impressively Wyatt. Tracing the history of editing Wyatt, Hughes shows that an orthodoxy for conformity very quickly established a defusing of the frissons in the famous poem 'They flee from me'. 'In fact, Wyatt's hand-wrought, gnarled, burr-oak texture owes more than a little to the alliterative tradition' (356). This, in turn, draws Hughes back to a 'speculative and provisional reconstruction of the music of *Gawain*'s unknown metre through Hopkins's known practice', pointing to the parallels in 'distorting syntax to achieve rhythmical effects' (360). The importance of all this is that a modern reader 'is accustomed to reading almost all verse in casual, conversational style, as if it were metrically simple … as if it were a line of "free verse"' (364), thus missing the effects upon meaning of the original rhythms. In a return to his starting point, Hughes gives an insight into how he hears his own 'unsayable' line, admitting that 'again, scansion marks seem inadequate to score the shape of the phrase as I hear it', including 'a stress of sense that falls partly in silence', until the final stress of the last word 'endure', 'is held into the blue distance, like the recession of horizons behind horizons on the Pennine moorland being described' (365). For Hughes, the music, like the mythos, is ultimately attempting to communicate a subtle and lived experience of an actuality.

In a rather remarkable 'Postcript', Hughes gives a rapid overview of the history of English poetry in terms of an uneasy marriage 'in which the old or unorthodox tradition is the bride and the new, metrically strict orthodox tradition the groom' (369). The Celtic tradition is first displaced by Chaucer's rhymed iambics that 'naturalize in an English poetry the up-to-this-point alien culture of the Court class' (367). The hilarious story of this stormy and abusive 'marriage' provides a framework by which to see how Hughes positions his own poetry in this clash of musical traditions with the older, much suppressed tradition. But what is also telling is how serving this bride brings many poets into embattled, sanity-threatening territory. It is ironic that a Poet Laureate writing this in 1993 feels that the official poetic orthodoxy is always seeking to 'resume control of the highways' against his own poetic journey. It is as though, late in life, he needs to understand his own trajectory by getting to the bottom of the poetic forces at work in Shakespeare, Hopkins, Wyatt and Coleridge where ecstatic celebrations of his own roots are to be found in consolation.

This becomes particularly evident in his essay on Coleridge's poetic journey, 'The Snake in the Oak', where Hughes is at his most explicit about the sanity-threatening shamanic call and its difficult negotiations with the Goddess in her various forms that produce the healing effect of the poetry. Any reader of Hughes's poetry who wants to understand his poetic quest and the central role of the female figures in that poetry will find a full account of its dangers and enlightenments in what Hughes writes about Coleridge's brief acceptance of the poetic call and its ultimate rejection, with disastrous consequences. Quite apart from the detail of the scholarship in this essay, the passion and subtle understanding evident in this brilliant account of a poetic journey indicates that Hughes knew from personal experience, and a life-time's study of shamanic practice, that Coleridge's engagements with the Goddess shared much with his own more conscious quest. As his final long prose reflection on the roots of his key poetic elements, this essay has the weight of a final statement of his own inner creative trajectory. After reading this essay it becomes clear why Hughes had to publish both *Birthday Letters* and *Capriccio*, his final accounts of negotiations with female figures.

The first motifs Hughes identifies in Coleridge's life are familiar to readers of both the preceding essay on metre and *Shakespeare and the Goddess of Complete Being*. In a Notebook entry Coleridge admitted that, since a boy, his pious Christian self had been undermined by 'an aching in the heart' where it might have been bitten by a snake and remained his 'unleavened Self' (377). A moralising Christian intelligence is thus in tension with an intuitive apprehension of an other life which Hughes capitalises as Coleridge's 'Unleaven Self'. It is this latter self that is 'besotted with woman', as Hughes puts it, from his mother, his sister, his first lost love, his wife Sarah, Dorothy Wordsworth, his second Sarah, to the terrifying women of his nightmares. In confronting his imaginative powers, Coleridge again notes, he lacks the necessary strength: 'the heart of Oak is wanting'. But in the first six months of his relationship with the Wordsworths, Coleridge finds himself able to address these tensions in what Hughes calls the three acts of a tragic opera: 'Kubla Khan', 'The Rime of the Ancient Mariner' and 'Christabel' Part I. The snake in the oak is actually the figure of Geraldine who emerges to 'rape' Christabel in the most horrific and mysterious moment of the 'opera' that produces Coleridge's ultimate rejection of his muse and withdrawal from poetry into an unsatisfying downhill life in prose.

It would be impossible to summarise briefly the detail with which Hughes demonstrates that all of the essential elements of the following acts of the opera are present (even in their absence) in the first. But the heavenly upper world and the liquid forces of the underworld in 'Kubla Khan' are geographically explained in their mythically charged dynamics. Each poem, Hughes suggests, 'revolves around the otherworld female' who in the first is 'the love-sick mesmeric bringer of ecstatic joys' that threaten 'the Christian values of the Intellectual Self' (391). At the crux of 'The Ancient Mariner' she is Coleridge's personal 'Nightmare Life-in-Death' whom the Mariner at first mistakes as evil, but who is the fearful force Hughes calls 'the Goddess at the source of things', beyond good and evil. At the moment of recognition the Mariner is able to transcend his Christian Intellectual Self and see the divine beauty of all life, 'to give himself wholly to that female' (432). In the remainder of the poem Coleridge struggles to reconcile this apprehension with its implications for his desire to become a Unitarian Minister. 'The triumph of the Pagan Great Goddess', writes Hughes, 'has told him that his Christian life, and the limited cognitive system that goes with it, is a lie. The pious end of the poem is his hollow refusal of a "call" he is too late to refuse' (433). The writer of this sentence had published *Gaudete*, his own playful exploration of 'the call', and the poem addressed to Plath, 'You Hated Spain', but had not yet decided to publish *Birthday Letters*.

Rather than see Christabel and Geraldine as Eve and Lilith, the two contrasting consorts of Adam in Hebrew mythology, Hughes believes that

Coleridge saw both Eve and Lilith in Geraldine. Indeed, he argues that 'the sum of her manifestations throughout the development of the visionary poems' culminates in 'the Great Goddess of the putrefying, oceanic grave and the radiant cauldron of abounding new life ... converged ... into the coiled power of Geraldine' (440). 'Her corpse-like and reptilian bosom identifies a *divine* beauty', writes Hughes, that Coleridge must celebrate wholly at whatever risk to the resistances in himself and his sanity. Hughes describes this as a 'biological' necessity that is 'a commonplace of the mystical life', even, he suggests, for a scientist who perceives an awesome 'ultimate reality' as an apprehension of divine beauty (441). From his long anthropological cultural reach, Hughes sees the archetype of the Serpent Woman as an aspect of 'mankind's psychological evolution' manifested here in the 'psycho-biological life' of the poet shaman who journeys into the otherworld to bring us back a healing vision of wholeness and the experience of living it. This 'is one reason why we value "The Ancient Mariner" as we do' (453).

In his Note on his sources at the end of 'The Snake in the Oak' Hughes mentions a book which he reviewed for *The Listener* when it was first published in 1964 – a review which is also included in *Winter Pollen*. Mircea Eliade's *Shamanism* not only remains the best introduction to the subject thirty years later, but is an example of the consistency of Hughes's interests, the continuity and importance of his study of anthropology since Cambridge. This reference also indicates how early, and for how long, he has nurtured and guarded his particular poetic gift. Even from the selection in *Winter Pollen* it is easy to see, looking back, the significant influence of the books he chose to review, at a time when this was a significant part of his income. The Introductions included here to collections of the poetry of Popa, Pilinszky and Douglas have often been seen as identifying features in their work that Hughes would hope to achieve in his own. In addition, the themes, language and insights of the longer essays on Baskin, Plath and Eliot can each be seen to be exploring elements that would contribute to the final integration of the vision in 'The Snake in the Oak', his most significant reflection on the materials of his own poetic vision.

When, in 1991 Hughes developed shingles, he mentioned to Andrew Motion that he believed his immune system had collapsed because he had spent too many years writing prose (Feinstein 2001: 237). Certainly Hughes wrote to Sagar just before he died that he had written for '5 or 6 years nothing but prose – nothing but burning the foxes' (*Letters* 719). Heaney takes a different view: 'His critical prose, in spite of recent insinuations to the contrary, was never at odds with the flourishing of his creative impulse' (1999/2000: 32). But in the year of the publication of *Winter Pollen* Hughes wrote to a correspondent that:

> These last years I've begun to feel that the hidden background of my poems is so unfamiliar to most likely readers, that there's more and more of a possibility that they might become wholly incomprehensible. When I looked at [*Winter Pollen*] it occurred to me that they provide a sort of background – in terms most readers would understand easily. So the book is a patch of jungle reserve for my poems to survive in – a

piece of the forest in which they evolved and are at home. That's how
I justify the book to myself now.

(T.H. to Dr Gillespie, 22. 2. 1994, MSS 644, Box 54, FF2)

It seems clear, however, that the exploration of this 'piece of the forest' that is
'background' to the poems has helped the poet himself understand where his
own poetic project is situated in the history of the major tensions in English
literature and English culture more generally. This may well have also helped
him to understand the very wide range of responses to his work and the
strength of feeling with which they have often been expressed.

The publication of *Letters of Ted Hughes* in 2007 not only confirmed the
enquiring and wide-ranging intellect behind the essays and reviews, but con-
stituted in itself a serious contribution to a huge variety of debates in English
culture. Edited with tact and invaluable notes by Christopher Reid, the *Letters*
provides a glimpse into a major writer's intellectual and emotional auto-
biography. Reid is right in saying that their dominant spirit is one of generosity,
offering family, friends and complete strangers alike an uncompromised and
fully developed train of thought drawing from a grasp of a surprising range of
esoteric forms of knowledge and experience. The direct form of address from
an enquiring intellect and an honest emotional self-examination provides a
volume of letters like no others in our culture. The integration of personal
experience – of responsibility for challenging relationships, for his art, for the
environment and for contemporary culture – with a wide range of reading and
reflection, reveals the whole person in continuous struggle with what is ultimately a dissatisfaction with the choices made in his life.

Reid admits that the lengthy contextualising annotations required prevented
him from including letters engaging with environmental issues that would have
revealed Hughes's full commitment 'to the research and lobbying that were
necessary. As he amassed evidence and read the scientific papers, he became a
true expert, well able, for instance, to face interrogation at public inquiries'
(*Letters*: xi). This present book has attempted to give some indication, especially in its 'Life and context' section, of what Reid might have included to
represent this neglected aspect of Hughes's 'work' in all its senses.

Translations

Ted Hughes wrote to his sister, an accomplished linguist, from his honeymoon
with Sylvia Plath in Benidorm in the summer of 1956 that on the train down to
Madrid he had been drinking wine and 'communicating with a compartment
full of "obreros" [workers] via my tiny Spanish dictionary' (MSS 980, Box 1,
FF4). From the tiny traditional fishing village of Benidorm he reports that he is
learning Spanish from a teacher, in return for teaching her English, and that he
intends to return to Madrid to live for a year teaching English. Hughes clearly
had an interest in learning foreign languages after having studied French and
Latin at Mexborough Grammar School. It was natural that he would play a
major part in bringing foreign poetry into the notoriously insular British poetry
scene in the 1960s and 1970s through his work on behalf of translation projects.

Of course, Hughes's own translation of Eastern European poets was to influence his poetry, particularly in the reductive language of the *Crow* project (1970). But also, late in his life, his translations of a body of plays and of *Tales From Ovid* (1997) were to become major achievements in themselves. Recent recognition of Hughes's work as a translator is indicated by one authority's claim that he 'must be regarded as among the major poetry translators in the English tradition' (Weissbort and Eysteinsson 2006: 521).

The Movement poets of the 1950s and 1960s were famously scathing about 'abroad' and their insularity was a part of their proud scepticism about anything European. When Philip Larkin was asked in a 1964 interview whether he read foreign poetry he replied, 'Foreign poetry? No!'(Morrison 1980: 60). So when Hughes first suggested to his Cambridge University friend Daniel Weissbort in 1963 that they might start a literary journal for translated poetry from around the world this was a radical idea for its time, although also somewhat of the zeitgeist. *Modern Poetry in Translation*, which Hughes edited with Weissbort for the first ten issues (1965–71), was a cornerstone of a movement in English poetry that included their friend and *Observer* poetry editor Al Alvavez. It was Alvarez who brought 'Iron Curtain' poets into the series *Penguin Modern European Poets* which had begun with a selection of translations of the poetry of Yevtushenko in 1962. In the *Observer* Alvarez had published the first translated poems by Zbigniew Herbert in September 1962, and by Miroslav Holub in June 1963. The first, unsigned, editorial of *Modern Poetry in Translation* (1965) indicates the radical intervention in the British poetry scene that the new journal intended to make by declaring: 'This poetry is more universal than ours. It deals with issues universally comprehensible. It does not fight shy of philosophy. It does not hide behind perverse imagery. As compared with our poetry it comes out into the open.' If this were not a clear enough critique of the Movement poets and others dominating British poetry at the time, the editorial of the fifth issue (1969), which focused upon Czech poets, compared Eastern European poets with 'Western poets': 'There is a tendency for the Western poet to become isolated and turn inwards, whereas the poet of the East is in tune with the rhythms of his people in a much more direct and dynamic way.' In his introduction to extracts from these editorials in *Ted Hughes: Selected Translations* Weissbort says that, although jointly written with him 'the views and intentions expressed are those of Hughes' (2006: 200).

Some of the Eastern European poets introduced by Hughes and Weissbort to the British audience reading *Modern Poetry in Translation* were to become key influences on Hughes's own work. From Poland, for example, Zbigniew Herbert produced simple political allegories that outflanked the sensors, while from Czechoslovakia Miroslav Holub used humour and his knowledge as a research scientist to point out the ironies of the conditions in which he lived. In 1968 there was published a selection of poems by the Israeli poet Yehuda Amichai in which the translations were credited to Assia Gutmann, but on which Hughes had collaborated (see Life and contexts, **p. 18**). This collection was the first of a series of books of translations that Hughes was instrumental in bringing to a British audience. It was followed by his writing Introductions to Anne Pennington's translations of the work of the Yugoslavian Vasko Popa (1969 and 1978) and the co-translation of the Hungarian János Pilinszky (1976).

The Hungarian poet János Csokits collaborated with Hughes on the work of Pilinszky and has written about their process in *Translating Poetry: The Double Labyrinth* edited by Weissbort (1989). Hughes preferred to hear the poetic idiom of the Hungarian and the poet's personal style in Csokits's literal renderings into English, however odd and awkward this first text might seem. But Csokits recognised a special quality to Hughes's reworkings of his originals that he described as 'X-ray versions':

> It was almost as if he could X-ray the literals and see the original poem in ghostly detail like a radiologist viewing the bones, muscles, veins and nerves of a live human body ... The effect is not that of a technical device; it has more to do with extra-sensory perception.
>
> (Csokits 1989: 11)

Weissbort has written that 'Hughes was struck by the way these [literal] versions powerfully conveyed material of great urgency, which was apparently dissipated in more polished ... versions' (Weissbort and Eysteinsson 2006: 521). The paradox remains that despite his desire to remain close to the literal versions and retain a sense of their 'foreignness', his translations are unmistakably Hughesian. This is true for translations as diverse as the Middle English of *Sir Gawain and the Green Knight* (which appeared in *The School Bag* edited by Hughes and Seamus Heaney, 1997) and the highly sophisticated Russian verse of Pushkin's 'The Prophet' that was the last poem he prepared for publication (1999). Hughes wrote in the editorial to the third issue of *Modern Poetry in Translation*:

> A man who has something really serious to say in a language of which he knows only a few words, manages to say it far more convincingly and effectively than any interpreter, and in translated poetry it is the first-hand contact – however fumbled and broken – with that man and his seriousness which we want.
>
> (Weissbort 2006: 201)

In his translations of the Greek and Roman classical plays Hughes preferred to use the dual language texts of the Loeb Classical Library, which he referred to as his 'Victorian crib'. The first of these was an adaptation of Senaca's *Oedipus* (1969) commissioned by Peter Brook for a performance at the National Theatre in March 1968. In his Introduction to the Faber edition of his adaptation Hughes wrote that he was guided by Brook 'to make a text that would release whatever inner power this story, in its plainest, bluntest form, still has, and to unearth, if we could, the ritual possibilities within it' (1969: 7–8). The text uses spacing and line breaks instead of punctuation, producing a poetic, epic, but stark, ritualistic effect. The translator David Turner, whose originally commissioned translation had been rejected by Brook, graciously described the first reading of the new text by Hughes to the cast as achieving 'inspiration, elegance, fire, poetry. It was all magic. And all the magic was Ted's' (1969: 9). This collaboration with Peter Brook led to work on the play *Orghast* which was written by Hughes in an invented language of sounds to communicate across cultures in a performance at Persepolis in what was then Persia. Hughes shared with Brook an interest in the possibilities of communication by the most minimal means. This recalls Pilinszky's desire to write poems about the Holocaust 'as if I had remained silent' (Weissbort 2002: 91).

This reductiveness characterises Hughes's translations, late in his life, of a series of classic plays from European drama, described more fully below under 'Plays' (see Works, p. 92). These translations have been variously described as 'terse' (*Spring Awakening*, 1995), 'direct' (*Blood Wedding*, 1996), 'robust' (*Phèdre*, 1998) and 'pared-down' (*The Oresteia*, 1999). Typical of the immediate admiration for these translations was Michael Billington's praise in the *Guardian* for Hughes's translation of *Blood Wedding* for 'capturing Lorca's mixture of starkness and lyricism … which faithfully captures Lorca's mix of earthiness and beauty … The stark, sensual power of the play emerges through Hughes's language' (*Guardian* 12. 10. 1996). The final and the best play of this series, *Alcestis* (1999), was a remarkable translation that was heard posthumously in the Yorkshire accents, as Hughes had intended, of Barrie Rutter's company, Northern Broadsides, performing in the bowels of an old mill in Halifax. That it is the only translation in this series of plays that was not originally commissioned, and that it is half as long again as the original, indicates its choice as a story of grief and redemption that had a personal significance for Hughes. The language of suffering in this text is both deeply and directly communicated, yet the play ends with the formidable challenge to accept each misfortune as an opportunity. From a minor play by Euripides Hughes found the modern language for not only a moving and profound insight, but a personal and sadly posthumous vision of redemption.

Tales From Ovid: Twenty-four Passages from the Metamorphoses (1997) was the most acclaimed translation project undertaken by Hughes, winning the Whitbread Book of the Year Award in 1998, the year of his death. It is characteristically much freer with the original than his early approach to literal translation. Asked to contribute four passages to an anthology titled *After Ovid* being edited by Michael Hofmann and James Lasdun in 1993, Hughes had become interested in doing more, obviously attracted by the mythic material that had always held a power for him in its direct, economical language, its emotional range and its narrative versatility. Hughes easily drew upon the earliest simple narrative style for children that he had found for his radio plays and creation stories. He also deployed a similar playful delight in his modernisation: 'But now Phoebus anointed Phaethon / With a medicinal blocker / To protect him from the burning' (1997: 32). But by now he also had in his repertoire the ability to deal with shocking violence and deep emotion with surprising images, revealing a depth of understanding from a lifetime of experience and his imaginative engagement with it. Published the year before his death, *Tales From Ovid* explores two significant themes, one of which dominates the early work and the other his last work.

The first might be characterised as the recurring paradox of the early animal poems in which the very qualities that give life and individual strength to a being might be the source of its vulnerability and its fatal flaw: 'Her own gaze flamed and hurt her' (1997: 226); 'Niobe, of all mothers / Would have been most blessed / If only she had not boasted // That she, of all mothers, was the most blessed' (1997: 212). The second theme is that of the late plays and of *Birthday Letters*, and that is the question of at what point a character's fate is sealed, or the degree to which choice is possible once events are underway. In these tales early and often impulsive choices determine the pattern of a whole lifetime.

In 2006 Hughes's original collaborator in establishing *Modern Poetry in Translation* in 1965, and correspondent about translation all his life – Daniel Weissbort – edited *Ted Hughes: Selected Translations* which revealed for the first time the full range of translation undertaken by Hughes. Beginning with the *Bardo Thödol* from 1960, this selection includes translations of more poets than were represented in published translations in Hughes's lifetime, including a section from Homer's *Odyssey*, the Portuguese of Mário Sá Carneiro and Helder Macedo, the Hungarian of Ferenc Juhász, the French of Yves Bonnefoy, Paul Eluard and Georges Schehadé (the latter an opera commissioned and performed by Sadler's Wells in 1974), the Italian of Lorenzo de' Medici and the Spanish poems of Lorca. Excellent notes and appendices of a selection of the texts from which Hughes worked make this book a powerful demonstration of his fascination with translation throughout his life. In addition, an appendix collects statements made by Hughes at various times on his approach to translation, including a substantial essay written in 1982 on the *Modern Poetry in Translation* project. It is this volume that makes the case for Hughes as 'among the most important poetry translators in the English tradition' (2006: vii).

Apart from Weissbort, the only critic to give a considered response to this aspect of Hughes's work is Neil Roberts, who comments in detail on Hughes's use of original texts with some interesting conclusions. One is that Hughes's translations are not only consistent with the linguistic and thematic agendas of his own poetry, but that they make changes from the originals in order to enhance their contemporary relevance as Hughes sees it:

> Hughes's whole *oeuvre* can be seen as a struggle to articulate spiritual experience in a vacuum of religious forms. A key feature of *Tales from Ovid* is that, despite the 'obsolete' and often corrupt nature of the religious 'paraphernalia', Hughes several times enhances the religious sentiment of the text.
>
> (Roberts 2006: 188)

Roberts's use of the word 'religious' here includes an emphasis on ecological harmony that, in the case of *Tales from Ovid*, is 'much weightier and more distinctive' than in the original text (2006: 190) (see Criticism, **p. 123**).

Daniel Weissbort argues that not only was Hughes keen to promote the influence of translations in English culture and to take some of those influences into his own work, 'translations were an integral part of his own oeuvre' (Weissbort 2006: viii). Weissbort believes that it was translation that got Hughes writing again after the death of Sylvia Plath and that it was translation, rather than a focus on critical prose as Hughes believed, that deflected the flow of Hughes's own poetry at the end of his life: 'While translation was, perhaps, a saving grace for Ted in the early '60s, it became at the end of his life a hard taskmaster' (Weissbort 2002: 106).

Plays

It was natural that an English poet struggling to make a living to support a family in the 1960s should turn to playwriting since this was an era in which drama was the leading mode of literary activity and was offering greater financial opportunities for young writers than poetry ever could. Many of Hughes's contemporaries at Cambridge were making a name for themselves in the theatre, with Peter Hall, for example, directing the Royal Shakespeare Company and seeking new work from young writers. In his letters Hughes mentions seeing some of the major new works in the theatre such as John Whiting's *The Devils*, Arnold Wesker's *Roots* and John Arden's *Serjeant Musgrave's Dance*. This was an age of theatrical experimentation in which there might be opportunities for Hughes to explore his interest in the inner world, and its suppression and distortion by social conventions.

There is a little-known photograph of Hughes on stage at Mexborough Grammar School in a performance of *Thunder Rock* (about a man who withdraws from the world into a lighthouse), but his experience as a performer did not extend beyond school (*Sheffield Star* 20. 12. 1984). Hughes began an apprenticeship in playwriting early in his career, when writing for educational and adult radio was his main source of income. After an important period of collaboration with Peter Brook there was a gap of nearly twenty-five years before the final flourishing of a series of translated stage plays that together form a surprisingly unified body of late work. In all of his playwriting for radio and theatre Hughes was working as a poet with an intense interest in the effects of language and there is a clear relationship between the stylistic qualities of the plays and the stages of his poetic stylistic development. There is also a dynamic relationship between Hughes's poetic themes and the plays he chose to work on that is consistent with his central preoccupation with human perception and choices in relation to inner and outer nature. It is perhaps true to say that the discoveries Hughes made in his playwriting have been underestimated in their importance to the development of the poetry, and that the final body of translated European plays have not yet been given the attention they deserve in contrast to the reception of *Birthday Letters*.

Diane Middlebrook writes that 'Literary history will not remember Ted Hughes as a playwright, yet it was his principal occupation and the chief supplier of his income during the 1960s' (2004: 135). She describes the earliest work as 'incoherent and unmarketable plays in which Hughes promoted the esoteric ideas he was hooked on' (2004: xvi). At first Hughes was interested in reviving the mode of verse drama, with the supportive interest of its most recent master, T. S. Eliot himself. Although a libretto for the *Bardo Thödol* (*The Tibetan Book of the Dead*), which Hughes worked on before leaving America, did not see the light of day (see Works, **p. 74 and p. 91**), a short verse drama *The House of Aries* was broadcast on BBC radio in 1960. Encouraged by this, Hughes then wrote for radio 'The Wound', the strange dream play which was published in *Wodwo* (see Works, **pp. 37–9**). Peter Hall requested a stage play from Hughes for 1962 which resulted in his working on 'The Calm', although this came to nothing and the manuscript sheets of the play were used for drafting poems by both Hughes and Plath. In 1963 BBC radio broadcast a play titled 'Difficulties of a Bridegroom' (not to be confused with the stories later collected under this title) which, like 'The Wound', shifts between a rationally accountable reality and dream-like psychic states.

The Coming of the Kings and Other Plays (1970) collected four of the plays written for the BBC Schools English radio series *Listening and Writing* and *Living Language* in the 1960s. These plays are condensed retellings of myths and folktales with the simplicity and power of ballads. Every word counts and the charge of the storytelling lies in capturing emotions in a style that can be both lyrical and stark. These plays evoke a mystery beyond the narrative itself that has the effect of the reverberations of poetry. Their success in their role in the educational setting is that they demand discussion. The texts were made available free to teachers using the broadcasts (usually live) in the classroom. These plays clearly contributed to the development of Hughes's first mythic style in the poems collected in *Wodwo* (1967) and to the interest in narrative in that collection of poems and stories. During this period Hughes obviously thought of his writing poems and stories to be explorations of common themes in closely linked modes and there is no reason to doubt that his plays for younger audiences were not also part of this project.

At the heart of experimentation in what could be achieved by theatrical performance at this time was Peter Brook. When Hughes heard that Brook wanted to commission a new version of Senaca's *Oedipus* (1969) he realised that he could be a part of this experimentation in language and performance with a director who shared his thematic interests. Moreover, Hughes would have noted that Brook's work also attracted funding that would pay a writer better than publishing poetry ever could at that time. From the classical text Hughes produced a hard-hitting script for vocal effects that anticipated the next stage of experimentation with Brook in which words would be abandoned altogether.

The climax of Hughes's collaboration with Peter Brook was the famous performance of *Orghast* (1970) at the Shiraz Festival in Persia which is documented in A. C. H. Smith's *Orghast at Persepolis* (1972). Brook believed that drama could communicate across cultures and languages if it was reduced to its most basic and powerful forms. For this performance Hughes devised a language of sounds that obviously had an influence on the reduced language of *Crow* (1970). The play was based upon the Prometheus myth and one spin-off from it was the poem sequence *Prometheus on his Crag*, published in *Moortown* (1979).

In the last four years of his life Hughes produced new translations of five plays from the world canon of classic play texts from Germany, Spain, France and ancient Greece (see Works, p. 90). Their common themes of passion and violence, of repression and guilt, of sexual impulses and social responsibility, suggest that Hughes was making drama that explored the very dynamics he had identified at the core of Shakespeare's work in *The Goddess of Complete Being*. Keith Sagar (2005) has represented these dynamic tensions as 'the crime against nature', by which he means both external and inner nature. To the extent that these new versions of famous plays explore the consequences of 'the crime against nature' they have much in common with Hughes's own poetic dramas *Gaudete* (1977) and *Cave Birds* (1978) in which neglect and suppression of sexual and emotional life have different forms of self-destructive consequences from which escape and redemption are hard-won. The language of these late plays is tight and reductive, in the manner that Hughes had learned from his translations of the Eastern European poets (see Works, **p. 88**). The Faber texts of these plays characterise this style with the words 'terseness and bite' (*Spring Awakening*), 'marvellous directness' (*Blood Wedding*), 'vivid and robust' (*Phèdre*) and 'pared-down and powerfully driven' (*The Oresteia*). In the final and probably the best play of the series, *Alcestis*, Hughes embedded what he must have known to be his last poetic statements and redemptive, hopeful release.

It is easy to understand why Hughes would be attracted by Tim Supple's commission for him to write a new translation of Frank Wedekind's 1891 play *Spring Awakening* for the Royal Shakespeare Company in 1995. The play demonstrates the destructiveness of sexual prudery in church and family culture to young people coming into puberty. In this respect the play has much in common with Hughes's early work, exemplified by 'Egg-head', satirising the protections raised in human culture to resist the natural charges and elemental forces in both emotional life ('Secretary') and the lives of animals ('Thrushes') and landscapes ('Wind'). In Wedekind's play a mother cannot bring herself to go beyond the story of the stork to explain to her daughter how her sister has come to have a baby. The passing of information concerning human reproduction between adolescent boys is a crime deserving expulsion from school. A boy who 'murders' his lust for famous paintings of naked women by tearing up pictures of them and flushing them down the toilet eventually commits suicide under the pressure not only of his sense of guilt, but his failure to gain 'academic' knowledge by passing his exams. The girl, meanwhile, who had been given only the traditional story of the stork, is raped by one of the boys. Hughes's translation is both modern and direct: 'Then along comes Mother Schmidt's abortion technology – and there she is in the grave with her dead foetus'. The brutal intervention and its hubris is brilliantly conveyed by the word 'technology'. Hughes's translation has a characteristic ironic power in the indirectness of the conversations about sexual knowledge and instincts that is compassionately indignant about cultural repression. In the final scene of the play a 'Masked Gentleman' intervenes in a dialogue between the ghost of the boy who has committed suicide and his friend, Moritz, who is on the run from the Reformatory in which he has been placed. The Gentleman explains that morality is a negotiation between 'duty and inclination'. 'Why didn't somebody tell me that?' asks the ghost boy. Moritz is offered the choice between death and life and chooses what the Gentleman offers: 'the hopes of having everything to come – insatiable, overwhelming, doubtful'. Again, this translation conveys the tensions and difficulties ahead that underlie that notion of youthful 'hope'.

A year after the Wedekind translation Hughes was commissioned by Tim Supple to write a version of the play *Blood Wedding*, written in 1933 by Federico García Lorca, for the Young Vic theatre. In the middle of her wedding the bride elopes on horseback with her former lover who is from a family responsible for deaths in her bridegroom's family. She has realised that she is about to marry the wrong man, although she knows that this elopement will end in violence. In a moonlit wood, with the bridegroom and followers closing in, the bride declares her passion, but pleads with her lover to leave her and escape.

Hughes's translation poetically conveys the stark paradoxes of her emotions and the relationship: 'I want to be with you. / You drag me back with you. / You tell me to go back / And I come after you through the air / Like a leaf torn off'. Later we are told that 'Two men who were in love / Killed each other'. A play that began with the preparations for a wedding ends with the image of a knife 'In the quivering / Dark / Roots / Of the scream'. Hughes invests Lorca's poetic drama with as lucid expressions of complex emotions as it is possible to hear on the modern English stage. At the end of the play the Bride tries to explain to the bridegroom's mother how she had wanted to resist her former lover, who had since himself married, and was committed to her son: 'My whole hope was your son and I haven't deceived him. But the other's arm dragged me like a wave from the sea. And it would always have dragged me, always, even if I'd been an old woman and all your son's sons had tried to hold me down by my hair'. Theatre critic Michael Billington was especially impressed by Hughes's translation 'which captures Lorca's mixture of starkness and lyricism' (*Guardian* 12. 10. 1996).

Before his death, Hughes agreed that Tim Supple should adapt his translation of *Tales from Ovid* for a Royal Shakespeare Company production, although Supple found that little needed to be changed from the drama of the verse already published. 'Ovid met his match in Ted', says Supple.

> I think he shared the Roman's interest in the moments when we lose contact with our rational selves and become possessed with extreme states, such as desire or anger. He wanted to know where you go, spiritually, when that happens.
>
> (*Daily Telegraph* 15. 4. 1999)

At the time of his death Hughes was planning a further collaboration with Supple, but only had time to write what Supple called 'one brilliant set of notes' for *The Epic of Gilgamesh* before his illness overwhelmed him (Tim Supple, email to T.G., 27. 2. 2008). This was, Hughes wrote to Sagar four months before his death, 'an old ambition' (BL ADD 78761, f. 3).

But after *Blood Wedding* British theatre directors were aware that Ted Hughes was fascinated by and had a facility for translations of plays concerned with the tensions of responsibility and passion, or the notions of 'duty and inclination' as Hughes himself puts it for a character in *Spring Awakening*. Jonathan Kent of the Almeida Theatre Company commissioned a version of *Phèdre* by Jean Racine (Hughes having rejected Kent's invitation to translate Racine's *Medea*) for a star-studded performance in the year of Hughes's death of a classic from French drama that retold a Greek myth. Abandoning Racine's famous complex verse forms, Hughes again simplified, tightened and tensioned the dialogue so that it achieved both a modern colloquialism and an archetypal power.

Again a story of the conflicts of infatuation, loyalty and honour is driven along towards tragic outcomes more bleak, if possible, than the previous two plays. Just at the moment when Hippolytus, the proud son of the famously heroic King Theseus, brings himself to confess his love to the daughter of his family enemy, Aricia, to his horror his father's second wife Phèdre confesses her love for him. Since Theseus, who has been missing in a bold journey to the underworld, is declared dead, the way seems open to Phèdre for her to marry her love and place him on the throne of Greece. Unexpectedly Theseus returns and Phèdre's maid attempts to save her mistress by getting to Theseus first to accuse Hippolytus of declaring his love to Phèdre. Theseus calls in a favour owed to him by the gods and demands that vengeance be exacted upon his son. This is enacted too late for Theseus to realise his mistake as Phèdre, having taken a slow poison, tells Theseus the truth. The only redemption at the end of this play is that Theseus makes his peace in grief with the grieving Aricia and adopts her as his daughter. 'The error of my judgement,' says Theseus, 'is so monumental and plain.' These are the very qualities of the language of this play in which errors of judgement are hard to avoid under the pressure of unsought passions that unravel into violent tragedy.

Now Hughes wanted to make his own choice of plays and he wanted to return to the original Greek drama. 'He regretted not having accepted the Almeida's invitation to write a new version of *Medea*' (Olwyn Hughes, letter to T.G., 14. 2. 2008). In many ways the National Theatre's acceptance of his new version of *The Oresteia* by Aeschylus was the climax of this series of new translations of classic plays that Hughes undertook in what were to be the final years of his life. Although originally a commission for another theatre, the play was first performed in 1999, the year following his death, under the direction of Katie Mitchell. *The Oresteia* consists of three plays telling one epic story of honour, violent revenge and self-destructive hubris. This is a monumental work that Hughes drives along with his terse and direct writing.

A father, Agamemnon, sacrifices his daughter to the gods in order to gain a fair wind on his journey to sack Troy for the taking of Helen, his brother's wife. Upon his triumphal return Agamemnon is killed by his wife in revenge, which results in her being killed by her son, Orestes, to avenge his father's murder. Troubled by having broken an archetypal taboo, Orestes appeals to the goddess of justice, Athene, to be pardoned for his matricide. Athene creates a jury of twelve citizens of Athens to try Orestes, but has to make a casting vote in his favour. The terrible wrath of the Furies this judgement produces has to be given a subterranean home within the city, 'the fortress of understanding', so that their wisdom is also available within the 'whole mind' of the society. Only by accommodating and venerating 'the powers of darkness / Who have risen from the earth / To watch over the ways of mankind' can the cycle of pride and revenge be redeemed. Indeed, the search for possible redemption for human hubris is the impulse at the conclusion of Hughes's last two plays.

Alcestis was the only one of the translated plays which Hughes wrote late in his life that was not a commission. It was his last work, although he had begun translating it in 1993, and he knew that his cancer was terminal as he completed the final draft. Watching the first performance of Hughes's version of Euripides' play at Dean Clough, Halifax, was like hearing a posthumous message from the underworld. We were deep in the bowels of a former textile mill in West Yorkshire, the home of Barrie Rutter's company, Northern Broadsides, which gives all its performances in a broad Yorkshire accent. Hughes had offered this company his translation, writing to Rutter, 'After translating *Phèdre*, I realised that my tuning fork lies somewhere in the Calder Valley' (*Times*, 11. 9. 2000).

The resonance of the West Yorkshire location and voices, combined with Hughes's death only months earlier and his choice of this play as his final work, were to give this performance a charged significance. This sense was not simply a matter of the context of the performance. In 1993 Hughes had obviously been attracted to the play for its dramatic themes, returning to complete it only months before his death. Since much of the play is a debate about the nature of death, and alternative stances towards it, and Hughes must have known that he was gravely ill despite his battle with his cancer, the sheer courage and deep poignancy of the text underlies the tensions of the narrative and the insights of the translation.

King Admetos is fated to die young, but his appointed slave Apollo has found that in rare cases Fate will accept a substitute. Apollo has sought volunteers among the family of Admetos, but even his parents, who are themselves near death, will not relinquish their lives to save their son. The one person unasked, Admetos's wife Alcestis, has offered to give up her life out of love for her husband and is now dying as Death calls at the house to claim her. The Chorus are friends of Admetos who have come to support him with the poignant words, 'In every marriage / One must mourn the other'. Hughes uses a line from a Wilfred Owen poem for Alcestis, 'Carry me into the sun', which brings her onto the stage where she dies. The Chorus comments in simple language upon a profound truth: 'Alcestis welcomed her death / When first she welcomed her life. / She has merely unwrapped / The gift her mother gave her'.

At this moment Heracles arrives to stay with his friend Admetos on his way to perform another heroic challenge in the series of tasks for which he is famous. Admetos keeps the truth from his guest in order to offer hospitality, as though under a test of their friendship. Here Hughes injects into the original play a comic drunken enactment of the tasks of Heracles, including the insertion of the story of Prometheus and the vulture. In these scenes Hughes seems to be suggesting that heroic courage is absurd in the face of the recurring success of death, that it is, indeed, a way of enacting death, in which Heracles actually delights. All that Prometheus has been protecting by his resistance to the daily return of the vulture is a secret that he eventually has to give to Heracles in return for his freedom from the chains which Heracles breaks. This turns out to be the secret that God's son will depose him. But now it is no longer a secret, God can avoid his fate. The narrative twist, which echoes, or rather historically anticipates, the crux of *The Winter's Tale*, is that Heracles chases after Death and returns with a veiled woman whom he asks Admetos to look after while Heracles continues to perform his next task. This is the test of Admetos's promise never to be tempted by another woman. The resistance of Admetos earns him the unveiling and return of his wife. Thus the compassionate courage of Heracles resolves the play, which ends with the line: 'Let this give man hope'. The Chorus comments that 'God has accomplished / What was beyond belief', apparently because the loss of hubris in grief by Admetos has enabled him not only to express a 'greatness of spirit' in the generous courage towards a guest and the refusal of the woman, but in the recovery of his own soul through listening to God's 'corrections', which are the consequences of his actions.

This translation immediately conveys a sense of its contemporary relevance by Hughes's use of language such as 'I killed the electro-technocrats, those

Titans' and 'A nuclear bomb spewing a long cloud / Of consequences', together
with references to 'the dark maze of the atom'. At the heart of Hughes's text is
the most explicit indication of the importance he attaches to the Prometheus
myth in a dialogue between Prometheus and God. 'I freed [man] to be human,'
says Prometheus. 'I broke the chains / That made him a slave to your laws.' But
God's reply indicates that the stolen gift of fire (and subsequent technology) to
man by Prometheus gave him the opposite of illumination: 'You freed him / To
grope his way into the dark maze of the atom / With no more illumination than
a hope.' This 'freedom' was actually also an inner loss, as God explains: 'You
cut the nerves / That connected him to his own soul.' This 'soul' was the
intuition that enabled man to hear God's 'corrections'. Hughes chooses to end
this play, and the whole of his life's work, with the offer of that small hope.

3

Criticism

Reputations

'When Ted Hughes died in 1998,' recalled the poet Simon Armitage in 2006,

> he was as valued as at any time in his career, and his two final col-
> lections, *Tales from Ovid* and *Birthday Letters*, had met with resounding
> acclaim. During the 1970s and 80s, however, to speak up on his
> behalf, whether as a reader or a writer, was to take a position. To
> support Hughes's poetry was to support the man himself, a man
> whose ideologies could have been described as unfashionable, and
> whose poetic style was seen by some as stubborn and entrenched.
> (*Guardian* 18. 2. 2006, Saturday Review, p. 22)

This is a good generalised summary of two phases of the reputation of Ted
Hughes. What it omits is the immediate and forceful impact of the first phase in
the 1950s and 1960s. But what it indicates is not just the roller-coaster ride of
the cultural status of the writer in his life-time, but the vehemence with which
opinions have been expressed about his work that have, somehow, also been
about what he stands for as a writer. In 1995 Sean O'Brien wrote: 'Hughes
could be forgiven for feeling that, at times, he undergoes the kind of eviscerat-
ing inquiry and judgement normally reserved for the dead' (*Sunday Times* 5. 3.
1995). It is clear that some critics have felt threatened by the writer's cultural
project, as he came to understand that they always would, since his work was
an intervention in the continuing history of tensions in English culture (not just
English literature), as his writing about Shakespeare, and later Coleridge, confirmed to him (see Works, p. 80).

The best survey of the critical reputation up to *Wolfwatching* (1989) is the
late Leonard M. Scigaj's 'Introduction' to his *Critical Essays on Ted Hughes*
(1992) and, until Neil Roberts's book (2006), this remained the only collection
of criticism covering each of the major collections of poetry. Scigaj's introductory survey can be recommended for his own rebuttals of the critics following his even-handed summaries of their views. A useful anthology of critical
work under major themes is provided by Sandie Byrne's book (2000). Reviews
for each book published by Hughes are listed in Sagar and Tabor's *Ted*

Hughes: A Bibliography 1946–1995 (1998). Books of critical essays on various aspects of the work have been published following conferences on Hughes (Sagar 1983; Sagar 1994; Moulin 2004; Schuchard 2006; Rees 2009) and the leading Hughes scholars have published monographs which will be referred to in the appropriate sections following this one. What are charted here in general terms are the fluctuations in the critical reputation of the major work as reflected in the reviews. The detail of the specific debates will be recounted in the following theme-based parts of this chapter.

In 1957 *The Hawk in the Rain* burst upon the English poetry scene with a bold vigour and sustained intelligence that immediately challenged the urbane incumbents of the Movement with a vitality, agenda and technical dexterity from which they barely recovered. Sniping about 'the myth-kitty' (Philip Larkin), mental instability (Donald Davie), imprecision (John Wain) and the desire for 'something sublimer than thinking' (Kingsley Amis) indicates how much the Movement poets felt under threat (Morrison 1980: 194, 278, 147). Reviewers recognised a new force in English poetry, Robin Skelton, for example, predicting 'the emergence of a new talent' (*Manchester Guardian* 4. 10. 1957). Graham Hough identified a penetrating and transformative 'poetic intelligence' that 'runs all through' the poem (*Encounter*, November 1957) in contrast to the epigrammatic conclusion of the current poetic mode. A. E. Dyson admired the exploratory, meditative quality of the poetry and was already predicting on the basis of the first collection that 'he will be one of the select few to be read a hundred years from now' (*Critical Quarterly* 1, Autumn 1959). It was Al Alvarez who made the rather startling observation that Hughes 'hardly *thinks* at all' in the poem 'The Thought-Fox': the poet 'apprehends the unwritten poem not as an idea or a feeling or a form, but as an ominous physical shock' (*Observer* 27. 3. 1960). Alan Brownjohn was one of the few reviewers who had reservations about 'self-consciously turbulent diction' and 'sex-and-violence imagery' (*Listen* 2, Spring 1958).

Lupercal (1960) was seen as an advance and elicited reviews that were sharper about the poetic qualities of the writing and its project. Al Alvarez, an important early champion as poetry editor of the *Observer*, countered Brownjohn's reservations by asserting that now the violence in Hughes's poetry was 'wholly contained by his artistic resources' (*Observer* 27. 3. 1960). But there remained a few doubters, John Press worrying, for example, that Hughes might have a 'preoccupation with power and violence regarded almost as ends-in-themselves' (*Sunday Times* 3. 4. 1960). Again Graham Hough was perceptive in identifying a structural balancing within the volume of animal predation with human dignity and compassion without resolving explicitly how they informed each other (*Listener* 28. 7. 1960). Frederick Grubb, in a chapter in his 1965 book *A Vision of Reality*, produced the most understanding commentary on the first two collections: 'He greets the intellect as in league with, though not subordinate to, nature, and his poems are often models of the ordering of experience'. Objectivity in treating death in animals and people evokes the pity and the terror, Grubb argued. From the observations of the attractions and traps of instinct in animals, 'the assertion of free will is born'. Grubb titled his chapter with an assertion of the thinking poet's integration with nature: 'Thinking Animal: Ted Hughes' (1965: 214–25).

In 1962 the reputation of Hughes was given a major endorsement, not so much from the inclusion of his poems in Al Alvarez's *The New Poetry*, as from the way the introductory essay, titled 'Beyond the Gentility Principle', was widely read as championing Hughes against Larkin. Alvarez's argument for his anthology in this essay set itself as a counter to Robert Conquest's Movement anthology *New Lines* (1956). Alvarez argued that the evidence of 'mass evil' that emerged from the Second World War, together with the continuing nuclear threat during the Cold War, could no longer be separated from individual anxieties underneath 'the pretence that life ... is the same as ever, that gentility, decency, and all the other social totems will eventually muddle through': 'the forceable recognition of a mass evil outside us has developed precisely parallel with psychoanalysis; that is, with our recognition of the ways in which the same forces are at work within us' (1962: 23).

In many ways this form of advocacy for Hughes's poetry had the effect of splitting the critics, many of whom wanted to admire the poetry for entirely different reasons. Those who objected to Alvarez's arguments used Hughes's poetry as the means to do so. Within a year David Holbrook began the first of a series of attacks on what he saw as the 'histrionic indulgence in a despisal [sic] of life' (1963) in the work of first Hughes, and later Plath, that culminated in his book *Lost Bearings in English Poetry* (1977). Scigaj writes, 'By the mid-1960s Holbrook and [Philip] Hobsbaum had articulated the central critical response to Hughes's poetry: corner Hughes on the violence question and insinuate the biographical fallacy' (1992: 11).

Wodwo (1967) elicited an interesting review from the young Seamus Heaney who admired the 'quest for a farther country of the mind', especially in the 'large, rhetorical poems' of Part III – 'powerful operatic gestures which indicate rather than express the crisis and compulsion behind them'. Although Heaney found some poems 'strident' and 'overwritten', he defended Hughes from rumours of his poetry 'going off' by commending 'a man exploring and pushing the limits of his achievement' (Heaney 1967: 50–52). *Wodwo*'s 'single adventure' of a radio play and stories dividing two sections of poetry reflected the artistic and economic life of a writer whose anthropological training had given him a broad sense of culture. Most critics, like Heaney, reviewed the poetry and ignored the rest. While P. Straus contrasted animal determinism with humans' self-determining freedom in the poetry (*Theoria* 38, May 1972), Derwent May (*Times* 13. 7. 1967) and Graham Martin saw the animal poems as 'metaphors for a particular human vision' as Martin put it (*Listener* 6. 7. 1967). Anthony Hecht identified ritual initiations in the structure of the volume in which 'the initiate was made dramatically and terribly to confront his deepest animal nature' (*Hudson Review* 21, Spring 1968). Daniel Hoffman went the furthest in perceiving that this shamanic quest did not lead as far as it might. What he called the missing 'healing power' was denied by the protagonist's isolation from any tribe or community; 'nor does Nature offer any consolatory unifica-tion of experience' (*Shenandoah* 19, Summer 1968).

Every one of the first three volumes by Hughes had been noted as a new contribution to contemporary English poetry, but *Crow* (1970) became imme-diately famous as the most original and challenging intervention of all. It remains a keystone in Hughes's reputation after his death: John Carey chose it as his book of the century, declaring *Crow* 'Hughes's most powerful work' (*Sunday Times* 24. 10. 1999). The debates around this volume not only hardened the positions of the critics in relation to Hughes, but defined the terms of the debate for the rest of the 1970s: 'the main areas of conflict included the violence, the unfamiliar style and form, authorial control, and whether myth constitutes a retreat from history' (Scigaj 1992: 14). Of course, all of these are linked in the poetry, as demonstrated by an amazing essay by J. M. Newton which began by asserting the moral concerns of the humour and ended by celebrating the music and regretting the reservations of his reviews of previous volumes (*Cambridge Quarterly*, 5(4), 1971). The continuing debate about violence in Hughes's poetry, with which Newton engaged, came to be discussed in relation to nihilism and morality. Ian Robinson and David Sims argued that 'actually the violence in these poems isn't shocking enough: it seems to come too easy, and it pays diminishing returns' (*The Human World*, 9, November 1972). Neil Roberts, on the other hand, suggested that *Crow* bravely confronted 'the struggle to understand what it means to be human, and to affirm that it does mean something, in the face of the conditions which cause some to lapse into the comfort of nihilism'. In the process Roberts saw 'the acquisition of a soul' and 'the implications of moral awareness for the sense of what one is', in conditions that one cannot change (*Delta*, 50, Spring 1972). Against Terry Eagleton's view of *Crow* as a use of myth to escape reality (Eagleton 1972), Charles Fernandez offered an analysis of myth used to critique the failures of Western Christian, technological civilisation to contain the demonic, which in this volume Hughes managed to 'reformulate and revitalize' with an alternative creativity (*Modern Poetry Studies*, 6, Autumn 1975). In 1975 the first book-length monograph, *The Art of Ted Hughes*, was published by Keith Sagar and stood for seven years as the only study of Hughes.

The appearance of *Gaudete* (1977) confused most Hughes critics on both sides of the debate about his poetry and it is significant that some critics have wanted to revise their readings in later years, as in the cases of John Bayley (cf. *Listener* 2. 6. 1977 and *London Review of Books* 21. 2. 1980) and Neil Roberts (cf. *Delta* 57, 1977 and Roberts 2006). Four exceptions stand out. Hermann Peschmann emphasised the 'cumulative effect' of the different parts of the book: 'the whole work ... is of great strength and originality' (*Times Educational Supplement* 10. 6. 1977). Irvin Ehrenpreis wrote at length about the whole work as a 'myth of death and resurrection' (*New York Review of Books* 17. 8. 1978). Oliver Lyne praised the 'fine writing' of the central action (*Times Literary Supplement* 1. 7. 1977). J. M. Newton continued his accommodation to Hughes's work by responding to the religious 'ferocity' by which Hughes conjured for the first time a divine female figure with 'a great and powerful though not at all a vague mystery' (*Cambridge Quarterly*, 7(4), 1977). Meanwhile, previous admirers of the poetry struggled to balance their enjoyment of the 'craft' (Thomas Lask, *New York Times* 19. 7. 1978; Philip Toynbee, *Observer* 22. 5. 1977) with the 'smash and bash' of the results (John Bayley, *Listener* 2. 6. 1977) in which 'the whole enterprise fails if rationality is invoked' (Martin Dodsworth, *Guardian* 19. 5. 1977). Dodsworth's frustration is a typical response: 'Hughes is a genius, a Samson in his strength, but lacking wisdom'. Ultimately *Gaudete* came to be thought of as an important opening stage in the poet's direct engagement with the Goddess of Complete Being, Roberts suggesting that 'the exploration of guilty masculinity in *Gaudete* ... is among his most enduring, and most humanly significant, achievements' (2006: 113).

The 'mythically challenged' critics were to be further extended by *Cave Birds* (1978). The clear internal narrative of its 'alchemical drama' was too much hard work for reviewers more used to collections of lyric poems that were situated, descriptive and experiential. Scigaj rather wickedly lists those reviewers who complained about a lack of narrative or unifying schema (1992: 36). Julian Symons rejected 'lines that seem impenetrably obscure' (*Sunday Times* 26. 11. 1978), as did Robert Nye for 'such persistently unreflecting savagery that it removes all need for thought' (*Times* 7. 9. 1978). Edwin Morgan did grudgingly see a 'more hopeful than one might expect' trend to the narrative (*Listener* 7. 9. 1978), but only Craig Raine (*New Statesman* 5. 1. 1979), Martin Booth (*Tribune* 13. 10. 1978) and Hughes's old friend Richard Murphy saw the thrust of the book towards 'giving up the false pride of our male technical mastery ... to become true to the most powerful feminine nature of our inner selves' (*New York Review of Books* 10. 6. 1982). It was left to scholarly books on Hughes to rescue the reputation of *Cave Birds* in the 1980s (Gifford and Roberts 1981; Hirschberg 1981; Sagar 1983; Scigaj 1986).

Two rather different collections were published in the year following *Cave Birds*. *Remains of Elmet* (1979) and *Moortown* (1979) might have been expected to provide some relief for reviewers overwhelmed by mythic sequences since here were poems anchored in the landscapes of the Calder Valley and north Devon respectively. But by now many reviewers simply looked for their established expectations to be fulfilled. Scigaj summed up the problem: 'In the late seventies, caricature often replaced criticism as shopworn critical clichés about the violence in Hughes's poetry substituted for honest readings of poems by a poet undergoing major stylistic changes' (1992: 24). Geoffrey Grigson, among others, was 'repelled by the extreme ordinariness of the language' of *Remains of Elmet* (*Listener* 26. 7. 1979), while, to the contrary, Peter Porter complained about being 'consistently battered by language' and 'excessive use of the pathetic fallacy' (*Observer* 15. 7. 1979). But by now some reviewers knew how to read the work, Glyn Hughes writing that 'without a shred of posturing, a thrillingly-described world is set in a myth that explains it' (*Guardian* 24. 5. 1979), Martin Booth seeing 'a modern attempt at a similar task as Wordsworth sought to present in *The Prelude*' (*Tribune* 22. 6. 1979) and Richard Murphy receiving the message 'that the world must be resacralized' (*New York Review of Books* 10. 6. 1982). Gifford and Roberts identified Hughes's method of doing this by giving their review the title 'Social History as Natural History' (*Delta*, 60, 1980).

By commenting only on the poems in the first part of *Moortown* that were later separately published as the *Moortown Diary* (1989), some critics were able to avoid the mythic sequences in the book. Thus John Carey was now able to say that 'Hughes is easily the most powerful poet writing in English' (*Sunday Times* 9. 12. 1979), Charles Causley to declare this part of the book 'a major triumph' (*Guardian* 29. 11. 1979) and John Bayley to prefer to 'turn back to the all too recognisable world'. Bayley felt that readers would not 'take much interest in the metaphysical world' constructed by the mythic sequences (*London Review of Books* 21. 2. 1980). Only Keith Sagar (*Literary Review* 16. 11. 1979) and John

Harvey relished engaging with the relationship between the material and mythical worlds in their reviews of *Moortown*, Harvey seeing the animal links, but regretting the lack of a 'sympathetic human drama where the experience of many people could meet' (*Listener* 17. 4. 1980). Both Terry Eagleton (*Stand*, 21(3), 1980) and Peter Scupham found in this volume what Scupham called 'a rape of the intellect' – that 'the throne of reason stands untenanted' (*Times Literary Supplement* 4. 1. 1980). It was an old complaint and a misunderstanding that, again, more considered studies by Robinson (1989) and Scigaj (1991) would clarify.

In response to *River* (1983) Edna Longley wrote: 'The real task confronting critics of Ted Hughes's poetry is not one of exegesis but of discrimination' (*Poetry Review*, 73(4), January 1984). She detected 'prefabricated Hughes-speak: bold enjambment, terse monosyllables, the omitted verb, the Lawrentian exclamation, the heaped adjectives'. Blake Morrison's review stated: 'Hughes is a baggier, more hit-and-miss writer than he used to be and some of his mannerisms have grown over-familiar' (*Observer* 4. 9. 1983). In fact, the scholarly work of exegesis was exactly what Hughes's poetry needed in order to facilitate discrimination, as book-length studies were to demonstrate. But it was clear that positions had now become entrenched and the 1980s were typified by two reviews in 1981 that characterised those undertaking such work as either 'devotees' (Graham Martin, *New Statesman* 26. 6. 1981) or 'humourless exegetes' (Roger Garfitt, *Times Literary Supplement* 24. 7. 1981). The regular 'devotees' wrote reviews that were positive about the awe and authenticity of the poetry (Martin Booth, *British Book News*, February 1984; Glyn Hughes, *Guardian* 25. 9. 1983), while the regular sceptics, such as Calvin Bedient, still found evidence of nihilism (*Parnassus*, 14(1), 1987).

Wolfwatching (1989) did not excite the critics who failed to connect the sense of loss in poems about family members and about animals that were unified by the tone of elegy underpinning cultural and ecological conservation (see Gifford 2006). John Lucas detected 'notes for a poem rather than a poem itself' (*Times Literary Supplement* 20. 10. 1989), while Mick Imlah and Jo Shapcott both sensed a loss of power in the poetry (*Observer* 17. 9. 1989; *New Statesman* 27. 10. 1989). Peter Forbes and Bernard McGinley praised the old empathy and sharpness of the animal poems (*Independent* 23. 9. 1989; *Financial Times* 23. 9. 1989) and James Aitchison (*Glasgow Herald* 23. 9. 1989) agreed with Carol Ann Duffy that the family poems, as 'moving acts of reclamation', brought a new humanity to Hughes's work (*Guardian* 19. 10. 1989). Perhaps the most significant review was from Derek Walcott who, while acknowledging an eclipse in Hughes's reputation during the 1980s, a period of preference for 'the ordinary ordinarily recorded', saw the poetry as cultural intervention in ecologically desperate times:

> the power of Hughes's work is that it preserves its own archaicness, that it shows us an England besieged by a rising sea of trash. It sometimes snarls back at us like a hounded, embayed beast, cornered and bleeding. Its width is massive, its ecology desperate.
>
> (*Weekend Telegraph* 21. 10. 1989)

The publication of *Shakespeare and the Goddess of Complete Being* in 1992 brought almost unanimous disapproval. In the *Independent on Sunday* Michael

Hofmann called it 'tedious to read and sometimes ridiculous' – it 'looks like maths written out' (19. 4. 1992). Tom Paulin in the *London Review of Books* was more generous, praising the writing as expressing 'a tragic energy that has all but disappeared from critical practice' (9. 4. 1992). But it was John Carey's derisive review ('his preposterous pick 'n' mix myth-pack is an act of grotesque, donkey-eared vandalism') in *The Sunday Times* (5. 4. 1992) that stung Hughes the most, and elicited a response in the newspaper two weeks later (19. 4. 1992). Sagar believes that 'the book was received with such virulence by the academic Shakespeare scholars that it seemed these reviewers were more interested in jealously protecting their territory than in exploring Shakespeare's imaginative process' (2004: 644). To be fair, Carey itemised in his response to Hughes's letter what he felt to be absurd distortions of the plays (*Sunday Times* 19. 4. 1992).

Hughes himself reflected in a letter to Keith Sagar at the time:

> Reviews were interesting. The Academics identified themselves to a man (with a kind of naivety) with the Adonis character in his Angelo phase – confronting my argument as the brothels of Vienna, Juliet's pregnancy, Isabella's appeal. How right Shakespeare was!
>
> Women were wiser – but still tended to identify themselves with the plaintiff Goddess, disturbed by what they saw as my puritan assault on them.
>
> No single reviewer transcended the quarrel, and observed the transformations of both. Mariner [*sic*] Warner nearest, by far.
>
> (9. 7. 1992, BL ADD 78759, f. 169)

Also in 1992 Hughes published *Rain-Charm for the Duchy and Other Laureate Poems* which did not enhance his reputation. Such few reviews as there were ranged from confused to derisory, one asking, 'Is this book, perhaps, a brilliant literary hoax?' (*Literary Review*, June 1992). Attempts at occasional political verse met with equal disdain. 'A Poem for Polling Day' in *The Times* titled 'Lobby from Under the Carpet' was attacked by D. J. Taylor in the *Guardian* as from a Laureate 'producing official poetry that does neither himself nor the form any favours' (20. 4. 1992). Dennis Walder, an admirer of earlier work, had to refer to the Laureate poems as 'often weak, blustering verse' (in Niven 1999). On the publication of the Laureate's poem for the Queen Mother's ninety-fifth birthday, the *Guardian* interviewed three poets and ran their responses under the headline 'Birthday verse gets worse and worse' (5. 8. 1995). *Winter Pollen* (1994), however, was widely welcomed for 'the extraordinary concentrated energy of his mind' (Caroline Moore, *Times* 10. 3. 1994), its insights into his own poetry (Blake Morrison, *Independent on Sunday* 6. 3. 1994) and its 'felicitous coherence' (Adam Thorpe, *Observer* 6. 3. 1994).

In reviewing *New Selected Poems 1957–1994* Sean O'Brien made reference to a factor in the literary reputation of Hughes that had nothing to do with the quality of his writing:

> It has become difficult to read the poems of either Hughes or Plath without overhearing reports from the continuing war of biographers, critics and executors. Whatever the biographical facts, Hughes could

be forgiven for feeling that, at times, he undergoes the kind of evis-
cerating inquiry and judgement normally reserved for the dead.

(*Sunday Times* 5. 3. 1995)

Since her death in 1963, Sylvia Plath's admirers had complained about the
slowness of her estate, controlled by Hughes, to publish her work. A succession
of Plath biographers publicly objected to the changes in their manuscripts
demanded by the estate if permission to quote from the poetry was to be
granted. Occasionally Hughes publicly explained the legal and moral responsibilities driving his actions (for example, *Observer* 29. 10. 1989). In 1995 O'Brien
may have had in mind two recent and much-discussed accounts of encounters
with the Plath estate, one negative and one positive: Jacqueline Rose's *The
Haunting of Sylvia Plath* (1991) and Janet Malcolm's *The Silent Woman: Sylvia
Plath and Ted Hughes* (1994). Some balance was restored by Diane Middlebrook's even-handed biography of the creative relationship, *Her Husband*
(2004). But it was this, coupled with the extreme feminists' sustained accusa-
tions of Hughes as the cause of Plath's suicide, that Simon Armitage refers to as
the situation in which, to defend the poetry was implicitly to defend the man.
Indeed, some fellow-writers did both in letters to the newspapers (for example,
Times Literary Supplement 6. 3. 1992).

In the USA the consequences of all this for Hughes were sadly disastrous,
denying him for a lifetime the lucrative lecture offers open to his friend Seamus
Heaney. More seriously, generations of students have been prevented from
studying his work since their professors have, in effect, been denied a crucial
platform for their scholarship at the annual Modern Language Association
meetings (Scigaj 1992: 29, 27). The negative stances towards Hughes by two
leading women poetry specialists in the USA, Marjorie Perloff and Helen Vendler,
have endorsed the almost total absence of the work of Hughes from the academic
curriculum there, in contrast to the popularity of his work from the beginning
of his career at all levels of the UK curriculum. Indeed, the continued presence
and influence of Hughes's work in British culture, whatever the fluctuations of
his reputation with the critics, has largely been sustained by his popularity in
schools and universities. In 1979, for example, the magazine *New Poetry* launched a poll for 'best UK poet' and found that Hughes beat Larkin and Heaney
with 'the core of his support coming from the teaching profession' (*Daily Telegraph* 2. 3. 1979). What should also not be forgotten was the power and
popularity of Hughes's rare poetry readings. Alistair Niven, Director of Literature at the British Council, said when Hughes died, 'He was without question
the finest verse reader I have ever heard ... Ted Hughes was a great poet partly
because his ear for the music of language was so perfect' (Niven 1999: 2). That
Hughes himself recognised this is evidenced by the important legacy of recordings that he systematically built up during the last decade of his life.

The last two books published by Hughes revived both his popular and literary reputations. *Tales from Ovid* (1997), the most acclaimed translation project undertaken by Hughes, sold in large numbers and won the Whitbread Book
of the Year Award in 1998, nine months before his death. Then came the
bombshell of *Birthday Letters* (1998). In one sense *Birthday Letters* changed
everything in terms of the popularity of Hughes's poetry, but in a deeper sense

it changed nothing for the reputation of Hughes's most challenging work. Unknown for a volume of poetry, it went into the bestseller lists and stayed there for weeks. The paperback was the hundredth best selling book of 1999 and the only book of poetry (*Guardian* 8. 1. 2000). It immediately spawned a book about the background to the book (Wagner 2000). 'Unmistakably the work of a great poet', wrote John Carey (*Sunday Times* 25. 1. 1998), but 'fatalism is relentlessly endorsed'. 'The aura of predestination is this book's strongest texture,' agreed James Wood: 'Revenge and self-justification are inherent in this enterprise' (*Prospect*, May 1998). But justifying oneself 'must be a legitimate aim of poetry', wrote James Fenton in one of the most considered reviews (*New York Review of Books* 5. 3. 1998). Indeed, in *Birthday Letters*, 'Hughes is an active protagonist inside the myth – like the minotaur in the labyrinth' wrote Blake Morrison. 'The poems are unappeasing, but by getting them out, something in Hughes will have been appeased' (*Independent on Sunday* 1. 2. 1998). Some Hughes scholars felt that because *Birthday Letters* was atypical of the *oeuvre*, calling it 'his greatest book', as Andrew Motion immediately did, would detract from a proper evaluation of his larger poetic project (*Times* 17. 1. 1998). Edna Longley smelled a rat: 'Is Hughes's reputation being talked up in some mysteriously collective way, and to hell with critical judgement, to hell with poetry?' (*Thumbscrew* 10, Spring/Summer 1998, p. 30) (see Criticism, p. 138).

Although at the end of his life Hughes was recognised by many, as Motion had said, as 'one of the most important poets of the century', or at least as 'the greatest living English poet' (Sarah Maguire, *Guardian* 22. 1. 1998), discussion of his work has often failed to engage with the new challenges it has offered with every new volume of poetry. Indeed, the variety of poetic challenges Hughes left us is an important aspect of his achievement. 'His overriding merit may well be seen eventually as his own dissatisfaction with the self-definitions he has at different times achieved in verse. More than most other poets of his generation, he has mistrusted any comfortable point of rest' (Robert Nye, *Literary Review*, March 1995). Perhaps for this very reason, reviewers have often fallen back on standard positions when faced with new work. The guides to modern literature that represent a summary of his work are also no exception to this tendency. In the *Guide to Modern World Literature* (1973: 323) Martin Seymour-Smith wrote that Hughes began as 'an elemental poet of power ... Then he began to assume a mantic role; he has now turned into (*Crow*, 1970) a pretentious, coffee-table poet, a mindless celebrant of instinct'. The 1988 edition of the *Cambridge Guide to Literature in English* edited by Ian Ousby (1988) identified Hughes's critique, but misread his solution: 'He directs us to the distance of civilized society from its vital organs. His portrait of female character as devouring and fearful apparently connects with his praise of isolation in a kind of lonely masculinity' (484). In Hughes's poetry the hubris of isolated aloof masculinity is repeatedly confronted by the goddess in her awesome, threatening aspect in order, if the negotiation is successful, for a humbling reconnection with the feminine to take place.

The lack of careful reading that has dogged Hughes's career is typified by a review by Ian Sansom, who recognised the poet's 'exploration of the role of poet-shaman and healer', but went on to make the amazing accusation that his poetry 'does not distinguish between the power to kill and the power to heal'.

More careful reading would reveal that all of the work has been driven by an awareness that the power to heal requires an often dangerous confrontation with destructive powers, and, indeed, the killing of some hubristic aspects of the self and a self-destructive society. Yet this same review could conclude positively, with reference to the poetic projects, anthologies for children, translations and both narrative and critical prose, that 'if there is a unity and purpose to all this activity and output, it's that Hughes is engaged in a huge work of re-education and re-imagining. He wants to shock us, to make us think again (why else would he have become Poet Laureate?)' (*Poetry Review*, 97(3), Autumn 1997). Why else, but to contine to provoke crucial debates on the following important themes?

Language

It was a distinctive use of language that first attracted critical attention to the work of Ted Hughes and also that drew the earliest negative criticisms of his poetry. After his death critics were still arguing about the language and tone of *Birthday Letters* (1998). Indeed, linguistic experiment and stylistic shifts were what characterised each new volume of poetry. Many of the essays in *Winter Pollen* (1994) indicate how much he had thought out his own theory of language from an overview of the history of English poetry, most fully in the far-reaching and detailed analysis of 'Myths, Metres, Rhythms' (1994: 310–72) (see Works, **pp. 82–84**). His collaboration in making theatre with Peter Brook gave him the opportunity in the *Orghast* project to experiment with communication across cultures in pure sounds (Smith 1972). On the other hand, his later translations of classic plays, together with *Tales from Ovid* (1997) were noted for being in a distinctively Hughesian language: 'It could be Ted Hughes translating Ovid, or it could be Ted Hughes' (Nigel Spivey, *Guardian* 28. 8. 1997). So what is Hughesian language? Or rather, what have been the modulating languages of Ted Hughes? And what have been the critical debates concerning language in his work?

Keith Sagar's first study argued that the task Hughes had set himself was, in itself, one inescapably concerned with language: 'His most difficult task is to remove the obstacles, the clichés of thought, feeling and expression to bring himself into a state of full awareness, openness, excitement, concentration' (1975: 3). About *The Hawk in the Rain* (1957) Sagar wrote:

> To watch an animal, particularly a predator, about its business; to watch a pair of lovers, or a woman in labour, or a man dead, dying, or at great risk, is, clearly, to be a watcher of violence, but not a voyeur. Hughes watches, and makes us watch such violence, not for frisson, but for estrangement. He wants to undermine our sense of the ordinary and let in a sense of the miraculous, a shock of recognition of ourselves as animals, as killers, as new-born babies or as corpses. If the violence we are made to confront is reality, or even a fundamental part of it, then the reality most of us think we inhabit must be relatively or wholly unreal. For Hughes, the poet cannot see too much or

experience too much. He tries to find 'words that live in the same dimension as life at its most severe, words that cannot be outflanked by experience', and out of them to forge a vision which evades as little as possible and which the soul must learn to bear as best it can.

(1975: 32–33)

It was Calvin Bedient who first used the phrase 'voyeur of violence' in his 1974 book *Eight Contemporary Poets*:

If Hughes is a voyeur of violence in *The Hawk in the Rain*, in *Lupercal* (1960) he is a fearful lover of the will to live – a far profounder thing. Wading out at last beyond the froth of violent escapism, he is abruptly stunned by the elemental severity of his subject. His manner contracts at once, thoroughly penetrated by the ancient cold. Now he knows – where before he had been too glutted with sensation to enquire – that the tooth is the clue to existence. He hardens himself, he prepares for battle. Better to speak of *this* subject, he seems to have told himself, in a style as sharp and as naked as an incisor.

(1974: 108)

Gifford and Roberts felt that these qualities were present in some poems in the first collection, but that the word 'violence', which Hughes himself had used for 'any form of vehement activity' (Faas 1971: 9), was not helpful.

The reason for the problem about 'violence' in Hughes's work is his determination to acknowledge the predatory, destructive character of nature, of which man is a part, and not to moralize about it. His work can be regarded as a prolonged confrontation with Manichaeism [the opposition of] spirit and matter, light and darkness, good and evil ... St George is the Christian equivalent of the Manichaean hero. Throughout Hughes's work we find a rejection of the self-sufficient ego, in the guise of spirit, or of intellect, or of heroic endeavour, and of the embattled, suppressive attitude to matter and darkness that is figured in the myths of Primaeval man and St George.

(1981: 14–15)

The problem was that many critics felt that the poet's ego was too fully present in the vehemence of the language in the early work. J. M. Newton, for example, wanted to be encouraging, but noted 'overdone virility and overdone violence' that resulted in conveying a sense of 'flogging his inspiration' (*Delta* 25, Winter 1961). But two new volumes later, Geoffrey Thurley wrote: 'It cannot be too strongly emphasised that to speak of Hughes's strength and power is in no way to suggest any deficiency in fineness' (1974: 174).

Sagar later wrote that, like Lawrence and Eliot, Hughes:

had the same lesson to learn, the need for self-abnegation by a famous poet of the pyrotechnics, the 'old heroic bang', on which his fame depended ['Famous Poet']. He admired a generation of East European poets such as Popa and Pilinszky whose work was purged of rhetoric, deliberately impoverished, 'a strategy of making audible meanings without disturbing the silence' (Hughes 1994: 223). He sought a simplicity not of retreat or exclusion but on the far side of experience and complexity.

(2000: 21)

Nick Bishop, in *Re-Making Poetry* (1991), suggested that many of the poems in the first collection – 'A man seeking experience', 'Meeting', 'Six Young Men' – had a 'didactic tendency' (56) to set up simple oppositions from an apparently 'objective' stance that was clearly exposing the weaknesses of one side of the dualism through the poem's rhetorical strategies. He called these 'structural accounts of the psychological dualism within the volume' (56). The shock of self-discovery for the reader was not generated by the text as it was in the title poem, together with 'The Jaguar' and 'The Thought-Fox'. 'Although the formal *content* of the poems like "Meeting" appears to accuse the abstract Ego, Hughes's *attitude* of superiority consolidates it' (57). In 'The Thought-Fox', 'the ideal of language in which words displace experiences with their own meaning *as* words, and the poet's assumption of his absolute control over the process of literary creation, the act of writing, are both humbled' (63).

'The commonest criticism,' wrote Sagar of the first collection, 'was that so many of the poems were derivative. This is of course true, and to be expected in a first book. These influences are not diffuse, but tend to be concentrated in single poems, as if Hughes has consciously attempted to write in the manner close to that of Hopkins, Dylan Thomas, Yeats, the Jacobeans, Frost or Wilfred Owen, for the space of a poem or two, and why not? He had much to learn from all of them' (1975: 33).

But as early as 1959 A. E. Dyson compared the language of *Hawk in the Rain* to that of John Donne:

> As in Donne, one finds explosiveness of utterance; imagery which is developed intellectually, but assimilated at every point to the central emotional experience; vividness and even grotesqueness of phrase and metaphor; metre which twists and turns in its wrestling with meaning … and a general sense of being at the white-hot moment of experience: directly involved, so that the experience of the words is inseparable from the insight with which they grapple, and is, indeed, the high point of awareness itself.

(1990: 118)

M. L. Rosenthal, also an early admirer, argued that:

> ['Wind', rather than 'The Thought-Fox'] was more representative of Hughes in the sense that it presents literal reality (though through the distortion of metaphor) rather than an abstraction made tangible. Nevertheless, it takes on symbolic meaning through the very accuracy and intensity of its literal presentation.

(1967: 225)

The way that language in Hughes's poetry is simultaneously charged with both 'the white-hot moment of experience' in Dyson's phrase, and the deeply symbolic in which 'the world itself is speaking' in Jung's phrase, was considered in detailed examples by Gifford and Roberts, who quoted this phrase from Jung (1981: 34):

> Hughes appears to hold a similar view of language, and this theory can be used to provide a synthesis of the two aspects of language's relation to the physical world: the ability of language to represent the spirit or essence of things-as-they-are (as opposed to cataloguing attributes) derives from its origins in that 'layer of the psyche' which is 'things as-they-are' itself ... In the first volume Hughes most obviously attempts to create poetry with a material body by employing language which, when spoken, demands a conscious physical effort, dense with dental, plosive and guttural consonants, and with alliteration and assonance. The opening lines of the title poem are an example of this ... The best early poems often seem to centre on a moment of stillness, which in some cases gives meaning to the bluster that goes on around it.
>
> (1981: 34–37)

Gifford and Roberts also drew attention to the roles of narrative and humour:

> Hughes's writing for children was an important factor in the change in his poetry between *Lupercal* and *Wodwo* (1967) ... There are formal parallels between the children's stories and the poetry of *Wodwo*, as can be shown by a comparison between 'Still Life' and 'Why the Owl Behaves as it Does' from *How the Whale Became* (1963) ... In both the story and the poem the narrative structure and the final image indicate that the complacent Owl and stone are finally outdone in a beautiful ironic reversal.
>
> (1981: 46–47)

This narrative structure was not unconnected to humour:

> Few of his best poems are entirely without humour, and in many of them it belongs to the shock of registering something in the natural world and establishing a relationship with it. It is there in 'a sag belly and the grin it was born with' of 'Pike' ... This mode emerges more strongly in the nature poems in *Wodwo* ... In each case anthropomorphism is an important element in the humour.
>
> (1981: 50–51)

Nick Bishop's *Re-Making Poetry* (1991) is a sophisticated and well-researched discussion of the work up to the publication of *River*. Bishop was prepared to be critical of some linguistic tendencies in the poetry and to use other critics to make his own points. His focus was on the qualities of the language in relation to the evolution of the self through work that increasingly used religious mythologies. He gives, for example, a useful analysis of the four voices in *The Hawk in the Rain* and *Lupercal* (1991: 71ff.) that establishes his critical terminology. He also quotes from letters to himself from Hughes on devotional metaphors (5), conscious and unconscious stages of writing a poem (75) and on *Crow* (110).

Referring to Hughes's writing about the *Orghast* experiment, Bishop notes Hughes's belief that 'the "audial-visceral-muscular" base of language – as opposed to its "visual-conceptual" tendency – is indeed responsive to the presence of the whole human being, not just a rationalized abstract one' (18). Thus Hughes followed the example of Shakespeare by 'breaking Latinisms on the wheel of Anglo-Saxon/Norse/Celtic ... an aspect of the self's willingness to explore the vocabulary belonging to its real mental life' (19). Also 'a *symbolic* language is necessary to resist the self-enclosure of the Ego-Personality and "objective" verbal structures alike' (20). Bishop argues that:

> Just as the struggle to regain the 'totality of self' was frustrated by the intervention of the Ego-Personality and false gods, it is likewise obstructed by the nature of language, which could be described as the formal mechanism of that personality.
>
> (15)

Bishop's reservations about the poetry concern a tendency to be assertive or didactic rather than experiential, together with a rather self-conscious rhetorical flourish. But in *Lupercal*, Bishop argues, Hughes himself critiques the 'superego-stylist self' of his previous collection. On the 'tirade of critical abuse which greeted "Hawk Roosting"', Bishop wrote:

> Lacking that flexible, ironic attitude to their own fictions which characterised the Central European response to similar revelations, the only way the critics could at the same time acknowledge the human context and yet 'separate off' from its negative implications (the consistent development from 'objectivity' to militant Egoism) was to brand it as 'Fascist', irredeemably evil, 'beyond the pale'. The poem, meanwhile, goes on doing away with the deceptive surfaces of the 'verbal centre', including 'sophistry', 'manners' and 'arguments'. The 'material' organisation of the poem perfects its irony on a phrase like 'the allotment of death', in which the democratic even-handedness of the (Latin-based) *word* is replaced by its grim consequences in *reality*. The counter-attack on language's capacity for the 'mystification of experience' (the term is R. D. Laing's) is an extension of the poet's counter-attack on his superego-stylist self, which he also accomplishes in the present poem through a forefronting of 'colloquial prose readiness' (Hughes 1994: 215) in the last three stanzas in particular.
>
> (79–80)

Gifford and Roberts quote Hughes's statement to Egbert Faas that 'the first idea of *Crow* was really an idea of a style ... with no music whatsoever, in a super-simple, super-ugly language' (1981: 102).

Hughes's statement about the origin of *Crow* tells us several important things: that it is a stylistic experiment, that it is not an absolute apocalypse but a 'stage' of the poet's 'adventure', that in at least one sense the experiment is reductive. On the other hand it dangerously over-simplifies the range of technique to be found in the poems. A study of the style of *Crow* will certainly not find unrelieved ugliness or a complete absence of 'music'. Hughes is in fact describing a prominent but not predominant part of the style: the deliberate use of crude colloquial and journalistic language in unexpected contexts ... It is, however, difficult to find poems that are written entirely in this kind of rock-bottom language, and the ones that are written like this are among the worst ... What we more commonly find, and invariably so in the best poems, is that language has a specific function in a context of more complex and often quite literary effects. Even the simple humour of 'The Battle of Osfrontalis' becomes more interesting and sharper when Hughes juxtaposes, with minimal statements of Crow's reactions, a fanciful and satirical yoking of the languages of warfare and phonology.

(102–4)

After a detailed discussion of 'Crow on the Beach' Gifford and Roberts demonstrate what they mean by 'complex literary effects' in a long comment on Crow's final uncomprehending question about the sea, 'What can be hurting so much?':

It is true that there is an element of apprehension in the heightened awareness of the opening lines, but the apprehension becomes detached and elaborated until, in the final line, Crow is unwittingly asking a question about himself. The simplicity of the final question is clearly an expression of Crow's limited consciousness, contrasting strongly with the language of the opening. This is not to say that Hughes is simply mocking Crow. The poem is sympathetic about the inevitability of conceptualisation, and the difficulty and even suffering that it entails. Maintaining this sympathy in a poem that celebrates the awesome unapproachableness of the natural world is a remarkable achievement.

(107)

Nick Bishop is especially good on *Crow*, seeing 'Crow and the Birds', for example, as:

a seminal moment in Hughes's imaginative progress: the final replacement of natural images and a language 'from above' with a bird, and a style culled 'from below'. Crow, who exists literally at the bottom-most point of the poem, is the foundation-stone from which reconstruction can begin; both the dance of the poetry's ritual music, and the dance of the false self associated with it, come to an end in the moment of realization of this moment. It is not too difficult to see

Hughes in this poem exorcising the demons of his own past, attempting to throw off the prejudices of attitudes to the self and poetic language, and to some large-scale cultural relativisms, all at once. When
the 'attentive' man begins to feel that reality has been converted
defensively into discourses 'not his own', and that the whole psyche
has started to fossilize into a false personality, he needs a figure as
explosive as Crow to shed those 'containers', that machinery. Hughes's descent into a new idea of style in Crow not only highlights the
suspect double-nature of language he singled out so lucidly in *Poetry
in the Making*, it casts the linguistic problem at its most encompassing,
and yet concise form: Hughes goes straight to the heart of the matter
when he claims that the God of *Crow* ... 'bears about the same relationship to the Creator as, say, ordinary English does to reality' (*Crow*
record sleeve notes). Only here do we see the poet struggling with
language in its true dimensions – that the assault on the abstract ideal
of conceptual language is the same as the psychological, or Metaphysical, assault. Thus several poems in the volume image this assault
directly: 'A Disaster', 'Crow and the Birds', 'Crow's First Lesson',
'The Battle of Osfrontalis'.

(1991: 116)

On the other hand, Veronica Forrest-Thomson quoted the opening of 'Crow
and the Birds' before commenting: 'These lines ... give us a glimpse of what Mr
Hughes's talent might have led him to, if he had not fallen victim to the stance
of "visionary"' (1978: 151). David Holbrook's objection to the 'visionary' mode
of *Crow* was the most sustained. He was appalled by the gap between the
'creativity rooted in love' (1975: 35) of 'Full Moon and Little Frieda' in *Wodwo*
and 'the breakdown of poetic language' (40) in *Crow*: 'Such fastidious attention
to the true nature of human existence would, however, seem "pallid and artificial" beside the falsifications and exaggerations of *Crow*' (35). Holbrook failed
to find any distance between Ted Hughes and Crow, 'the embodiment of ego-
tistical nihilism': 'While posturing as "the contender", Hughes also tries to lock
us in the reductionist vision of man, as seen by the ironical (and "realistic")
Crow' (39). For Holbrook this was a sign of the times. He was, after all, con-
tributing a chapter on *Crow* to a book that took its title from it, with an
unequivocal subtitle: *The Black Rainbow: Essays on the present breakdown of
culture*. Holbrook responds to the language of 'Fragment of an Ancient Tablet'
as though it were a political agenda:

> After so many words thrusting on us guts, blood, impossible pain,
> distortion, dismemberment, and vile images of the inside of the body,
> nothing is left but a mental rage, that is encapsulated within itself ...
> There is nothing in *Crow* for which to have respect[,] or for which to feel
> care or concern: it belongs to the 'racking moment' of smashing every-
> thing to pieces: in one's head, at least. There is no one to whom to
> render account: there is no respect for 'community'. Today our culture
> is nihilistic in this ... way – with no social or personal goals in view.
> (33)

The reservations about Hughes's poetry expressed by Antony Easthope are concerned with a language and mode that he describes as pre-Modernist. In his discussion of the poem 'The Horses', for example, Easthope writes:

> Two generations after Eliot's 'Preludes' it should give us pause that 'Horses' seems ready to reactivate a traditional poetic structure almost as though Eliot and Pound never happened. These horses are natural objects taken as symbols in a menagerie which stretches back to include through [sic] Yeats' swans, Hopkins' hawk, Keats' nightingale to Shelley's lark – they are *symbolic* horses ... Hughes's poem is not concerned to annotate or observe horses as a phenomenon in nature since as natural objects they vanish almost immediately into what they mean for the speaker and his attempts to catch their relation to something beyond them – megaliths, the light of the sun, sculptured horses with 'stone manes', 'hung heads' which are 'as patient as the horizons', horizons themselves said in the last line to 'endure'. Such metaphors seek out an identity between the horses and what they mean for the speaker in the sense in which de Man points out that 'symbol is always a part of the totality that it represents' (a conception of symbol that goes back to Coleridge and the German Romantic writers) ... In this respect the language of 'Horses' – and arguably of Hughes in general – aims for transparency. This may seem implausible given the manifestly *worked* character of sound and diction ('The curlew's tear turned its edge on silence'), its repetitions ('making no move', 'making no sound'), but valid in sofar [sic] as the poem sub-scribes to what de Man refers to as 'an aesthetics that refuses to distinguish between experience and the representation of this experi-ence'. Sound, diction, trope (especially anaphora), intonation and metaphor would efface themselves before the represented, symbolised meaning and the intensity with which it is envisaged.
>
> (1999: 17–18)

Easthope goes on to include examples from *Crow* (1970) and *Birthday Letters* (1998) in his essay before concluding with, 'Sensibility has been altering rapidly since the start of [the twentieth] century. How much has Hughes's expression altered?' (23).

Paul Bentley's focus on language in his book *The Poetry of Ted Hughes: Language, Illusion and Beyond* (1998) draws upon the French theorists Julia Kristeva (on *Gaudete* and *Cave Birds*), Roland Barthes (on *Remains of Elmet*) and Jacques Lacan, as in his use of the Lacanian 'Real' in his discussion of *Moortown* (1979):

> After the 'experimental' volumes of the 1970s (*Crow, Gaudete, Cave Birds*), *Moortown* can be seen to represent a transitional stage between these and Hughes's more accessible recent work: the com-paratively short 'mythic' sequences of the book suggest Hughes's use of myth as a way of conceiving a Real beyond the ken of consciousness to be near exhaustion; the poem 'No God – only wind on the flower',

from the *Prometheus on his Crag* sequence, constitutes a kind of hole in the mythic frame that exposes the *provisional* status of this frame ... For all the poet's attempts to make metaphoric tracts into this 'unutterable' Real, to decipher possible meanings with the aid of myth, the Real nonetheless stays firmly and silently in place: Buried behind the navel'.

The flexible, open-ended style of the *Moortown* sequence (the poems were originally journal entries) seems to attest to the difficulty of finding any stable meaning in a world posited as indifferent to human concerns, a difficulty thematicized by focussing on Hughes's own experience of farming in Devon. Just as the farmer wrestles with and makes 'manageable' 'the world of half-ton hooves, and horns,/ And hides heedless as cedar-boarding' ('Hands'), so the poet tries to wrench some sort of meaning from a world that resists human projections. In the poem 'Tractor' a frozen tractor is 'an agony/ To think of'. In the poem the farmer's attempt to start a frozen tractor is directly analogous to the poet's attempt to make 'tracts' into an obstinate Real with language. Lacan writes: 'The real is the impact with the obstacle; it is the fact that things do not turn out all right straight away, as the hand that is held out to external objects wishes'. The recalcitrance of the object provides the impetus for much of Hughes's poetry. The technique is self-reflective: the poet can only make the experience with the object mean anything by personifying it – in response to the speaker's attempts to start it up the tractor 'just coughs./ It ridicules me'. In so far as the poem's speaker thinks, he meets only his own projections, his capacity for illusion. Yet despite the illusory, self-reflective quality of the imagery here, there is something heroic about the whole procedure: in being humanized life is made more manageable, as if it were in this very process of imaginative projection (against the odds) of human meaning (onto a void) that our humanity as such resided: the frozen tractor of the poem finally comes to life, 'Raging and trembling and rejoicing'; man and machine have merged in a kind of primordial exultancy at overcoming the intractable.

(1998: 102–3)

Other Lacanian approaches to Hughes can be found in the collection of papers originating from the Hughes conference in 2000 in Lyon edited by Joanny Moulin, and in particular those of Christian La Cassagnère (2004) and Axel Nesme (2004). Postmodern approaches to Hughes's use of language have been neglected. In *The Poetry of Postmodernity* (1994) Dennis Brown refers to 'the prophetically postmodern character of *Crow*' (78), explaining: 'despite its shock effects and at times its affected superficiality, I take Hughes's *Crow* to be morally prophetic' (86), adding '*Crow* reads like some checklist of postmodern techniques as identified in accounts of recent prose fiction' (80). The potential fruitfulness of such approaches might be indicated by the way Craig Raine has taken a phrase from a letter from Hughes about Raine's own collection *A Martian Sends a Postcard Home* – 'double exposure of comic and horribly real' – to represent the way a Hughes poem appears to be about one thing, but is actually about something quite different – the 'farce and the frightening' in 'Football at Slack', 'Sunstruck' or 'Full Moon and Little Frieda', for example (*Times Literary Supplement* 24. 11. 2006, pp. 11–13). Further approaches are suggested by Paul Muldoon's detailed account of the intertextuality of the *Birthday Letters* poem 'The Literary Life' that goes beyond Plath and Marianne Moore to Yeats and Shakespeare (2006).

Myth

Any reader of the work of Ted Hughes must respond to his sense of the importance and potency of myth as a vehicle for engaging with cultural and personal realities. There are those critics, to be considered below, who are deeply sceptical about Hughes's use of myth to make such engagements with lived realities. Larkin's early sneer about the 'common myth-kitty' (Morrison 1980: 192) came from the Movement poets' suspicion about pretension, as opposed to Sean O'Brien's later accusation of Hughes's use of myth as evasion of history (O'Brien 1998: 37). But the pioneer of interpreting Hughes's developing sense of myth, Keith Sagar, was always scrupulous about clearly demonstrating the poetry's insights into the human condition. Of course, from the start of his work on Hughes (Sagar 1972), Sagar had a correspondence with the author, however uneasy Hughes was about this at the start of what were to become 145 letters to a trusted friend and critic. It is through the mythic framework of Robert Graves's *The White Goddess* that Sagar first read *Wodwo* in *The Art of Ted Hughes* (1975). In these poems Sagar found the triple goddess of nature as violent, motherly and vulnerable, all rejected by the mechanical hubris of the abstracting logos of contemporary civilisation. For Sagar the *Wodwo* poems tried out a variety of stances towards contemporary culture's conflict with nature, including, as he later put it, 'whether it is possible to accept Nature as a whole, to worship it, perhaps even to love it' (2006: 14).

In fact, this became the theme of *The Art of Ted Hughes* which is dominated by Graves's mythic framework. By the time of writing his latest work on Hughes, *The Laughter of Foxes* (2006), Sagar had completed his magnum opus *Literature and the Crime Against Nature* (2005) in which he had read Western literature backwards from the mythic agenda he identified in the work of Hughes. So it would be true to say that Sagar is not only the earliest, but the most far-reaching commentator on myth in the work of Ted Hughes. Indeed, *The Laughter of Foxes* is an attempt to trace the over-arching mythic structures through the whole work. Its opening chapter is titled 'The Mythic Imagination' and it represents the core argument of *Literature and the Crime Against Nature*: the ultimate function of serious literature has always been to attempt to heal the wound that culture has inflicted upon nature.

> The crucial factor that makes the healing process potentially mythic is that the wound is self-inflicted, so that the healing process is simultaneously the trial and correction of a criminal. Hughes once said at a reading that he was always astonished by 'the extraordinary assumption

by the critics that they were the judges of literature, rather than
criminals merely reporting on the judgements passed on them by
literature'.

(2006: 16)

Sagar suggests that in the early work 'it is a crime committed by others, the
eggheads and egotists', but in *Crow* it is the culture at large and in *Cave Birds* 'the
writer hauls himself, as Everyman, into the dock of his own imagination' (18).

Sagar has always believed that Hughes reached a redemptive vision in the
mythic journey of his shamanic trials which Sagar characterises as a journey
'from world of blood to world of light' in a chapter of this title in *The
Laughter of Foxes*. 'Given the landscape of mud and blood, the vast no-man's
land, which is the world of Hughes's early poems, it is not easy for him to say
how men should try to live in such a world. It is easier to say how they should
not' (109). Thus critique and suffering dominate until giving way to the turning
point of the marriage in *Cave Birds*. But Sagar treats this pivotal poem ('Bride
and Groom Lie Hidden for Three Days') as a *Crow* poem and regards *Cave
Birds*, like *Prometheus on his Crag*, as leaving the protagonist 'still to learn how
to live in terms of his new ego-free self in the substantial world' (136). For
Sagar the crucial turning point is actually the volume *Moortown* that opens
with practical farming responsibilities and concludes with *Adam and the Sacred
Nine*, that is with 'Adam's affirmation of his total dependence on Nature, a
Nature whose only god is a god of mud, but with miracles enough' (137).

The process of achieving and renewing this vision Sagar finds in the Epilogue
poems to *Gaudete*, but its ultimate enactment is to be seen in the poems of
River. Glimpsed in the shafts of occasional light in *Remains of Elmet*, which is
'entirely about the crime against nature' (2006: 153), the light in which to
attempt to live a redeemed life is, for Sagar, to be found in the fishing poems of
River. Hughes 'describes fishing as a "corridor back into the world that's made
us as we are". Every fishing trip, like every myth, is a journey in search of this
primeval self reconnected to the "divine flux"' (2006: 162). If the poems of *River*
offer 'the reassurance of one who has been there, in the full flow of grace', for
Sagar this mythic journey challenges us and our culture to a crucial moral
choice: 'Even if the covenant held, and man had the option of life "among the
creatures of light", would he choose the goddess for his bride and nature for his
home?' (2006: 168).

In 1970 Terry Gifford wrote an undergraduate thesis titled 'The Anthropologist Learns to Sing' in which Hughes's own undergraduate switch from
English to Social Anthropology was seen as a crucial influence on the progress
of his poetry into the voice of myth. The anthropologist/poet was to use this
new voice as a vehicle for a critique of contemporary values and attitudes that
fully emerged in the songs of *Crow*. The notion of the anthropologist/poet fed
into a consideration of Hughes's continuing interest in folklore and the shama-
nistic social role of story and poetry in Terry Gifford and Neil Roberts' *Ted
Hughes: A Critical Study* (1981) which began by suggesting that Hughes had
learned a story-telling skill in his narratives for children that had formal parallels with the voice of myth that first found its strength in *Wodwo*. Also
important to Hughes's use of myth was the playful and profound use of

humour to highlight both provisionality and vulnerability, together with a serious critique of the absurdities produced by suppression and distortion of deep instincts and emotions, especially in *Crow* and *Gaudete*. Roberts went on to write an important chapter on Hughes's mythic narrative technique in his book *Narrative and Voice in Postwar Poetry* (1999). Gifford and Roberts established, through discussion of specific poems such as 'Still Life' and 'Ghost Crabs', the way Hughes had learned from shamanism to create a sense that 'recall[s] Jung and Kerényi's remarks about "the world speaking" through symbols and myths' (Gifford and Roberts 1981: 46). Indeed, the shaman's annihilation of self that is the key to this process, achieves, in a number of poems about death, a

> unity of the inner self and 'external' nature which he [also] attempts to express in his poems celebrating intense life. Perhaps the finest expression of this unity, combining an uncompromising statement of the material body's fate with a religious honouring of the earth to which it returns, is in 'The Knight' [from *Cave Birds*].
>
> (100)

It is in their discussion of the mythic structure and poetic achievement of *Cave Birds* that Gifford and Roberts's book has come to be best known.

> The 'living, suffering spirit, capable of happiness' (Hughes's Introduction to Vasko Popa's *Selected Poems*) emerges from the reductive questioning of *Crow* as a subject of celebration, and the metaphysical discovery hinted at in *Crow*'s final poems, such as 'How Water Began to Play' – the discovery of the universal in the self – is the basis of *Cave Birds*.
>
> (199)

Even without reference to Hughes's letter to the authors that they included as a footnote (now in *Letters* 395–97), explaining the original idea behind *Cave Birds*, Gifford and Roberts argued that a close reading of the text would reveal the mythic narrative of the complacent cockerel protagonist's trial, ritual disintegration and 'alchemical' transformation following a symbolic marriage of his now humbled spirit with his newly sensitised body that is also a marriage with his female creator. Thus the cock is transformed into a falcon, anchored in mud and dirt, 'fondled' by a wind that also 'scours' and 'empties', yet a living Blakean divinity. 'The bird achieves its divinity by being subjected to its divinity – just as the bird-beings to whose terrors the hero was subjected were all aspects of his own nature' (Gifford and Roberts 1981: 230–31). Yet the provisionality of myth in the work of Hughes is registered by the poem's final couplet and by the 'goblin' waiting in the wings that will require the engagement of the next mythic sequence. Gifford and Roberts conclude by demonstrating that the force of the archetypal and the symbolic continue to be used by Hughes in the apparently more 'realistic' and 'autobiographical' sequences of *Remains of Elmet* and *Moortown*. They were not to know in 1981 that the final 'goblin' to appear would be the mythologising sequence of the apparently autobiographical *Birthday Letters*.

The late Leonard M. Scigaj, for decades the only American scholar championing Hughes's work, produced, in his first book on Hughes, what remains the most thorough documentation of the sources and background to Hughes's use of myth. *Ted Hughes: Form and Imagination* (1986) is also an exemplary application of scholarship to the interpretation of the poetry. Scigaj's strength is his relation of Hughes's widespread Oriental influences to the traditions of Occidental folklore and myth in which the poetry is embedded. After the early work of the first two collections Scigaj sees the effect of Hughes working upon a libretto for the *Bardo Thödol* (*The Tibetan Book of the Dead*) as opening up a second phase of work that explores a mythic surrealism in *Wodwo* and *Crow* which in turn leads to a third phase of mystic landscape poetry that has its apotheosis in *River*.

Scigaj traced the influence of Hughes's readings in Sufi fables, Tamil *vacanas* and Indian and Chinese mysticism to the inner spiritual journeys of the poetic sequences that lay within the outer temporal journeys of Western folklore.

> Though Oriental philosophies and religious systems do not value Western notions of the individual's uniqueness or of impassioned engagement with temporal experience in the interests of realizing one's own self-responsible destiny, the goals of the self-absorbed Oriental ascetic and the action-orientated Western quest hero are ultimately the same. According to Joseph Campbell, both inner and outer journeys end ideally in exulted states of spiritual illumination.
>
> (1986: 5)

For Scigaj this was the purpose of Hughes's poetry from *Gaudete*'s Epilogue poems, through *Cave Birds*, *Remains of Elmet*, the Prometheus poems of *Moortown* until it was most ecstatically achieved in 'the Taoist light' of *River*.

> The mortality inscribed in the salmon egg and human egg, a major theme of *River*, becomes an opportunity for a Taoist immersion in the concrete and the immediate, a reconciliation with natural processes that yields visionary moments. Like Eschenbach's Parzival or the Bodhisattva of the *Panchatantra*, the great lord achieves Reality, the goal of his quest, by enduring suffering, transmuting pain into vision, and imbuing his daily life with love and compassion for all created beings.
>
> (7)

All of the scholarship of *Ted Hughes: Form and Imagination* informs the more condensed interpretations of Scigaj's later book *Ted Hughes* (1991) which takes the metaphysics of myths into an analysis of Hughes's sense of our ecological responsibility. Crucial to this link is Scigaj's emphasis on the self-challenging moral role of myth in the work of Hughes:

> In Hughes's very able hands these sources serve to convince us that we are not passive *tabulae rasae* moved by empirical forces that determine our fortunes, but generators of our own perceptions and potentially in

full control of what values we choose to posit on external phenomena. All of the Oriental and occult sources Hughes brings to bear upon his poetry ... have in common an emphasis upon the subjective self as an active component in determining what is real for that self.

(19)

One should note that Ann Skea has made the point that, in his concern for Oriental influences, Scigaj can overlook the Englishness of Hughes's world (Skea 1994: 208).

Like Sagar and Scigaj, Neil Roberts in *Ted Hughes: A Literary Life* (2006: 2) traces Hughes's interest in myth to his sense not only that 'humanity had catastrophically lost connection with the sacred', but that this had led directly to the ecological crisis that emerged during his lifetime. In characterising the roles of myth and the esoteric disciplines of other cultures in Hughes's poetic search for an adequate stance towards nature, Roberts uses the word 'religious' for what Hughes was seeking:

He became a kind of religious *bricoleur*, drawing on Robert Graves for the idea of the Goddess, the antagonist of the masculine intellect and patriarchal Puritanism, but also on a range of mystical, archaic and anti-rational discourses such as astrology, alchemy and cabbala. This was emphatically not in the spirit of 'New Age' faddishness, but a disciplined attempt to resist the seductions of the intellect (he himself had a formidable intellect), and keep open communications with an inner life, which was also the life of the natural creature in him.

(3)

In an interesting insight into Hughes as a translator of myths Roberts comments:

Hughes's whole *oeuvre* can be seen as a struggle to articulate spiritual experience in a vacuum of religious forms. A key feature of *Tales from Ovid* is that, despite the 'obsolete' and often corrupt nature of religious 'paraphernalia' [Hughes's own terms], Hughes several times enhances the religious sentiment in the text.

(188)

In the 'Four Ages' section, for example, Roberts points out that in the age of bronze, 'the highly general and almost desultory note of the original and the prose translations is turned into something much weightier and more distinctive' (190). In fact, Hughes has introduced a clear reference to the modern ecological crisis in the lines Roberts quotes: 'Mankind listened deeply / To the harmony of the whole creation'. That Roberts suggests that in this Hughes 'intensifies the religious tone of the original', indicates Roberts's intention that the word 'religious' should evoke the disciplined awe and respect for nature that Hughes sought to find through the voice of myth.

Stuart Hirshberg's *Myth in the Poetry of Ted Hughes* (1981) is concerned with the mythic figures of shaman, trickster and scapegoat, largely in *Crow*, *Gaudete* and *Cave Birds*. Drawing attention to the poet's education in the

'Cambridge School' of Social Anthropology with its attention to structures and icons in mythology and folklore, Hirschberg charts a development from the use of 'primordial animal totems' to 'becoming a shaman' in the latter *Wodwo* poems, to the self-defeat of the trickster in *Crow*, to his redemption as Prometheus the voluntary scapegoat in *Prometheus on his Crag*, to 'the revenge of the White Goddess in *Cave Birds*', to the 'Closing of the Circle: Dionysus to Parzival in *Gaudete*'. If this sounds programmatic, it does not distort subtle and alert readings of individual poems and is ultimately convincing as far as it goes.

From the Cambridge School's interest in James Frazer's *Golden Bough* and Hughes's own interest in Robert Graves's *The White Goddess* Hirschberg describes a movement that enacts the archetype of the dying and reviving god through mythic patterns of the dismemberment of the ego, the internal fight between aspects of the self that makes possible a redemptive reunification of the male and female aspects of the self. In 1981 Hirschberg had to conclude his analysis of these mythic patterns with *Gaudete* and its Epilogue poems. He was aware that there was an ongoing mythic but also psychologically demanding struggle

by an extremely powerful intellect that has surveyed and has an excellent grasp of literature, history and philosophy. Indeed, one has the very strong impression of a mind that increasingly must improvise, almost with every phrase or word, to capture and express a reality that is sensed but ungraspable. One feels the presence of a mind that has exhausted everything within reach, legends, myths, folklore of many nations, literature itself, a mind that now gropes, distrusting anything not under its control and strong enough to control everything except itself. This in turn produces that peculiar quality of moral alertness, the stylistic equivalent of perpetual vigilance, that is so much a part of the heart-rending simplicity of Hughes's poetry.

(1981: 214)

Nick Bishop's approach to myth in *Re-Making Poetry* (1991) is a psychological one:

Crow is the first of Hughes's books to deepen the inward exploration far enough that it begins to take on the structural hardness of a mythology ... A mythological language not only realizes the fundamental patterns of the psychic 'whole', it also inaugurates the effort to integrate all the voices within the self which are artificially isolated from one another as a formal consequence of the lyric.

(109)

For Hughes, the levelling and re-construction of self, language and Creator-image – in which myth participates – *is* a cultural, historical necessity, though its sense of history manifested in the individual and collective *psychology* is scarcely congruent with a Marxist understanding of the term.

(130)

Bishop took from Hughes's essay on Shakespeare the notion of two versions of the Creator and that Hughes's work was driven by the conflict between them: the male Puritan Jehovah of the Logos and 'objective imagination' who attempts to suppress the Goddess of Medieval Nature, the *Imago Dei* as Bishop called her, referring to Jung's image of 'the loving and terrible mother' (10–12). 'The current status of the Mother-symbol, and its potential for transformation, could really be used to plot the moral position of every poem in *Crow*' (138). 'It is possible to speculate that the synthetic effort of *Cave Birds* is Hughes's attempt to re-align or marry the "experience" of *Crow* with the "argument" of *Gaudete*' (140). 'It is not until *Remains of Elmet*, *Moortown* and *River* that a successful return to the "outer" – social, cultural and Natural – world is engineered, and the benefits of the invisible quest begin to be registered in everyday life' (174). In *River* Hughes is using what Bishop, using Jung's terminology, calls 'the collective imagination' (244) and '"exulting" memorably through language' (246) in 'a renewal, not an abolition of Lyricism' (243).

Craig Robinson in *Ted Hughes as Shepherd of Being* (1989) points out that Hughes is attracted to myths in his later work in which 'convention and habit' as a protective readiness for experience have previously been exposed as inadequate in the earlier work. What is needed is:

> a vigilance on the difficult dividing line, that which runs between the Wodwo's faculties of openness to experience, tentative and wise insecurity on the one side, and a disastrous unreadiness on the other. Keeping these two pairs apart, readiness from habit, and openness from unreadiness, is health, and part of the maturity Hughes offers.
>
> (156)

Joanny Moulin makes a similar point rather differently:

> Hughes's basic monomyth is the basic, Orphic scenario of an excursion from physics into meta-physics, or from the realm of *techne* to that of *tyche*, or again what Hughes would call the outer world of things to the inner world of spirits.
>
> (1999a: 163)

Moulin's argument in his book *Ted Hughes: New Selected Poems* (1999) is that:

> myths had already been made up in the earlier stage of his poetry, which found it necessary to master the technical machinery of mythic writing. But from *Crow* on, mythmaking is more a tool, for it develops into a whole vision of the world, a cosmology, which is also a theology ... a Poetry of Presence entirely aimed at sustaining some metaphysical transcendence.
>
> (1999a: 164)

Ann Skea's scholarly interest in Hughes's wide-ranging use of myth has focused in her book *Ted Hughes: The Poetic Quest* (1994) upon the structures of his work derived from his knowledge of alchemy and latterly, on her website, on magic in his work, and on the patterns of the Tarot and Cabbala underlying *Birthday Letters* and of Cabbala underlying *Howls and Whispers* and *Capriccio* (www.ann.skea/THHome). The depth and detail of Skea's analysis in her book is hard to indicate briefly, but is perhaps best summarised as indicating:

> Hughes's use of myth as a framework in which to explore, and to some extent control, the Energies, ... moving away from distancing and alienating personas (such as Crow and Lumb) towards the adoption of an Everyman/Hero figure with which both he and the reader can readily identify.
>
> (1994: 237)

Observing that Hughes follows a quest common to all Gnostic texts, 're-union with the Source for healing and renewal' achieved through 'repeated sacrifice, suffering, humility and love', Skea makes the point that 'his path is not the Eastern mystic's path of retreat inwards, away from reality, but the very Western path of confrontation with the Energies: a confrontation which is, however, presented in Hughes's poetry as an inward journey' (237–38).

Many of the critics mentioned above discuss the central significance of a female goddess – the White Goddess, the Goddess of Complete Being – in the mythology of Hughes. The Indian Hughes scholar, V.T. Usha, has focused especially upon human women in the early work of Hughes as 'the earthly representatives of the Moon Goddess, the fertility principle' (1998: 202). While recognising 'the masculine tone, manner and language' in his poetry, Usha observes that it 'highlights the role of women and envisages a holistic universe' in which the female potential is no longer suppressed and distorted. 'Their degraded state will, according to him, be disastrous for civilization' (202). In this gendered account of Hughes's central myth Usha notes that male humility and recognition of the goddess in her healing form comes partly through male engagements with 'semi-mythical creatures', tough, terrifying, but potentially transforming male arrogance in the realm of what Usha calls 'the imaginary world'. Angels associated with a mother figure, for example, can be frighteningly dangerous, or the epitome of goodness, Usha points out, depending upon the outcome of the male's negotiations with them – that is whether he is able to see that his humbled help is needed to revive the Goddess to a harmonising role. In the children's book *What is the Truth?* Usha sees a model, or at least a linking figure of the innocent and the divine, in God's son, practical, hopeful and outward-looking in negotiations with all the (gendered) elements and forces of the world.

Some critics have expressed reservations about Hughes's use of myth. Sean O'Brien, for example, has suggested that it has been a device to enable Hughes to side-step history. In arguing that Hughes omits engagement with politics and history in his poems, O'Brien asks, 'Are they a result of choice or incapacity?' (1998: 37). He seems to suggest that the answer is both, in that by choosing the time frames of myth, 'real time is a source of real anxiety' (40). O'Brien quotes Hughes's notes on a Laureate poem in *Rain-Charm for the Duchy* suggesting that the Crown's symbolic significance lies not in 'historical time', but in 'natural time' as Hughes puts it. That O'Brien sees nothing of politics, history or a concern for the future, in the poetry of Hughes, despite an acknowledgement of *Shakespeare and the Goddess of Complete Being* where the role of all three are fully explained as defining Hughes's poetic context, reveals a fundamental misunderstanding of the fact that from the beginning Hughes's poetry has been a social intervention in a historically understood rationalist culture. To accuse Hughes of 'rural conservatism' (40) is to ignore the way his work has contributed to environmental politics, the history of our treatment of nature and our responsibility for the future quality of life on the planet, all of which have been explored through mythic narratives, symbols and dramas.

In an essay titled 'Ted Hughes's Anti-Mythic Method', Joanny Moulin has suggested that Hughes's use of 'myth' is the reverse of that used by, say, T. S. Eliot:

> As Eliot saw it, myth was still very much a tool to be used in a method, that is to say as a means to an end. Eliot's 'mythic method' can be read as an extension and a variant of the 'objective correlative' ... Hughes's definition of myth is very close to that of a referent, that is to say an extra-linguistic fact, of which a given group of people may have a common experience, or mythology.
>
> (2004: 96)

Moulin argues that Hughes's sense of myth is not only different, but that it is 'actually anti-myth' in being against the idea of myth as a fantasy structure selected by a writer as a kind of scaffolding or parallel narrative, such as Joyces's use of the *Odyssey* in *Ulysses*. For Hughes, Moulin argues,

> myth is not a method, it is the target. That is because, for Hughes, there is no real solution of continuity between words and things, any more than between physics and metaphysics. *Mythos* is for him the connective side of *logos*.
>
> (97)

Moulin goes on to discuss a range of work by Hughes that is specifically anti-Christian in its critique of what Hughes called, in the first 'Myth and Education' essay, 'the neurotic-making dynamics' of Christian myths such as Saint George which Hughes countered with *The Iron Man* ('Myth and Education' 1970: 66).

Graham Bradshaw has raised the essential challenge to the reader of Hughes's poetry by his insistence upon the term 'creative mythology' when discussing it. Bradshaw argues that literature manipulates mythology with originality and power in a manner that implicitly asks of that mythology 'how well does this help us to manage our lives?' (1983: 217). Writing about the *Cave Birds* poem 'The Baptist', Bradshaw says:

> the poetry itself controls and concentrates such associations, as it projects the central idea of some mysterious healing process ... An elaborate exegesis may uncover *analogies*, in helpful or off-putting ways, but can no more explain the source of the poem's unnerving

power than we can explain Ariel's songs in *The Tempest*, which provide one of the more obvious analogies.

(232)

Indeed, Bradshaw's conclusion, quoting Hughes's definition of the function of myth, is that the creative mythology of *Cave Birds* demonstrates 'the lack of a sustaining communal myth, and the need to find some "realm of management between our ordinary minds and our deepest life"' (238).

Laureateship, history and politics

While Sean O'Brien accuses Hughes of omitting any engagement with politics and history from his poetry (1998: 37), he describes the Laureate poems as 'Hughes's most nearly political work' which were unequivocally 'poetically unsuccessful' (38) (see Criticism, p. 107). For Tom Paulin, however, the poetry of Hughes was, throughout his life, both political and historically positioned. In the 1970s in particular, Paulin writes, the poetry 'speaks for the freebooting private sector' (1992: 270) and 'belongs to a type of Protestant discourse' (255) that is very much historically located. In his essay titled 'Poet of the Free Market?', Paulin develops a characteristically idiosyncratic line of argument. All 'nature poetry is always a form of disguised social comment' and this must be the case for a Poet Laureate who has 'aligned his poetry with the British state' (252). 'The apparently natural forces he celebrates are symbolic metaphors for a series of historical struggles – Reformation, Industrial Revolution, First World War' which combine in the 'radically unsettled imagination' of a poet who is 'a patriot who dislikes the British Empire, a domineering Anglo-Saxon Protestant drawn to a relaxed Catholic Celticism, a monarchist fascinated by the molten energies of the free market' (252).

The evidence for these views is drawn from a very wide range of sources in the work of Hughes. 'The animal theme in Hughes's verse is an expression of his wish to exit from history ... But he immediately re-enters history and exposes the hidden ideology of the natural and elemental' (255), which is that of 'an unfallen, new and natural world that predates society and ideology' (254) – a 'utopian primitivism' (260) expressed in his memorial oration for the Nazi sympathiser Henry Williamson (Sewell 1980). Paulin identifies an 'insistent feudalism' in *The Hawk in the Rain* and suggests that 'Hughes would revive the age of chivalry', citing the 'kitsch language and imagery' of the Laureate poems: 'For Hughes, salmon, prize bulls, falling leaves, bees and thistles are naturally royal' (258–59). If this seems to be a strange series of connections and leaps of argument, they are actually presented just as fluently as this.

Typical of Paulin's treatment of the poetry is his assertion that its 'entrepreneurial energy and puritan striving' produce 'a myth for individual private enterprise':

> His outlook has in many ways the solitary, committed toughness and risky certainties of the self-employed, and his unique ability to locate a North American type of wilderness poetry in England endorses,

however unconsciously, Thatcher's famous remark when she was Prime Minister that 'there is no such thing as society'.

(260)

An admiration for the improvisational language of Shakespeare is evidence of this, apparently, and an interest in regional vernacular forms of English 'against standardisation and state centralisation' can be found in surprising places: 'his obsessive images of caged wild animals express that struggle' (261). The poem 'A Motorbike' is compared with 'Hughes's fascination with elemental energy as expressing an impatience with the post-war consensus', that is with 'what are now regarded as the "fudge and mudge" policies of the 1970s. Hughes speaks for the freebooting private sector, with its hostility to state interference and control' (270).

Paulin seems to miss the irony, ambivalence and critique in the poetry as he seeks to move from association to association in pursuit of his argument. He moves from a pond 'as deep as England' in 'Pike' to the statement, 'This occult nationalism is the subject of "Crowego"' (264). But Paulin sees, underlying this nationalism, a historical Protestant guilt that is exultant in advocating, in the poems 'The Warriors of the North' and 'Gog' for example, 'a nationalist mythology which glorifies and justifies political violence' that comes close to that of Yeats, were it not for the fact that 'Gog' 'colludes with its own obscurity' (267). What all this comes down to is that Hughes's private sector 'economic philosophy expresses itself in a type of elemental super-realism', a 'superbright puritan aesthetic' that finds its form in 'Hughes's most assured, most perfect work', the *Moortown Diary* poems (271). Here 'the forces – the "struggle" – which have created capital' find expression in 'a celebration of the absolute newness of commodity production' in the poem 'Birth of a Rainbow' (272). Less satisfactory because it 'draws attention to its saleability, its existence as commodity' (275) is *River*, an 'ambitious wish to draw together history, the natural environment and human enterprise' (274). Quite how this volume engages with history might be as puzzling as how it engages with city life were it not for Tom Paulin's offers of half-truths in his discussion of Hughes's poems: 'By pretending to look away from the packed cities of Britain and continental Europe, they tell many uncomfortable truths about our civilization' (275).

John Lucas has also written about Hughes as a 'post-Imperial' Laureate of a Thatcher government. Lucas discusses many of the same poems as Paulin ('Thistles', 'Warriors of the North') to support his view of 'the authoritarian nature of Hughes's politics' (1986: 194). Quoting the Indian critic M. G. Ramanan, Lucas worries about the notion of nationalism Hughes projects. 'Much of Hughes's early work has worn badly', in the view of Lucas, because of its consciousness of a masculine, tough, Anglo-Saxon identity, although Lucas does admire his empathetic powers and his critique of 'rationalistic positivism' (196). In a more balanced and nuanced argument than Paulin's, Lucas seeks to introduce a more critical approach to the work than was common in 1986.

A decade later, the publication of a volume of Laureate poems, with its his-toricising Notes, provided an opportunity to observe Hughes qualifying his admitted 'boyhood fanatic patriotism', as Paul Bentley points out:

Much as Hughes qualifies his 'patriotism' by delineating its historical determinants, by finding the self to be continuous with – though never reducible to – such determinants, so any notion of national or ethnic purity that might cling to the word 'British' is undermined in the volume by Hughes's sense of the history of the British Isles, which in Hughes's vision have always been a kind of multi-cultural melting-pot, the British people 'genetically the most mixed-up gallimaufry of mongrels on earth' (*Rain-Charm for the Duchy*: 63).

(1998: 119)

Bentley senses in the volume of Laureate poems an 'uneasiness and precariousness of the parts that currently make up the "whole"' of the nation in the poem 'Solomon's Dream' that prefaces the collection. A new kind of vision of 'wholeness' is called for in these poems, according to Bentley:

In the context of the current climate of uncertainty about the role of the monarchy in a secular democracy, and given the increasingly isolated standing in a multicultural society of the Queen as head of the Church of England, there is a message here from the Laureate to his Queen.

(119)

This radical suggestion is not shared by Neil Roberts, who believes that the Laureate poems, supported by the long Note about Hughes's personal connection with both World Wars (*Rain-Charm for the Duchy*: 58–60), reflect 'a distinctive kind of history, both analytic and interior, both material and mythologising' (2006: 166). Roberts reveals a state of confusion, or rather personal tensions, in these poems and Notes. On the one hand is the desire for an archetypal, ahistorical, unifying, symbolic Crown, 'when many historical developments, most obviously devolution, European union and multiculturalism, threatened the concept of nationhood as a spiritual unity, which is the theme of Hughes's Laureateship', while on the other is a recognition that he writes from a generational historical context 'of the son of an infantryman of the First World War' as Hughes put it in the long Note 'that amounts to one of his most important and illuminating essays' (164, 165). Roberts originally welcomed the first Laureate poem as promising the 'challenge and excitement' of a pagan poet committed to 'the rival religion of Neumann's "Great mother", Graves's "White Goddess", the presiding deity of Hughes's three major mythological works, *Crow*, *Gaudete* and *Cave Birds*' (1985: 4). In his later book Roberts concludes that 'unlike Tennyson, Hughes is not creating "new forms for a new national consciousness" [as Tennyson's Laureate verse had according to Pitt 1962: 195], but constructing a personal myth, which may be shared by some, though I suspect not all, of his generation' (Roberts 2006: 166).

In his latest study of Ted Hughes, *The Laughter of Foxes* (2006), Keith Sagar is silent about the Laureate poems. In correspondence with the poet just after the publication of the poem for the Queen Mother titled 'The Dream of the Lion' Sagar raised questions about Hughes's view of the role of the monarchy for the tribe in relation to this poem. With characteristic generosity and grace Hughes wrote back a long explanation for Sagar, ending with the words:

You don't have to defend it, Keith. You only have to say that you don't like that kind of verse. And who can write in an amiable way to any member of the royal family without it looking like flattery? Can't be done.

(19. 1. 1986, BL ADD 78757, f. 159)

Hughes and Plath

In her pioneering study *Sylvia Plath and Ted Hughes* (1979), Margaret Dickie Uroff argued from a reading of the poems (the archives of both poets were not available at that time) that understanding their mutual influence on each other could avoid the reductive distortions of reading Plath only within an American tradition and Hughes in an English one. The result might offer insights that confound conventional expectations:

> Their poems read as parts of a continuing debate about the nature of the universe, in which Plath's reservations and Hughes's assertions play against each other. Strangely enough, as Hughes developed he began to retreat from the confident insights of his early poems and to question the laws of the universe.
>
> (Uroff 1979: 12)

Rather than see Plath as part of the contemporary movement of confessional poets such as Lowell and Sexton, Uroff sees Plath borrowing something of Hughes's dramatic mythologising: 'The very inflation of her experience in her poetry suggests, first, that she was searching beyond its private accidents for its larger meaning, and, further, that the impulse of her poetry is not confessional but visionary' (13).

Uroff observes that the later work of Plath may have adopted a role from Hughes's visionary repertoire: 'In creating the role of the vengeful female who rises against her oppressors, Plath had available as an aid Hughes's own myth of enraged and captive energies, and his own image of the creative-destructive female' (14). Meanwhile Hughes's later surrealism may well owe something to Plath's inward journeys:

> Even as early as 'Mayday in Holderness', he sounds like Plath (in 'Poem for a Birthday') ... If Plath's surrealistic imagery served to express states at the extremities of consciousness, states which she could formulate in no other way, Hughes was also able to use such imagery to break through the rigidity of rational coherence to a deeper level of the imagination.
>
> (15)

Although 'Mayday in Holderness' was almost certainly written before Hughes met Plath, their parallel need for the imagery of dreams is surely significant.

The meeting of the two young and ambitious poets provides the opportunity for Uroff to attempt to pin down immediate mutual influences and shared preoccupations, as in their treatment of passion, for example: 'The predatory woman of "The Shrike" may have inspired "Billet-Doux", or the panther "A Modest Proposal" [by Hughes]' (76). On the other hand, '"Spinster" and "Two Sisters of Persephone", both poems Plath included in *The Colossus*, are drawn from Hughes's "Secretary"' (76). In an enlightening discussion, Uroff's method is usefully displayed by her suggestion that 'Perhaps the poems that most clearly connect and distinguish Plath and Hughes at this time are "Black Rook in Rainy Weather" and "The Hawk in the Rain"' (77–78). Uroff's comparison concludes: 'The fear of total neutrality can be relieved by poetic vision, Plath claims, against Hughes's conviction that nature is anti-human' (78). The problem is that some of the weakest early poetry by both writers is being compared here, with the result, for Uroff, that Plath's poems are, 'as psychic explorations, more particular, more intense, more ominous, and more psychologically complex than Hughes's poems' (81).

A comparison of Plath's first collection *The Colossus* with Hughes's second collection *Lupercal*, which were worked on at the same time, produces some interesting insights into both shared and parallel preoccupations and results. Hughes 'began to use figures from literature and myth in his poetry at this time, perhaps following Plath's example' (Uroff 1979: 88). The title poems of their two collections invite comparison as a dialogue between the poets: 'In some ways they speak across the poems to each other and reveal a private argument: the wisdom Plath fails to find is cancelled out in Hughes's poem, and the anarchy Hughes celebrates is the subject of Plath's concern' (91). In their landscape poems Uroff notices that human observers feel vulnerable to the elements, although the poetry of Hughes exhilarates in this more than does Plath's: 'he thrills to the dangers that frighten her' (95). As they both 'probe depths that they identified with the world of magic, legend, folklore, and nature' they both explore submarine imagery as in Hughes's 'Pike' and Plath's 'Full Fathom Five', or 'An Otter', which Hughes was writing while Plath wrote 'Lorelei'.

Uroff makes the point that knowledge of Plath's suicide and father-fixation has tended to overshadow the parallel explorations of the two poets:

> Hughes's poems have never attracted the autobiographical and psychological readings that fascinate Plath critics, because he deals with animal spirits rather than fathers and sisters; but he, too, was beginning to explore life submerged beneath the mundane order, and he finds there the same attraction and treachery, fatal powers that must be confronted.
>
> (97)

Indeed, it can be argued that 'Hughes appears more fascinated with death and deadliness than does Plath' in the predators and 'dark, destructive gods' of his second collection (105). But her vulnerability appears to be greater: 'In general, Hughes's poems do not deal with the search for identity that fascinated Plath' (124).

Uroff compares Hughes's 'Lines to a Newborn Baby' and 'To F. R. at Six Months' with Plath's 'Morning Song' and 'Magi', noticing that, in contrasting 'Lines to a Newborn Baby' with 'Morning Song',

Plath's poem shows no concern for the child's place in the universe, although when she came to dwell on this subject in most of her other poems about children [see Criticism, **p. 135**], she could never summon Hughes's assurance that the child would be safe.

Arguing that Plath's 'Magi' picks up on Hughes's reference to the magi in 'To F. R. at Six Months', Uroff sums up 'the imaginative intimacy between the two poets': 'The parallels in these poems show how the two poets could penetrate each other's insights, draw on similar images and experiences, cast them in different molds, return again to redevelop hints from each other, and respond to the other poetically' (135). Plath's 'The Moon and the Yew Tree' is also compared with 'Full Moon and Little Frieda', although Uroff's failure to sense the irony at the end of Hughes's 'Pibroch' (as she also fails in her comments on 'Hawk Roosting') produces a surprise that the writer of 'Pibroch' could produce, in 'Full Moon and Little Frieda,' an 'affirmation of wonder [that] seems to contradict almost everything he ever wrote about nature' (178).

In the poems Hughes wrote in *Wodwo* following Plath's suicide, Uroff finds echoes of Plath's surrealism, imagery and 'defiant voice', while 'the strategies that Crow employs to survive in the world [his female creator] dominates are similar to Plath's: sardonic humour, caricature, hyperbole, parody' (223). The idea that Hughes's poetic developments in *Wodwo* and *Crow* are in any way still influenced by Plath's poetry seems less than convincing, as does Uroff's reductively neat conclusion to her book: 'In these late poems Hughes and Plath seem to have reversed their earlier positions: Plath is now triumphant, and Hughes, if not defeated, is at least aware of that possibility' (224).

The late Diane Middlebrook's book titled *Her Husband: Hughes and Plath – A Marriage* (2004) is largely a biographical work, although she, too, compares the two poets' poems about their first baby – Hughes's 'Lines to a Newborn Baby' and 'To F. R. at Six Months' – with Plath's 'Morning Song'. Hughes apparently believed that Plath's poem was based upon his own earlier poem and was 'much superior' (T.H. to Keith Sagar, 13. 3. 1981, BL ADD 78757, f. 54). Middlebrook quotes Hughes on the difference in approaches to composition by the two poets: 'My method was to find a thread end and draw the rest out of a hidden tangle', while 'hers was to collect a heap of vivid objects and good words and make a pattern' (Heinz 1995: 77). Middlebrook demonstrates the results of these processes:

> Working from Hughes's images of the reflected cloud and the hand gripping the head, Plath produces the startling condensation 'effacement at the wind's hand'. 'Effacement', a dreaded outcome of contact, is brilliantly deployed to suggest troubling self-discovery: the cloud produces its own mirror – the reflecting surface of pooled rainwater – as a woman has produced a simulacrum of herself in a child, and fears the loss of her former identity. In Hughes the image is shockingly violent: a beheading. The difference in the poems is Hughes's impersonality – he keeps the emotional charge of his metaphor out there in history, ancient history at that. 'Morning Song' works in the opposite direction: from emotional distance to joyful empathy.
>
> (2004: 154)

In a later essay, Middlebrook traces in more detail what she characterises as the 'call and response' of the 'marriage poems'. Noting that Hughes began drafting his poem 'Lines to a Newborn Baby' on the back of a typescript of Plath's poem 'Metaphors for a Pregnant Woman' ['Metaphors'], Middlebrook suggests that Hughes picked up metaphors from the natural world in Plath's poem. Then, like Uroff, Middlebrook argues that Plath's poem 'Magi' is prompted by a reference to the magi in Hughes's 'To F.R. at Six Months'. 'From the outset Plath counters Hughes's grim prognostications about the fateful star that hovers over the crib by insisting on the infant's own preoccupation with physical life' (Middlebrook 2006: 161). However, Plath's 'Morning Song', prompted by Hughes's 'Lines to a Newborn Baby', is then presented as the 'unmistakable' influence upon Hughes's 'Full Moon and Little Frieda' by the comparison of nine phrases common to both of them. 'Moreover, it seems significant that Hughes drafted "Full Moon" on the verso of a typescript of Plath's poem "Tulips", [which] rejects the burden of intimacy, of the family, [while] "Full Moon" affirms the attentiveness of parental love' (2006: 162).

Commenting on Hughes's belief that he and Plath worked so closely on their imaginative projects that they shared 'one single mind', Middlebrook's reading of these poems led her to agree that their 'total confidence in each other' was mutually beneficial 'at the level of dialogue between images', but that 'Plath's poem is conducting a secret life as well, in which Plath is responding with resistance to her most influential mentor's published work' (Middlebrook 2004: 157). This comment is based upon Hughes's observation that they were also each 'conducting a secret life of the imagination' during a joint BBC radio interview in a series called 'Two of a Kind' (18. 1. 1961). The interviewer, Owen Leeming, asked the two poets if theirs was 'a marriage of opposites'. Hughes replied that they were 'very different' while Plath said they were 'quite similar'. What Hughes meant was that, although they shared 'one single mind', their unconscious imaginative agendas went in different directions. Plath, on the other hand, explained that by 'similar' what she meant was not that the work was similar, but that they shared common interests, she opening up American poetry to Hughes and his interest in wildlife reconnecting her to her father's beekeeping scholarship, for example. Middlebrook opens her book with this remarkable interview, saying that 'just such a dance through the minefield of their differences characterized their partnership at its best. It succeeded because each of them invested wholeheartedly in whatever the other was working on, even when the outcome was of dubious merit' (2004: xvi).

Middlebrook's book is particularly good at demonstrating how the presence of Plath's work, which Hughes was later responsible for publishing as her estate-owner and editor after her death, continued to influence his own work as he 'found his way as an artist through the unfinished business of his marriage' (2004: 214). A discussion of the poem written in the days following Plath's death, 'The Howling of Wolves', leads to *Birthday Letters* and the wolves in the poem 'Life After Death' that evoke the image, from the Roman legend of Romulus and Remus, of two children lying beside their dead mother before being raised by wolves. Middlebrook points out that this image echoes that in Plath's last poem 'Edge' and hints at 'the children's rescue by a lupine care-taker – Hughes himself'. Thus Middlebrook introduces her central thesis: that after Plath's death Hughes 'began incorporating his family into a mythic auto-biography that accounted for his marriage' writing as 'her husband', 'a literary character who is telling the story of his life' (213–15).

Middlebrook is not only referring to the voice of the writer of introductions and notes to Plath's work, just as she is not only referring to the writer of *Birthday Letters*. The style of *Crow*, she argues, with some support from a late letter by Hughes, 'was, however improbably, the way he was finally able to write about his own experience of personal devastation' (230). But it is in the biographical notes to Plath's work that Hughes seeks 'to present himself in the character of Plath's working partner': 'By placing himself inside the story from its beginnings, Hughes suggests that neither could be written about, as poets, without reference to the other' (263). In fact, Hughes was Plath's work-ing partner after her death in more than his famously publishing a different version of *Ariel* from the completed manuscript he found (see Bundtzen 2001). In establishing the evidence for 'the call-and-response manner of their productive collusion', Middlebrook suggests that the ending of Plath's poem 'Child' echoes the line from 'Full Moon and Little Frieda': 'To tempt a first star to a tremor' (2004: 191).

Actually, in the manuscript of the obviously unfinished poem 'Child' that Hughes found after her death, the alternative endings that Plath crossed out do not include the last line 'this dark / ceiling without a star', which sounds like a Hughes line to Middlebrook because it is one, inserted so that the almost completed poem could be published in *Collected Poems*. This fact has been in the public domain since 1995 and indicates an additional dimension to the phrase 'working partner' (Gifford 1995: 150). Plath's biographer Ann Stevenson has told me that this is by no means the only example to be found of Hughes 'completing' a Plath poem for publication.

Diane Middlebrook concludes her book with the suggestion that the poem 'The Offers' from the limited edition *Howls and Whispers*:

> occupies an important position in Hughes's myth of the evolution of his poetic persona, her husband. It completes the story of his separa-tion from his family into the role of consort to his female opposite, that alchemical Bride of his imagination, in a tale of magical reunion.
> (2004: 280)

In the earliest poem of his first collection, 'Song', Hughes wrote, with accidental premonition, 'When will the stone open its tomb? ... You will not die, nor come home'. In the poem 'Visit' in *Birthday Letters* Plath is buried in her tomb but speaks to Hughes through the voice of her journals as he edits them for publication. Drawn from the same set of poems as *Birthday Letters*, 'The Offers' dramatises three appearances by Plath to Hughes, on the third of which she says the lines which end the poem: 'This is the last time. This one. This time / Don't fail me.' Middlebrook refers back to the lines from 'Song': 'That "you" who has always been and is not Sylvia Plath has come home, in the closing words of "The Offers". And he, on the occasion, is naked: vulnerable, undefended, receptive to her summons' (2004: 283). Published in January 1998 after being written over a period of twenty-five years, *Birthday Letters* was the very public, long-delayed, last-chance response to that 'This time / Don't fail me' that was itself 'hidden' in the very expensive limited edition book *Howls and Whispers*. By the end of October Ted Hughes was dead. Middlebrook presents this situation as a last-minute reunion of the poet with his muse.

Tracy Brain has complained that Hughes critics have largely failed to allow for the possibility of Plath's influence on Hughes (Brain 2001: 191). She then neatly side-steps the difficult issue of 'Which poem came first?' by arguing that when two poets live together 'conversations and influence can pass unrecorded' (192). 'It is less important to determine who or what came first, than to identify the reverberation and evaluate it; the poems are best regarded as fragments of a continuing conversation' (193). Brain goes on to make an interesting linguistic comparison between Plath's 'The Detective' and Hughes's 'Crow's Song About England'. One of the important contributions to the debate about the narrative of *Birthday Letters* is Brain's drawing attention to the way the poems raise questions about the reliability and partiality of memory: 'Hesitant words and questioning syntax are a striking feature of the first half of *Birthday Letters*, as if to emphasise Hughes's position as a witness who can only describe the way things appeared from one vantage point' (182). An important exception to Brain's complaint about Hughes critics must be an essay by Neil Roberts titled 'The Common Text of Sylvia Plath and Ted Hughes' (2003) which discusses a sharing of motifs from their first acquaintance to *Birthday Letters*.

Jacqueline Rose, in her book *The Haunting of Sylvia Plath* (1991) has much to say about Hughes's editing of Plath's work, but little about their mutual influences upon each other's work. She is critical of Robert Graves's conception of the White Goddess – 'woman as inspiration, woman as drudge' (154) – and the way, as she sees it, 'Both Plath's and Hughes's poetry suggest that this conception of femininity was being consciously or unconsciously negotiated between them' in their domestic arrangements, as well as 'more symbolically' in their poetry (155). As an example of this Rose goes on to discuss Hughes's radio play 'The Wound' in the light of the theories of Jung and Freud, to argue that Plath and Hughes 'battled out' in their work the concept of female transcendence. In this discussion Rose reveals that Plath was, in a letter to her mother, 'highly sceptical of Hughes's metaphysical interpretation of his own work' (163). Plath's emergent identity in her poetry, Rose argues, has to enact Graves's and Hughes's concept of the transcendent female figure, while at the same time wanting to subversively celebrate 'what this requires the woman to leave behind': 'Following back Plath's figure of female transcendence into its (male) origins, we find a grotesque fantasy of femininity as its underside and support' (162).

That Hughes's version of the feminine in his whole work is taken from 'The Wound' is itself somewhat limited. But to fail to grasp the salutary role of the female figures in this dream drama in relation to the complacent male ego is to fail to realise how radically Hughes is himself critiquing the male origins of grotesque images of the feminine. And to imply, as Rose does, that Hughes endorsed Graves's notion that woman cannot be a poet, in the light of his regard for Plath's poetry, is evidently absurd (154).

Strangely, the 'authorised' biography of Sylvia Plath by Ann Stevenson, while making passing references to Ted's suggestions to Sylvia on her writing, makes no assessment of their mutual influence on each other's work. Indeed, with the exceptions of Uroff, Brain, Middlebrook and Roberts (below) critics specialising in the poetry of either Plath or Hughes have largely failed to consider the contribution of Plath to the technical development of the poetry of Hughes. More common are studies – useful in themselves – such as Gayle Wurst's 'Words to "Patch the Havoc": The Imagination of Ted Hughes in the Poetry of Sylvia Plath' (2004). Perhaps an early and unexplored exception might be the suggestion of Gifford and Roberts that 'it seems to us likely that the greater rhythmical freedom, compression and elliptical language of Hughes's poetry from *Wodwo* onwards owes something to the example of Sylvia Plath's later work' (1981: 22).

Indeed, in his book *Ted Hughes: A Literary Life* (2006), Neil Roberts suggests that the poems Hughes wrote following the death of Plath, 'Song of a Rat' and 'The Howling of Wolves', may be borrowing a new tone, stance and form from the Plath poem 'Burning the Letters' which was written about her response to the discovery of Hughes's affair with Assia Wevill. Roberts quotes Lynda K. Bundtzen's description of this poem as 'an anti-thought fox', a rejection of 'poetic lyricism' and 'literary convention' in favour of 'the poetic efficacy of shrieks ... Something crude and sensational' (Bundtzen 1998: 442–43). Of the two Hughes poems Roberts writes:

> Both in feeling and in style these poems resemble 'Burning the Letters' much more closely than 'The Thought-Fox'. It would be rash to assert that Hughes had taken note of the rebuke to himself in 'Burning the Letters', and that in 'Song of a Rat' and 'The Howling of Wolves' he is not only mourning Plath but paying poetic tribute to her. Nevertheless, the resemblance of [what Bundtzen calls] the 'enervated tone', the 'misshapen' appearance, the supplanting of 'poetic lyricism' with 'something crude and sensational', is striking.
>
> (Roberts 2006: 67)

Also of importance in Roberts's book are his comments on Marjorie Perloff's influential essay first published in 1984, 'The Two *Ariels*: The (Re)Making of the Plath Canon'. Perloff accuses Hughes of abandoning Plath's plan for *Ariel* as she had left it in a folder at her death and removing, in his own words, 'one or two of the more openly vicious poems', which included poems about himself, and substituting the most recent poems (by many of which she subsequently became well known). Roberts demonstrates how even a reputable critic like Perloff not only distorts the evidence to support her argument, but slips from criticism of the collection into 'pass[ing] judgement with equal confidence on Hughes's private conduct' (Roberts 2006: 91). It is hard to escape the evidence, Roberts concludes, that Hughes was hounded, not only by partisan Plath 'supporters', but 'even by respectable critics like Perloff' (91). In his discussion of what he calls 'the Plath wars', Roberts distinguishes the limits of literary criticism, both here and in his comment on Hughes's decision to immediately destroy Plath's last journal when he read it after her death: 'The destruction of the journal was a private act on which I do not think a critic is qualified to comment' (94). Curiously, neither of these issues is discussed in Middlebrook's book *Her Husband* (2004), as they are not in Lynda Bundtzen's book *The*

Other Ariel (2001) in which the simplistic and judgemental phrase 'Plath's abandonment by Hughes' is used as biographical fact.

Of course, the reviewers' responses to *Birthday Letters* inevitably revisited the intertextuality of the work of Plath and Hughes. Some reviews have been quoted above (see Criticism, p. 109), but in this context one stands out. Edna Longley wrote that 'the languages of the poets were mutually entangled before her death, and Hughes does little to disentangle them', as though, first, inter-textuality is itself reprehensible and, second, Hughes's voice in *Birthday Letters* is indistinguishable from (presumably the later) Plath's, both of which are surely suspect assumptions. Longley's judgement of the poetry is that it is var-iously, 'tiresome and aggrandising', 'banal, obvious', 'not taking enough lin-guistic care', 'ugly and shrill' in tone, and has 'amazing bad taste', 'lack of poetic tact' and 'crude bad writing'. Amazed at the positive response from 'other poets and critics who should have known better', Longley asks, 'Is Hughes's reputa-tion being talked up in some way, and to hell with critical judgement, to hell with poetry?' (Longley 1998: 30).

A more sympathetic source of criticism of *Birthday Letters* came from the late Leonard M. Scigaj in an essay titled 'The Deterministic Ghost in the Machine of *Birthday Letters*' in which he argued that Hughes presents Plath's dead father in the role of the ghost that determined the course of their marriage: 'In her self-destructive indulgence in anger and emotional tirades, Plath apes her father as she becomes the Minotaur' (2004: 2). Then Hughes 'adds a second level of genetic and cultural determinism. Otto himself is infected with fascistic faith in an all-powerful Ruler', despite Plath's mother's statement in her Introduction to *Letters Home* that Otto was 'a confirmed pacifist' (2, 13). While Hughes admits his own errors in pressing for the move to Devon, the emphasis on genetic determinism in *Birthday Letters* 'eliminates all other possible causes of Sylvia Plath's actions in the last years of her life' (5). Scigaj's conclusion is that *Birthday Letters*, while sincere in its grief and regrets, still fails to take account of not only Plath's real medical condition, but also her struggle for career equality in the isolation and domestic work-load of life in Devon.

In the Introduction to his book *Myth in the Poetry of Ted Hughes* (1981) Stuart Hirschberg makes a tantalising suggestion that he has no space to pursue: that the poetry of Hughes and Plath

> are reciprocals of each other; each moves toward the condition of the other. In Hughes's recent work [Hirschberg writes in 1981] we see the tentative self-questioning so characteristic of Plath's early poetry, while in Hughes's first animal poems we can fully observe an absolute certainty achieved through imaginative fusion with universal forces that Plath finally attained only in her very last poems ... readers should be aware that the exact same process we will outline and explore chronologically operating in Hughes's poetry is duplicated, in reverse form, in Sylvia Plath's work.
>
> (7–8)

It is clear that there remains much to be said about the poetic relationship between the work of Hughes and Plath, as there is also much more to be said about Hughes's poems addressed to Assia in *Capriccio*. The latter work has been begun by Carol Bere (1999) who points out that by placing the poem 'Capriccios' both at the opening of *Capriccio* and at the end of the sequence addressed to Plath, *Howls and Whispers*, 'Hughes has deliberately created a circular pattern among the sequences, again suggesting the unpredictable, unmotivated nature of events, and, more important, the impossibility of fulfilment of transforming or completed myth' (37). Indeed, it is the incompleteness of the mythic cycle that might benefit from more exchanges of critical readings.

Ecology

Just as Hughes's work moved towards a more informed and radical engagement with environmentalism during his lifetime, so too has critical discussion of that work moved from terms such as 'nature poet' (Sagar 1972: 4) to 'ecopoet' (Usha 1999: 83). Indeed, during the poet's life there had sprung up the new school of environmentally aware 'ecocriticism' (see Glotfelty and Fromm (1996), Coupe (2000) and Garrard (2004)). Gifford and Roberts' chapter title from their 1981 book on Hughes, 'Man and Nature', now looks dated on both counts. Since the ecological relationship between human nature and external nature is the central subject of Hughes's *oeuvre*, the foregoing sections of 'Criticism' on other themes have inevitably also touched upon what critics have had to say about Hughes's representations of that relationship, so some overlaps are to be expected. It now seems appropriate to consider critical discussion of Hughes's treatments of the dynamics of the relationships within nature under the heading of 'ecology'.

Most early criticism was concerned with the language and stance with which Hughes approached internal and external nature. Keith Sagar's first defence of the work declared that Hughes's language was 'able to cope with the biggest things; it can generate energies equal to the great primary energies of the world' (1972: 9). Dismissing the early patronising labels of 'Nature Poet' and 'Animal Poet', Sagar points out that animals were metaphors for 'the most typical stresses and contradictions of human nature and of nature itself' (4). Around the time Sagar was writing, Ian Hamilton could still provocatively patronise the early poetry as 'ripplingly muscular neo-Georgianism' (1973: 165) and Calvin Bedient formulated his famous appellation 'voyeur of violence' (1974: 108). Actually, Bedient's attitude towards the early poetry's representations of nature was as much in awe as it was horrified: 'If Hughes is a voyeur of violence in *The Hawk in the Rain*, in *Lupercal* he is a fearful lover of the will to live – a far profounder thing' (ibid.).

Gifford and Roberts saw the early animal poems as 'the sustained attempt of the conscious mind to articulate continuities between the human self and the animal world; and an exploration of the creative-destructive nature of the material reality on which all life is founded' (1981: 80). Their book concludes with a discussion of the elegies for Jack Orchard in *Moortown*:

> It has been a long discipline of imaginative objectivity that has brought Hughes to the point where positive connections between man

and nature can be expressed, and in directly personal terms. For this sense of connection has always been one of the main criteria by which Hughes's work should be judged. Hughes's poetry has not been striving towards mystical transcendence or for some supposedly invulnerable stance. In it he is seeking a position of practical engagement with the world that is utterly honest, stripped of self-deceptions, humble and respectful but at home in the only world, that is our life and our death.

(252)

Some later critics did believe that mystical transcendence was what the *Gaudete* Epilogue poems and the *River* sequence were striving for. One of those was Craig Robinson, whose book *Ted Hughes as Shepherd of Being* (1989) is a clearly written, if somewhat simplistic book that focuses especially on *Cave Birds*, *Gaudete*, *Moortown* and *River*. Its strength is the way it takes its discussion of the poet's negotiations with the forces of nature embodied in the various forms of the Goddess into a detailed charting of the poetic sequences in *Moortown*. Robinson is inclined neither to express any reservations about the work of Hughes, nor to refer to the work of other critics. His focus is on a series of close readings in explication of the development in the poet of a psychological, religious and ultimately ecological responsibility. For Robinson this is a matter of restoring a more balanced view of Hughes's reputation:

> In the early 1960s Hughes earned from his detractors a reputation ... for proposing the resignation of the reasonable parts of the mind in favour of an unbridled licence for the instincts. Though Hughes's view has ... changed in some respects over the years, he has never been a straightforward anti-rationalist, but has stood against the tyranny of a diminished reason over the psyche, always seeking an augmentation, harmonising and attunement of its faculties.

(2)

In *Ted Hughes as Shepherd of Being* Robinson takes Heidegger's notion of Being as the deepest layer of reality from which scientific-technological culture has alienated us and applies Heidegger's possibility of 'the Turn' to Hughes's poetic project, which he characterises as 'the Hughesian attack on the excessively rational mind, on scientific-technological thinking and Cartesian dualism, on earth rape, and on psychological closure' (8). Robinson uses Heidegger's concept of 'man as shepherd of Being' to read the work of Hughes as bringing the reader back into contact with inner reality and the processes of nature by perceiving that they are connected. A respect for 'the spirit of Being', Robinson suggests, entails both a valuing of the inner life of an individual and a caring for the creative-destructive forces of nature. For Robinson the practical activities of fishing and shepherding in *River* and in *Moortown* indicate a connective caring for the environment that enacts the redemptive possibilities of *Cave Birds*, *Gaudete* and the poem sequences of *Moortown*.

On *Moortown* Robinson writes:

Man has increasingly come to appear in Hughes's more recent poetry
as the pinnacle of the evolutionary process – not in the sense of his
being lord over creation, able to use and exploit it at his whim, but as
life's latest servant, the current growing tip of a single urge. What is
special about man is that the directing and furtherance of that urge
seems to have been put into his own hands ... whereas throughout
pre-human evolution life developed as though automatically, now the
burden of further development has settled in part onto man's shoulders. He himself has been charged with the task of fulfilling nature in
himself. Hughes uses the rest of nature to remind man of his destiny,
[as in the] 'Adam and the Sacred Nine' sequence, for example.

(184–85)

Robinson is one of those who revere *River* as a religious text and his admiration leads him to the remarkable statement that 'Fish swim in a religious
trance'(205). But in a comment on the story 'The Head' Robinson was one of
the first critics to note 'that Hughes's goddess has an ecological aspect, as well
as a psychological and a religious [one]' (208).

The other critic who combines the ecological with a notion of transcendence
is the late Leonard M. Scigaj, whose second book *Ted Hughes* (1991) drives
towards making the case for Hughes as an ecological poet. But even in his 1986
book, Scigaj saw Hughes's poetry after *Crow* as enacting journeys 'toward a
restoration of equilibrium with the environment after exorcising demons within
the self and in the cultural context' (15). The later book makes larger claims,
especially for the *River* poem 'Salmon Eggs': 'Hughes has constructed a cathe-
dral of ecological vision to show readers how to enliven their imaginations and
save our planet' (1991: 144). This last phrase might appear to be a huge claim,
but Scigaj takes the environmental crisis seriously, as he believes Hughes does.
In his Introduction Scigaj outlines Hughes's belief in the shamanic healing
power of poetry for a species alienated from its natural home:

Though we are dimly aware of global ecological issues such as water
and soil pollution, the eroding ozone layer, and the greenhouse effect,
we are not alert to minute changes in our natural environment because
we have few worries about daily survival. So much the worse for us,
believes Hughes, for we have purchased our sophistication at great
cost. The progress of Western civilization ... has exiled us from our
rightful place in nature into the pseudosecurity of machines and
rational analysis. At the same time we have alienated ourselves from
our own nature and its healing powers.

(1991: 3)

In his best chapter, 'Language and Ecology', Scigaj demonstrates how basic
notions of ecology are at work in *Remains of Elmet*, *Moortown* and *River*.
From the 'energy transfer of trophic or feeding organisms' (1991: 109) in
Remains of Elmet, to the 'ecological animism' in Hughes's use of 'the hydro-
logical cycle' of *River* (136), Scigaj argues that scientifically observed processes
and networks are the poet's vehicle towards a mystical unity with nature: 'The

fisherman disappears into the river's great silence, swathed like a Zen adept in the allness of nature' (144). Because Scigaj is arguing that an animism is at work here, he can say that salmon after death 'return to a supratemporal Source' (135) and that a sea-trout can 'concentrate in a yogic trance' (137). His defence is that 'ecologists have for decades been pointing out the environmental soundness of this so-called primitive system [animism], for it promotes resource conservation and reverence for the natural world' (136). The poem 'Go Fishing', for example, 'is a triumph of ecological thinking that also synthesizes the advice of Patanjali's *Yoga Sutras* and most Zen and Taoist masters' (139). Scigaj's own awe at the achievement of this volume led him to write: '*River* will one day be recognized as one of the central literary masterpieces of the world; it should be required reading for all humans on our planet to help them attain responsible adulthood' (133).

In opening a chapter on 'Hughes and Nature' in his survey of criticism on Hughes, Sandie Byrne refers to Seamus Heaney's eulogy at the memorial service in Westminster Abbey in which Heaney associates Hughes with the first known English poet, Caedmon. Byrne points out that the difference between Caedmon and Hughes is that the first praises nature as a Christian, by assuming that it is created for human appreciation and consumption, whereas Hughes takes the opposite position: 'Hughes's poetry is not anthropocentric but biocentric (that is, it places at the centre of the universe not humankind but the bio-system of Nature of which humanity is just one part in a complex system of interrelations)' (2000: 85). Interestingly Byrne notes the limits of the biocentric in Hughes's poems: 'they emphatically do not advocate animal rights in the sense of condemning the killing of animals for food, "sport", research or other reasons' (85).

The use of the term 'biocentric' in literary criticism has followed the development of ecocriticism. Scigaj was the first ecocritic to forcefully argue that Hughes's work has been speaking all along to what has only latterly been recognised as our current environmental crisis. In his later writing on Hughes, Keith Sagar has made the same point:

> After Hughes reviewed Max Nicholson's *The Environmental Revolution* in 1970, environmental and ecological concerns came to figure more and more centrally both in his poems and in his life, and led to his working for such organisations as the Atlantic Salmon Trust, Farms for City Children and the Sacred Earth Drama Trust (which he founded).
>
> (2004: 643)

Sagar has since produced a book which seeks to demonstrate that all truly great literature, including that of Hughes, has always engaged with the issue of the relationship between our species and nature, *Literature and the Crime Against Nature* (2005). In his final chapter Sagar writes that:

> ecology needs imagination, and imagination's most articulate expression, literature. What has kept the old consciousness alive through the thousands of years of gradual rejection and persecution, in spite of the

obliteration of the beliefs and rituals of nature religions and the total desecration of modern life in the West, has been art, myth, and, especially, poetic literature. The literary imagination [of a poet such as Hughes] connects all the severed halves – inner and outer, self and other, male and female, life and death, man and Nature.

(371)

Neil Roberts has written of the *River* poems, especially in their revised form in *Three Books*, that they are 'more than any of Hughes's earlier poetic work, overtly engaged with ecological crisis' (2006: 141). Roberts draws attention to what he calls the 'strained' nature of the language in some of the poems before going on to discuss 'the representation of a disturbed and displaced subjectivity, through an intriguing shift in subject positions between poems' (143). The point is that the relationship with nature experienced by the speaker of the five poems Roberts goes on to discuss is not an easy one, and the 'paradisal' unity which is sought is not easily achieved:

> Several of the poems in *River* (especially in the *Three Books* version) are in the form of a loose autobiographical narrative in which the narrator enters the river or its environment and encounters there, in the river itself and its fish, something that calls to the hidden self who belongs to the natural world, and who is usurped in social existence. But the position of the speaker, the subject, of these poems, in relation to this hidden self, is unstable.

(146)

More than 'paradisal', as in 'That Morning', Roberts argues, 'the subject position is conflicted' in 'The Gulkana' and 'Milesian Encounter on the Sligahan'. This struggle to relate appropriately to the natural world, in both its internal and external modes, which includes the occasional experience of displacement, achieves what Roberts can only call 'religious' poetry: 'Hughes's whole *oeuvre* can be seen as a struggle to articulate spiritual experience in a vacuum of religious forms' (188).

The whole of Ann Skea's book *Ted Hughes: The Poetic Quest* (1994) tracks Hughes's quest to engage and represent what Skea capitalises as 'the Source of life' (202) and 'the Universal Energies at the source of everything' (207). Skea sees the presence of the Celtic goddess Brigantia in the *River* poems in a way that typifies Hughes's attitude to nature:

> Her presence gives the natural world which Hughes describes mythical and sacred dimensions, but it brings it, also, disruptive primitive and pagan energies, and because of this the uncompromising realism of Hughes's picture of Nature often seems excessively and disturbingly explicit. Yet, the constant and inseparable presence of life and death, the perpetual 'travail of raptures and rendings' which inform Hughes's perception of our mutable world ... convey the combination of beauty and horror in Nature which evinces the presence of the Goddess.

(209)

In the last lines of her book Skea suggests that Hughes's shamanic quest has been an exemplary journey that might reconnect his readers with the energies in nature to 'bring healing light and music into our darkened world' (239).

Some critics have commented upon the issue of gender in Hughes's representations of nature. Edward Larrissy in *Reading Twentieth Century Poetry* (1990) identifies a shift from early misogyny to 'an accommodation with the feminine' (131) culminating in the *Gaudete* Epilogue poems, 'the first of his poems to address or speak of an Other on the implied basis of a relationship, rather than describing or controlling or "capturing" objects or animals' (135). 'The disavowal of the ideology of masculine control and ruthless mechanical-bestial energy has consorted with the shedding of techniques which suggest the operations of an isolated, self-consciously ingenious and domineering mind' (136).

Reading the narratives of encounters with a female figure, especially in the children's stories, as a kind of 'skeleton key' to all of Hughes's works, Claas Kazzer argues that the 'mythic Equation' Hughes identified at the base of Shakespeare's plays was actually at the base of his own work. Hughes's narratives of the challenge of

> the ego's confrontation with the 'Goddess of Divine Love, the Goddess of Complete Being' [was] one that he saw at the base of humankind's abusive relationship with nature and at the base of one of the most disabling spiritual injuries: the suppression of one's 'inner world'

which is one's inner nature (1999: 187–88). Kazzer points out that for a crucial period from 1962 onwards Hughes used 'Difficulties of a Bridegroom' as an over-arching title for all of his projects, including his work for children. It is in the children's works, Kazzer argues, that Hughes is able to deal most directly with the problematic relationship between humans, God and God's Mother, and to come close to a redemptive accommodation with the complex and contradictory female and masculine aspects of nature that 'hold the promise of reconciliation, healing for the reader' (199).

The role of *The Iron Woman* (1993) is obviously crucial to Kazzer's identification of Hughes's agenda of reconciliation and healing. Christina Hardyment reads the novel as:

> an account of twenty years of women's struggle to adjust to a world which has slowly but inexorably sacrificed domestic and spiritual values; a story of feminist rage followed by an assertion of feminine values and concluding, perhaps a little tentatively, with a pointer to a new age of co-operation between the sexes, of respect for inner voices that teach us how to exist.
>
> (*Independent* 25. 9. 1993)

Calvin Bedient, a repeatedly negative critic of the work of Hughes from the earliest days, finally found himself being positive about the culmination of what he called 'attempts at self-greening' in *River* (1987: 150). '"People", here, are secondary to "river", which is now hero, now heroine, and ever a substance racing toward essence, a noun running into a verb' (153). An awed and fearful imagination saves Hughes from the sentimental and the theatrical, and an imagination 'that veers anyway toward extremity and bravura' (156). In *River* 'Hughes pursues, at least as a shadow does, the disappearing figure of the green man. And as a poet he is more or less instinctually one with inexplicable process, organic metamorphosis, gulping surprise' (159). 'The only certain philosophy of the volume ... is that of the unity and kinship of all that exists in the world, things and living beings alike' (162). With more passion and 'greater turbulent force' than Heaney, suggests Bedient, Hughes leaves something of himself in the 'singular and forceful style' of his poems that celebrate his apprehension of the goddess of nature.

It is interesting to note the influence of Hughes upon a later generation of poets who engage with the natural environment. Alice Oswald, a poet concerned with developing a new kind of nature poem in her work *Dart* (2002) and in *Woods etc.* (2005), has written:

> Hughes always finds some procedure for stripping away the protective layers – the soundproof ears, the double-glazed eyes – that prevents us making contact with anything outside ourselves. Right now, I can't think of anything more important than that kind of poem ... The disruption of comfort, the chance to concentrate utterly on what's there, to see it in its own way and to say so without disturbing its strangeness is what Hughes offers.
>
> (*Guardian* 3. 12. 2005, Saturday Review, p. 21)

It is significant that in contemporary Eastern culture the work of Hughes is noted for its environmental concerns and its ecopoetics. The Chinese critic Chen Hong compares the treatment of animals by Blake, Lawrence and Hughes in her book *Bestiality, Animality, and Humanity* (2005) and concludes that Hughes goes furthest in relating animal qualities to the animality in humanity and its problematics. She also notes the environmentalist concerns of Hughes that underpin the later poetry, drawing attention in particular to the two poems, 'If' and '1984 on "The Tarka Trail"', about water pollution added to the *Three Books* version of *River* (222). In India V.T. Usha has emphasised, in her book on the work of Hughes, 'a biocentric view that Hughes graduated towards through his poetry that was in [an] intimate relationship with nature and the natural habitat. It would be appropriate to call his poetic vision an *ecopoetics of complete being*' (1999: 83).

My own work on Hughes over the last four decades has tended to focus upon aspects of his representations of nature and engagements with ecology. *Green Voices* (1995, second edition 2009) compares the notions of nature underpinning the work of Hughes with those of other contemporary poets, placing each of them in a historical tradition of poetic attitudes to nature. For the chapter on Hughes I received from the poet a statement about his 'greening', together with an admission that the attempt to write 'semi-protest verses' on green issues had not resulted in 'the real thing' (1995: 131–32). In that book I offer a critique of the transcendentalist evaluations of *River* by Robinson and Scigaj (see Criticism, **p. 141**) and trace the development of Hughes's distinctive stance towards nature as moving from anti-pastoral to what I have called 'post-pastoral' poetry, using a term defined by six features of the work of Hughes first proposed in the essay 'Gods of Mud: Hughes and the Post-Pastoral' (Gifford 1994). The position of Hughes in relation to the long pastoral tradition is further contextualised in *Pastoral*, first within the anti-pastoral tradition (Gifford 1999a: 135–37) and then within a post-pastoral tradition (169–71).

The latter is illustrated with examples taken solely from *Cave Birds* which begins and ends with a critique of pastoral complacency (cockerel arrogance; and the desire to possess the falcon – 'But when will he land / On a man's wrist'). The first feature of post-pastoral is described as humility derived from awe at the forces of the natural world that the cockerel protagonist lacks. The second is the Knight's recognition of a destructive-creative universe of which he is a part. The third is the suggestion in 'Bride and Groom Lie Hidden for Three Days' that the processes of outer nature are paralleled in inner nature. The fourth is the apparently paradoxical notion of 'two gods of mud' at the orgasmic climax of this poem which represents culture (gods) as nature (mud), just as nature is culture in the word 'mud' (see Criticism, **p. 147**). The fifth is contained in the expression of consciousness as carrying the responsibility of conscience in 'The Risen' ('his each wingbeat – a convict's release'). Then that final temptation which creeps into 'The Risen' – of the resurgent desire of 'a man' to exploit nature in the form of the risen falcon on his wrist – echoes his historic desire to exploit the female and other human social groups (169–71). The whole of Hughes's writing about nature and the Goddess has been a recognition and a critique of his gender's exploitation of nature as deriving from the same mindset as his exploitation of the female, the sixth feature of post-pastoral literature.

This notion of exploitation raises the question of Hughes's interest in fishing, which only one other critic has ever raised (Moody 1987). Correspondence with Hughes about the issue of fishing and the poetry of fishing resulted in the essay '"Go Fishing": An Ecocentric or Egocentric Imperative?' (Gifford 1999b). A discussion of the linguistic effects in the poem 'Go Fishing' that take the reader on a journey towards a 'healing' biocentrism – a communion with layers of the self that pre-date language, as Hughes once put it – is juxtaposed with a poem about the killing of a salmon by fishing in the poem 'Earth-Numb'. It is argued that in the self-questioning poem 'The Gulkana', the insights gained are not those derived from actually killing fish, but from the attentive, vulnerable, respectful, fearful mode of hunting which is justified in Jungian terms in Hughes's letter to me (*Letters* 658).

Hughes's willingness to include human ecology, in the form of his own family, in his notion of nature is discussed in '"Dead Farms, Dead Leaves": Culture as Nature in *Remains of Elmet* and *Elmet*' (Gifford 2004). Not only are 'Dead Farms, Dead Leaves' in that poem's title, but the industrial revolution – the opposite of 'natural' to a writer such as D. H. Lawrence – is, in its death throes, characterised by Hughes's imagery as part of the creative-destructive cycles of nature. This is a radical conflation of a long-standing separation of first, civilisation and nature, of art and nature, then of industrialism and nature in English culture. But it is also a return to the earliest European sense of the grounding of human culture within nature that Hughes has evoked in his translation of Ovid: 'Mankind listened deeply / To the harmony of the whole creation, / And aligned / Every action to the greater order'. In 'Lumb Chimneys' and 'First Mills', for example, Hughes deploys a technique for the conflation of culture and nature which often ends with an image of culture as nature, falling back into earth after a cultural 'flowering'. But in the later book *Elmet* the natural individualistic flowering and decay of the lives of family members are also represented as embedded in the landscape they inhabited, just as their dead farms, dead mills, dead chapels are like dead leaves.

This argument for a recognition of Hughes's integration of culture into nature is extended in a discussion of *Wolfwatching* which leads into a summary of the poet's conservation activism in an essay titled 'The Ecology of Ted Hughes' (Gifford 2006). Most recently I have published previously neglected evidence from the archives of the link between the poetry of *River*, the children's story *The Iron Woman* and Hughes's environmental activism in relation to water quality in the rivers of the Southwest of England (Gifford 2008). This provides significant evidence in relation to the way we confront the current environmental crisis and shows that Hughes has bridged the Two Cultures (Science v. Arts) that were separated so disastrously in the education system of his youth – a separation which he might have appeared to have been promoting in his early attacks on scientific rationalism. For the evidence now shows that the poetry was informed by science and that Hughes used poetry and narrative for conservation purposes that might indeed contribute to healing the self-inflicted wounds of our relationship with our planet referred to by Sagar and Scigaj. As Jeanette Winterson says:

> What poetry prompts us to remember alters according to what we are most in peril of forgetting. The jargon of global warming and climate change brings no one closer to the planet that is melting under our feet. Reading Ted Hughes is a wild call to live 'where the night snows stars and the earth creaks'.
>
> (2008: 8)

Conclusion

Hughes defined poetry as:

> nothing more than a facility for expressing that complicated process in which we locate, and attempt to heal, affliction – whether our own or that of others whose feeling we can share. The inmost spirit of poetry, in other words, is at bottom, in every recorded case, the voice of pain – and the physical body, so to speak, of poetry, is the treatment by which the poet tries to reconcile that pain with the world.
>
> (*Letters* 458)

Hughes knew that he was in a tradition of poetic exploration of how the afflictions inherent in human nature can be understood and reconciled through considering its place within the wider natural world. But he needed to get clear of the complacent pastoral aspects of that poetic tradition to deal with the growing twentieth-century evidence of the pain arising from the failure of the relationship our species has with our home. And that journey towards reconciliation required an inward journey of transformation through first confronting the pain of the incomplete but complacent self.

Hughes himself felt that he had made mistakes, latterly writing too much prose and not publishing *Birthday Letters* earlier. Accepting the Laureateship was perhaps a mistake − although he did not think so himself − because we now associate him with the establishment before we think of his radicalism. But from the beginning and right through his work he challenged the status quo artistically, philosophically and socially. The *Letters* are full of nothing else. Ultimately, he used the Laureateship as a platform for his radicalism − in education, in widening the narrow British poetry world, in challenging literary scholarship, in increasing environmental awareness nationally and in local environmental activism. Each successive book of poems was an event of literary radicalism and risk-taking in the cause of reconnecting our inner life with the life we live on the planet. He challenged complacency in himself with each new book and each new book challenged our imaginative understanding of what kind of an animal we are and could be. The last line of his last play was: 'Let this give man hope'.

4

Chronology

Any chronology must be indebted, like this one, to the work of Ann Skea whose more detailed Timeline is available on her website: www.ann.skea.com/THHome

1930
Born 17 August, Mytholmroyd, Yorkshire, to William Henry and Edith (née Farrar) Hughes.

1938
September – Family move to Mexborough, Yorkshire. Own a newspaper and tobacco shop.

1943
Mexborough Grammar School.

1945
First poems written.

1946
First poems published in School magazine, *Don and Dearne*.

1948
Wins Scholarship to Pembroke College, Cambridge University.

1949
National Service in the Royal Air Force.

1951
Enters Pembroke College, Cambridge to study English.

1952
Parents return to West Yorkshire to live at The Beacon, Heptonstall.

1953
Fox dream: drops English to study Archaeology and Anthropology.

1954

Publishes poems in student magazines under pseudonyms Daniel Hearing and Peter Crew. Graduates from Cambridge.

1955–56

Living at 18 Rugby Street, London and in Cambridge at weekends. Rose gardener, security guard, washing-up at London Zoo, reader for J. Arthur Rank.

1956

26 February – At launch of *Saint Botolph's Review* meets Sylvia Plath.

25 March – Second meeting with Sylvia.

16 June – Marries Sylvia Plath at St George the Martyr's Church, Bloomsbury, London.

July/August – Honeymoon at 59 Tomas Ortunio, Benidorm, Spain.

November – Living at 55 Eltisley Avenue, Cambridge. Teaching English and Drama at Coleridge Secondary Modern School.

1957

April – First poem, 'The Martyrdom of Bishop Farrar', read on BBC radio.

June – To Plath's home in Wellesley, Massachusetts, USA, then on holiday in Eastham, Cape Cod.

August – To 337 Elm Street, Northampton, Massachusetts, where Sylvia teaches at Smith College.

September – *The Hawk in the Rain.*

1958

Spring semester – Hughes teaching at University of Massachusetts, Amherst as instructor in English Literature and Creative Writing.

May – Meets Leonard Baskin.

August – Rents flat at 9 Willow Street, Beacon Hill, Boston.

1959

Summer – Crosses America by car.

September – Yaddo Artists' Colony for 11 weeks. Meets Chou Wen-Chung and agrees to collaborate on *Bardo Thödol.*

December – Returns to parents' home in Heptonstall, Yorkshire.

1960

February – Moves to 3 Chalcot Square, Primrose Hill, London.

March – *Lupercal.*

1 April – Daughter Frieda Rebecca born.

May – First story, 'The Rain Horse', read on BBC radio.

1961

April – *Meet My Folks!*

August – Sells lease on London flat to David and Assia Wevill and moves to Court Green, Devon.

November – First radio play, *The House of Aries*, produced by BBC.

1962
17 January – son Nicholas Farrar born.
May – *Selected Poems* with Thom Gunn.
May – David and Assia Wevill visit.
June – Ted and Assia become lovers.
July – Hughes driven from Court Green (literally) by Plath to live in London.
September – Hughes and Plath visit Richard Murphy in Ireland and leave
   separately.

1963
11 February – Sylvia Plath's suicide.
November – *How the Whale Became.*
November – *The Earth-Owl and Other Moon People.*

1964
3 March – Ted and Assia's daughter Alexandra Tatiana Eloise Wevill (Shura)
   born.
April – *Nessie the Mannerless Monster.*

1965
Autumn – *Modern Poetry in Translation* (first editorial with Daniel Weissbort).

1967
May – *Wodwo.*
July – BBC broadcasts Poetry International '67 with Hughes speaking and
   reading; writing broadsheet and programme notes.
December – *Poetry in the Making* (broadcasts).

1968
February – *The Iron Man.*
The Arvon Foundation established by John Fairfax and John Moat.

1969
23 March – Deaths of Assia and Shura.
May – Death of Hughes's mother, Edith.
December – *Seneca's Oedipus.*

1970
August – Marriage to Carol Orchard.
October – *Crow: From the Life and Songs of the Crow.*

1971
July–December – Accompanies Peter Brook to Shiraz Festival, Persia to write
   Orghast.
Rainbow Press founded by Olwyn and Ted Hughes.

1972
October – *Selected Poems 1957–67.*

1973
Buys Moortown Farm (ninety-five acres) and runs it with Carol and her father, Jack Orchard.

1974
Awarded Queen's Gold Medal for Poetry.

1975
30 May – *Cave Birds* and *Lumb's Remains* performed at the Ilkley Literature Festival.
October – *Seasons Songs*.

1976
February – Death of Jack Orchard.
November – *Moon-Whales*.

1977
May – *Gaudete*.
Awarded OBE.

1978
February – *Moon Bells*.
October – *Cave Birds*.

1979
October – *Moortown*.

1980
Fishing in Alaska with Nicholas.

1981
February – Death of father, William.
March – *Under the North Star*.

1982
February – *Selected Poems 1957–81*.

1983
September – *River*.

1984
June – *What is the Truth?*
December – Appointed Poet Laureate.

1986
August – *Ffangs the Vampire Bat and the Kiss of Truth*.
October – *Flowers and Insects*.

1988
June – *Tales of the Early World.*

1989
September – *Moortown Diary.*
September – *Wolfwatching.*

1990
Spring – *Capriccio* (50 copies at $4,000 each).

1992
April – *Shakespeare and the Goddess of Complete Being.*
June – *Rain-Charm for the Duchy*

1993
June – *Three Books.*
September – *The Iron Woman.*

1994
March – *Winter Pollen.*
October – *Elmet.*

1995
March – *New Selected Poems 1957–1994.*
March – *The Dreamfighter and Other Creation Tales.*
August – *Spring Awakening* performed at the Barbican, London.
October – *Difficulties of a Bridegroom.*
October – *Collected Animal Poems* (four volumes).

1996
October – *Blood Wedding* performed at Young Vic, London.

1997
Late spring – begins treatment for cancer.
Tales from Ovid.

1998
January – *Birthday Letters.*
January – *Tales from Ovid* wins the Whitbread Book of the Year prize.
March – *Tales from Ovid* wins the W.H. Smith Literature Award.
Spring – *Howls and Whispers* (150 copies at $4,000 each).
August – *Phèdra* performed at Malvern Literary Festival and the Almeida Theatre, London.
October – Forward Prize for Poetry awarded to *Birthday Letters.*
October – Appointed member of the Queen's Order of Merit.
28 October – Ted Hughes dies.

1999

January – *Birthday Letters* wins T.S. Eliot Prize for Poetry.

Birthday Letters wins the South Bank Award for Literature.

Birthday Letters wins the Whitbread Book of the Year prize.

April – *Tales from Ovid* performed by the Royal Shakespeare Company at the Swan, Stratford.

13 May – Memorial Service at Westminster Abbey.

August – *The Iron Giant*, Brad Bird's animated film version of *The Iron Man*, is distributed by Warner Bros.

December – *The Oresteia* performed at the National Theatre.

2000

September – *Alcestis* performed by Barrie Rutter's Northern Broadsides Theatre Company at Dean Clough, Halifax, West Yorkshire.

Further reading

Biographical sources

The best original source of biographical information is *Letters of Ted Hughes*, edited, with brief biographical notes, by Christopher Reid. But Hughes began giving biographical information to the writer of the first book about his work, the critic who became his trusted friend, Keith Sagar. Much of the biographical information in *The Art of Ted Hughes* that is not directly quoted from Hughes is derived from his letters to Sagar. The only biography is Elaine Feinstein's *Ted Hughes: The Life of a Poet*, which, despite the inevitable errors in a pioneering book of this kind, does draw upon her interviews with many friends and collaborators. Feinstein's book is not an authorised biography and, given Hughes's apparent wish that there should be none, it is unlikely that an authorised biography will appear in the next decades. It is likely, however, that memoirs will continue to be published, in forms as varied as the warm prose of Lucas Myers (2001), the poignant poetry of Daniel Weissbort (2002) and the memoir poems of Frieda Hughes (2008). Nick Gammage's *The Epic Poise* contains a number of memoirs and tributes. Originally intended as a seventieth birthday present for Hughes, in the event of his death during its preparation it became a posthumous celebration of his life and work from his friends, collaborators and critics. On the relationship between Hughes and Plath, Diane Middlebrook's book *Her Husband* is an example of what can be produced by careful archival research and literary deduction. The availability of so much material in the archives and of living collaborators, family and friends suggests that new biographical work may yet be published. The 'Life and contexts' chapter of the present book has been checked and corrected by all the living main players, including the Hughes estate.

Sagar, Keith (1975, second edition 1978) *The Art of Ted Hughes*, Cambridge: Cambridge University Press.

Gammage, Nick (ed.) (1999) *The Epic Poise: A Celebration of Ted Hughes*, London: Faber & Faber.

Feinstein, Elaine (2001) *Ted Hughes: The Life of a Poet*, London: Weidenfeld and Nicolson.

Myers, Lucas (2001) *Crow Steered, Bergs Appeared*, Sewanee, TN: Proctor's Hall Press.
Weissbort, Daniel (2002) *Letters to Ted*, London: Anvil.
Middlebrook, Diane (2004) *Her Husband: Hughes and Plath – A Marriage*, London: Little, Brown.
Hughes, Ted (2007) *Letters of Ted Hughes*, London: Faber & Faber.
Hughes, Frieda (2008) *Forty-Five*, New York: Harper Collins.

Bibliographical

Two bibliographies have been produced by Keith Sagar and Stephen Tabor, the second edition of which represents the state of the art in the very interesting bibliographical history of Hughes publications, broadcasts and studies. There is clearly a need for an update of this work and the best source of currently available information are the websites devoted to Ted Hughes which archive reviews and information.

Sagar, Keith and Stephen Tabor (1998) *Ted Hughes: A Bibliography 1946–1995*, London: Mansell.

Websites:

www.earth-moon.org (managed by Claas Kazzer)
www3.sympatico.ca/sylviapaul/hughes_archives.htm (Centre for Ted Hughes Studies, managed by Sylvia Paul)
www.theelmettrust (The Elmet Trust)
http://ann.skea.com/THHome.htm (managed by Ann Skea)

Reviews of criticism

Scigaj, Leonard M. (1992) *Critical Essays on Ted Hughes*, New York: G. K. Hall. The 'Introduction' of this book provides a lively survey of criticism up to its publication, with Scigaj's personal commentary.
Byrne, Sandie (2000) *The Poetry of Ted Hughes: A reader's guide to essential criticism*, Cambridge: Icon Books. This book-length review of Hughes criticism includes long extracts from critical studies and a useful bibliography.

Critical studies

Sagar, Keith (1975, second edition 1978) *The Art of Ted Hughes*, Cambridge: Cambridge University Press. The first monograph on the work of Hughes, the second edition discusses each of the first eight books up to *Gaudete* in a clear style of explication.
Gifford, Terry and Neil Roberts (1981) *Ted Hughes: A Critical Study*, London: Faber & Faber. Under the headings 'Finding a voice' (including 'A utility

general-purpose style', 'The world speaking', 'Narrative' and 'Humour'), 'Man and nature', and 'Knowledge of death' a detailed evaluative approach is established before then applying this to the books from *Crow* to *Moortown*.

Hirshberg, Stuart (1981) *Myth in the Poetry of Ted Hughes*, Dublin: Wolf-hound Press. Hirschberg is concerned with the mythic figures of shaman, trickster and scapegoat, largely in *Crow*, *Gaudete* and *Cave Birds*. If this sounds programmatic, it does not distort subtle and alert readings of individual poems.

Bishop, Nick (1991) *Re-Making Poetry*, London: Harvester. This is a sophisticated and well-researched discussion of the work up to the publication of *River*. His focus is on the qualities of the language in relation to the evolution of the self through work that increasingly used religious mythologies. He has a useful analysis of the four voices in *The Hawk in the Rain* and *Lupercal* that establish his critical terminology.

Scigaj, Leonard M. (1991) *Ted Hughes*, Boston, MA: Twayne. Scigaj takes the metaphysics of myths into an analysis of Hughes's sense of ecological responsibility. This book was the first to make the case for Hughes as an ecological poet in the context of Hughes's belief in the shamanic healing power of poetry.

Skea, Ann (1994) *The Poetic Quest*, Armidale, NSW: University of New England Press. Skea focuses upon the mythic structures of Hughes's work derived from his knowledge of alchemy and magic, arguing that his quest was not inwards, but towards confrontation with suffering to achieve re-union with 'the Source'.

Bentley, Paul (1998) *The Poetry of Ted Hughes: Language, Illusion and Beyond*, London: Longman. Paul Bentley's focus on language in this book draws upon the French theorists Julia Kristeva (on *Gaudete* and *Cave Birds*), Roland Barthes (on *Remains of Elmet*) and Jacques Lacan, as in his use of the Lacanian 'Real' in his discussion of *Moortown*.

Sagar, Keith (2000; second edition 2006) *The Laughter of Foxes*, Liverpool: Liverpool University Press. An overview of the work of Hughes, thirty years after Sagar's impressive pioneering book *The Art of Ted Hughes*, including a theory of imagination underpinning the work and a study of Hughes's practice in the redrafting of one poem, 'The Dove Came' from *Moortown*.

Roberts, Neil (2006) *Ted Hughes: A Literary Life*, Basingstoke: Palgrave Macmillan. Full of new insights using archival research, this clear and lively book discusses the whole work, including chapters on translations and writing for children.

Collections of critical essays

Collections of critical essays on various aspects of the work have been published following conferences on Hughes (Sagar 1983; Sagar 1994; Moulin 2004; Schuchard 2006 (contains four essays only); Rees 2009).

Sagar, Keith (ed.) (1983) *The Achievement of Ted Hughes*, Manchester: Manchester University Press.

Dyson, A. E. (ed.) (1990) *Three Contemporary Poets: Thom Gunn, Ted Hughes & R. S. Thomas*, Basingstoke: Macmillan.

Scigaj, Leonard M. (ed.) (1992) *Critical Essays on Ted Hughes*, New York: G. K. Hall.

Sagar, Keith (ed.) (1994) *The Challenge of Ted Hughes*, London: Macmillan.

Moulin, Joanny (ed.) (1999) *Lire Ted Hughes*, Paris: Editions du Temps.

—(ed.) (2004) *Ted Hughes: Alternative Horizons*, London: Routledge.

Schuchard, Ronald (ed.) (2006) *Fixed Stars Govern a Life*, Atlanta, GA: Academic Exchange, Emory University.

Rees, R. D. (ed.) (2009) *Ted Hughes and the Classics*, Oxford: Oxford University Press.

Hughes and the history of ecopoetics

Gifford, Terry (1995; second edition 2009) *Green Voices: Understanding Contemporary Nature Poetry*, Manchester: Manchester University Press; Critical, Cultural and Communications Press.   *Green Voices* compares the notions of nature underpinning the work of Hughes with those of other contemporary poets, placing each of them in a historical tradition of poetic constructions of nature.

Sagar, Keith (2005) *Literature and the Crime Against Nature*, London: Chaucer Press.   Reading the history of Western literature backwards, as it were, from the insights of Hughes, Sagar traces the forms of hubris, the signs of regeneration, the false signs and the unintended signs of the possibilities of reconnection with nature, in works that are always read as imaginative encounters with forces beyond the writers themselves.

Selected works of Ted Hughes

BOOKS

The Hawk in the Rain, London: Faber & Faber, 1957.

Lupercal, London: Faber & Faber, 1960.

Meet My Folks, London: Faber & Faber,1961.

The Earth-Owl and Other Moon People, London: Faber & Faber, 1963.

How the Whale Became, London: Faber & Faber, 1963.

Nessie the Mannerless Monster, London: Faber & Faber, 1964.

Recklings, London: Turret Books, 1966.

Poetry in the Making, London: Faber & Faber, 1967.

Wodwo, London: Faber & Faber, 1967.

The Iron Man, London: Faber & Faber, 1968.

Seneca's Oedipus, London: Faber & Faber, 1969.

Crow, London: Faber & Faber, 1970.

The Coming of the Kings, London: Faber & Faber, 1970.

A Choice of Shakespeare's Verse, London: Faber & Faber, 1971 (second edition 1991).

Earth-Moon, London: Rainbow Press, 1976.

Moon-Whales and Other Moon Poems, New York: Viking, 1976.
Season Songs, London: Faber & Faber, 1976.
Gaudete, London: Faber & Faber, 1977.
Cave Birds, London: Faber & Faber, 1978.
Moon-Bells and Other Poems, London: Chatto & Windus, 1978.
Orts, London: Rainbow Press, 1978.
Moortown, London: Faber & Faber, 1979.
Remains of Elmet, London: Faber & Faber, 1979.
A Primer of Birds, Lurley, Devon: Gehenna Press, 1981.
Under the North Star, London: Faber & Faber, 1981.
Selected Poems 1957–1981, London: Faber & Faber, 1982.
The Rattle Bag (edited with Seamus Heaney), London: Faber & Faber, 1982.
River, London: Faber & Faber, 1983.
What is the Truth?, London: Faber & Faber, 1984.
Ffangs the Vampire Bat and the Kiss of Truth, London: Faber & Faber, 1986.
Flowers and Insects, London: Faber & Faber, 1986.
The Cat and the Cuckoo, Bideford, Devon: Sunstone Press, 1987.
Tales of the Early World, London: Faber & Faber, 1988.
Moortown Diary, London: Faber & Faber, 1989.
Wolfwatching, London: Faber & Faber, 1989.
Capriccio, Lurley, Devon: Gehenna Press, 1990.
A Dancer to God, London: Faber & Faber, 1992.
Rain-Charm for the Duchy, London: Faber & Faber, 1992.
Shakespeare and the Goddess of Complete Being, London: Faber & Faber, 1992.
The Iron Woman, London: Faber & Faber, 1993.
The Mermaid's Purse, Bideford, Devon: Sunstone Press, 1993.
Three Books (Cave Birds, Remains of Elmet, River), London: Faber & Faber, 1993.
Elmet, London: Faber & Faber, 1994.
Winter Pollen, London: Faber & Faber, 1994.
Collected Animal Poems: 4 Vols, London: Faber & Faber, 1995.
Difficulties of a Bridegroom, London: Faber & Faber, 1995.
The Dreamfighter and Other Creation Tales, London: Faber & Faber, 1995.
New Selected Poems 1957–1994, London: Faber & Faber, 1995.
Spring Awakening, London: Faber & Faber, 1995.
Blood Wedding, London: Faber & Faber, 1996.
Tales from Ovid, London: Faber & Faber, 1997.
By Heart, London: Faber & Faber, 1997.
The School Bag (edited with Seamus Heaney), London: Faber & Faber, 1997.
Birthday Letters, London: Faber & Faber, 1998.
Howls and Whispers, Lurley, Devon: Gehenna Press, 1998.
Phèdre, London: Faber & Faber, 1998.
Alcestis, London: Faber & Faber, 1999.
The Oresteia, London: Faber & Faber, 1999.
Collected Plays for Children, London: Faber & Faber, 2001.
Collected Poems, London: Faber & Faber, 2003.
Collected Poems for Children, London: Faber & Faber, 2005.
Selected Translations, London: Faber & Faber, 2006.
Letters of Ted Hughes, London: Faber & Faber, 2007.

UNCOLLECTED ESSAYS

'Myth and Education', *Children's Literature in Education*, 1: 55–70, 1970. (Importantly different from the revised version included in *Winter Pollen*.)

RECORDINGS

The Thought-Fox and Other Poems, read by Ted Hughes, Faber & Faber, 1994.
The Dreamfighter and Other Creation Tales, read by Ted Hughes, Faber/Penguin, 1996.
Ffangs the Vampire Bat and the Kiss of Truth, read by Ted Hughes, Faber/Penguin, 1996.
The Iron Woman, read by Ted Hughes, Faber/Penguin, 1996.
Nessie the Mannerless Monster and *The Iron Wolf*, read by Ted Hughes, Faber/Penguin, 1996.
Tales of the Early World, read by Ted Hughes, Faber/Penguin, 1996.
Ted Hughes Reading his Poetry, HarperCollins Audio Books, 1996.
By Heart: 101 Poems to Remember, read by Ted Hughes, Faber/Penguin, 1997.
Crow, read by Ted Hughes, Faber/Penguin, 1997.
How the Whale Became and Other Stories, read by Ted Hughes, Faber/Penguin, 1997.
The Iron Man, read by Ted Hughes, Faber/Penguin, 1997.
Tales from Ovid, read by Ted Hughes, Faber/Penguin, 1998.
The Spoken Word – Ted Hughes. Poems and short stories (a two CD set drawn from BBC Radio broadcasts), British Library Sound Archive, 2008.
The Spoken Word – Ted Hughes. Poetry in the Making *and* Season Songs (a two CD set of five BBC Radio broadcasts for schools, plus two programmes reading *Season Songs*), British Library Sound Archive, 2008.

MANUSCRIPTS

Not all of the papers of Hughes have been archived to date, but the collections of two libraries are essential for consultation by future Hughes scholars. The Department of Special Collections at the Robert W. Woodruff Library, University of Emory, Atlanta, Georgia, USA holds the bulk of Hughes's papers, which he sold to the library in 1997. New material is continuously being added to this essential collection. In 2001 the British Library acquired the letters of Hughes to Keith Sagar and also holds the papers of Al Alvarez, Leonard Baskin, Fay Godwin and Bernard Stone/Turret Press. Again, active acquisition of Hughes material continues at the British Library. King's College London has the archive of *Modern Poetry in Translation*. Cambridge University Library has the papers of Plath's biographer, Ann Stevenson, which, although closed, Elaine Feinstein, Hughes's biographer, was allowed to view. Other Hughes manuscript material is held in the libraries of the universities of Aberystwyth, Exeter, Leeds and Liverpool.

Bibliography

Alvarez, Al (1962) *The New Poetry*, London: Penguin.

——(1999) *Where Did It All Go Right?*, London: Richard Cohen Books.

Armitage, Simon (2000) 'Introduction', *Ted Hughes: Poems Selected by Simon Armitage*, London: Faber & Faber.

Bark, Ann Voss (1983) *West Country Fly Fishing*, London: Batsford.

Bassnett, Susan (2008) *Ted Hughes*, London: Northcote House.

Bedient, Calvin (1974) *Eight Contemporary Poets*, Oxford: Oxford University Press.

——(1987) 'Ted Hughes's Fearful Greening', *Parnassus*, 14(1):150–63.

Bentley, Paul (1998) *The Poetry of Ted Hughes: Language, Illusion and Beyond*, London: Longman.

Bere, Carol (1999) '*Birthday Letters*: Ted Hughes's Sibylline Leaves', in Joanny Moulin (ed.) *Lire Ted Hughes*, Paris: Editions du Temps.

Bishop, Nick (1991) *Re-Making Poetry*, London: Harvester.

Bradshaw, Graham (1983) 'Creative Mythology in Cave Birds' in Keith Sagar (ed.), *The Achievement of Ted Hughes*, Manchester: Manchester University Press.

Brain, Tracy (2001) *The Other Sylvia Plath*, Harlow: Longman.

Brown, Dennis (1994) *The Poetry of Postmodernity*, London: Macmillan.

Bryson, J. Scott (2002) *Ecopoetry: A Critical Introduction*, Salt Lake City: University of Utah Press.

Bundtzen, Lynda K. (1998) 'Poetic Arson and Sylvia Plath's "Burning the Letters"', *Contemporary Literature*, 39(3): 434–51.

——(2001) *The Other Ariel*, Amherst: University of Massachusetts Press.

Byrne, Sandie (2000) *The Poetry of Ted Hughes: A reader's guide to essential criticism*, Cambridge: Icon Books.

Cassagnère, Christian La (2004) 'Ted Hughes's Crying Horizons: "Wind" and the Poetics of Sublimity' in Joanny Moulin (ed.), *Ted Hughes: Alternative Horizons*, London: Routledge.

Conquest, Robert (1956) *New Lines*, London: Macmillan.

Coupe, Laurence (ed.) (2000) *The Green Studies Reader*, Abingdon: Routledge.

Cox, Brian (1999) 'Ted Hughes (1930–98): A Personal Retrospect', *The Hudson Review*, 52(1): 29–43.

Csokits, János (1989) 'János Pilinszky's "Desert of Love": A Note' in Daniel Weissbort (ed.), *Translating Poetry: The Double Labyrinth*, Basingstoke: Palgrave Macmillan.

Cushman, Keith (1983) 'Hughes' poetry for children' in Keith Sagar (ed.), *The Achievement of Ted Hughes*, Manchester: Manchester University Press.

Dawkins, Richard (1978) *The Selfish Gene*, Oxford: Oxford University Press.

Douglas, Ed (2007) 'Poet as Eco Warrior', *Observer*, 4 November 2007, Review section pp. 10–11.

Dyson, A. E. (1990) *Three Contemporary Poets: Thom Gunn, Ted Hughes & R. S. Thomas*, Basingstoke: Macmillan.

Eagleton, Terry (1972) 'Myth and History in Recent Poetry', in Michael Schmidt and Grevel Lindop (eds), *British Poetry Since 1960*, Chatham: W. & J. Mackay.

Easthope, Antony (1999) 'The Poetry of Ted Hughes: Some Reservations' in Joanny Moulin (ed.), *Lire Ted Hughes*, Paris: Editions du Temps.

Eliade, Mircea (1964) *Shamanism*, London: Routledge.

Faas, Egbert (1971) 'Ted Hughes and Crow', an interview, *London Magazine*, 10 (10 January): 5–20.

——(1980) *The Unaccommodated Universe*, Santa Barbara, CA: Black Sparrow Press.

Feinstein, Elaine (2001) *Ted Hughes: The Life of a Poet*, London: Weidenfeld and Nicolson.

Forrest-Thomson, Veronica (1978) *Poetic Artifice*, Manchester: Manchester University Press.

Gammage, Nick (ed.) (1999) *The Epic Poise: A Celebration of Ted Hughes*, London: Faber & Faber.

Garrard, Greg (2004) *Ecocriticism*, London: Routledge.

Gervais, David (1993) *Literary Englands*, Cambridge: Cambridge University Press.

Gifford, Terry (1978) 'A Return to "The Wound" by Ted Hughes', *Kingfisher*, 1 (2/3): 46–53.

——(1994) 'Gods of Mud: Hughes and the Post-Pastoral' in Keith Sagar (ed.), *The Challenge of Ted Hughes*, London: Macmillan.

——(1995; second edition 2009) *Green Voices: Understanding Contemporary Nature Poetry*, Manchester: Manchester University Press; Critical, Cultural and Communications Press.

——(1999a) *Pastoral*, London: Routledge.

——(1999b) '"Go Fishing": An Ecocentric or Egocentric Imperative?' in Joanny Moulin (ed.), *Lire Ted Hughes*, Paris: Editions du Temps.

——(2001) 'Interview with Fay Godwin', *Thumbscrew*, 18: 114–17.

——(2004) '"Dead Farms, Dead Leaves": Culture as Nature in *Remains of Elmet* and *Elmet*' in Joanny Moulin (ed.), *Ted Hughes: Alternative Horizons*, London: Routledge.

——(2006) 'The Ecology of Ted Hughes' in Ronald Schuchard (ed.), *Fixed Stars Govern a Life*, Atlanta, GA: Academic Exchange, Emory University.

——(2008) 'Rivers and Water Quality in the Work of Brian Clarke and Ted Hughes', *Concentric*, 34(1): 75–91.

Gifford, Terry and Neil Roberts (1981) *Ted Hughes: A Critical Study*, London: Faber & Faber.

Glotfelty, Cheryll and Harold Fromm (eds) (1996) *The Ecocriticism Reader*, Athens: University of Georgia Press.

Greening, John (2007) *Focus on Ted Hughes*, London: Greenwich Exchange.

Grubb, Frederick (1965) *A Vision of Reality*, London: Chatto & Windus.

Hamilton, Ian (1973) *A Poetry Chronicle*, London: Faber & Faber.

Heaney, Seamus (1967) Book review, *The Northern Review*, 1(3), Autumn: 50–52.

—— (1999/2000) St. Jerome Lecture. 'Fretwork: On Translating *Beowulf*', *In Other Words: The Journal for Literary Translators*, Autumn/Winter: 23–33.

Heinz, Drue (1995) 'Ted Hughes: The Art of Poetry LXXI', *Paris Review*, 134: 55–94.

Hirschberg, Stuart (1981) *Myth in the Poetry of Ted Hughes*, Dublin: Wolfhound Press.

Holbrook, David (1963) 'The Cult of Hughes and Gunn', *Poetry Review*, 54: 167–83.

——(1975) 'Ted Hughes's *Crow* and the Longing for Non-Being' in Peter Abbs (ed.), *The Black Rainbow: Essays on the present breakdown of culture*, London: Heinemann.

——(1977) *Lost Bearings in English Poetry*, London: Vision Press.

Hong, Chen (2005) *Bestiality, Animality, and Humanity*, Wuhan: Central China Normal University Press.

Hughes, Frieda (2008) *Forty-Five*, New York: Harper Collins.

Huws, Daniel (2007) 'Memories of Ted Hughes 1952–63', unpublished.

Kazzer, Claas (1999) 'Difficulties of a Bridegroom', *Q/W/E/R/T/Y*, 9: 187–201.

Koren, Yehuda and Eilat Negev (2006) *A Lover of Unreason: The Life and Tragic Death of Assia Wevill*, London: Robson Books.

Larrissy, Edward (1990) *Reading Twentieth Century Poetry*, Oxford: Blackwell.

Lucas, John (1986) *Modern English Poetry from Hardy to Hughes*, London: Batsford.

McCartney, Jenny (2007) Interview with Seamus Heaney, *The Sunday Telegraph*, 9. 9. 2007.

Malcolm, Janet (1994) *The Silent Woman: Sylvia Plath and Ted Hughes*, London: Macmillan.

Maslen, Elizabeth (1986) 'Counterpoint: Collaborations between Ted Hughes and three visual artists', *Word and Image*, 2(1), January–March: 33–44.

Middlebrook, Diane (2004) *Her Husband: Hughes and Plath – A Marriage*, London: Little, Brown.

—— (2006) 'The Poetry of Sylvia Plath and Ted Hughes: Call and response' in Jo Gill (ed.), *The Cambridge Companion to Sylvia Plath*, Cambridge: Cambridge University Press.

Moat, John (2005) *The Founding of Arvon*, London: Frances Lincoln.

Moody, David (1987) 'Telling It Like It's Not', *The Yearbook of English Studies*, 17: 166–78.

Morrison, Blake (1980) *The Movement*, Oxford: Oxford University Press.

Moulin, Joanny (1999a) *Ted Hughes: New Selected Poems*, Paris: Didier Erudition.

——(ed.) (1999b) *Lire Ted Hughes: New Selected Poems 1957–1994*, Paris: Editions du Temps.

——(1999c) *Ted Hughes: la langue rémunérée*, Paris: L. Harmattan.

——(ed.) (2004) *Ted Hughes: Alternative Horizons*, London: Routledge.

——(2007) *Ted Hughes: la terre hantée. Biographie.* Paris: Aden.

Muldoon, Paul (2006) *The End of the Poem*, London: Faber & Faber.

Myers, Lucas (2001) *Crow Steered, Bergs Appeared*, Sewanee, TN: Proctor's Hall Press.

Nesme, Axel (2004) 'Drives and their Vicissitudes in the Poetry of Ted Hughes' in Joanny Moulin (ed.), *Ted Hughes: Alternative Horizons*, London: Routledge.

Niven, Alistair (1999) *Literature Matters: Newsletter of the British Council's Literature Department*, No. 25.

O'Brien, Sean (1998) *The Deregulated Muse*, Newcastle upon Tyne: Bloodaxe.

Ousby, Ian (1988) *Cambridge Guide to Literature in English*, Cambridge: Cambridge University Press.

Owen, Jane (2003) *The Poetry of Ted Hughes: Author Study Activities for Key Stage 2/3*, London: David Fulton.

Paul, Lissa (1999) 'The Children's Ted Hughes' in Joanny Moulin (ed.), *Lire Ted Hughes*, Paris: Editions du Temps.

Paulin, Tom (1992) *Minotaur: Poetry and the Nation State*, London: Faber & Faber.

Perloff, Marjorie (1984) 'The Two *Ariel*s: The (Re)Making of the Plath Canon', *American Poetry Review*, 13: 10–18.

Pitt, Valerie (1962) *Tennyson Laureate*, London: Barrie and Rockcliff.

Radin, Paul (1956) *The Trickster*, London: Routledge.

Rees, R. D. (ed.) (2009) *Ted Hughes and the Classics*, Oxford: Oxford University Press.

Roberts, Neil (1985) 'Ted Hughes and the Laureateship', *Critical Quarterly*, 27 (2): 3–5.

——(1999) *Narrative and Voice in Postwar Poetry*, Harlow: Longman.

——(2003) 'The Common Text of Sylvia Plath and Ted Hughes', *Symbiosis*, 7 (1): 157–73.

——(2006) *Ted Hughes: A Literary Life*, Basingstoke: Palgrave Macmillan.

——(2007) *Ted Hughes: New Selected Poems*, Penrith: Humanities-Ebooks.co.uk

Robinson, Craig (1989) *Ted Hughes as Shepherd of Being*, Basingstoke: Macmillan.

Rose, Jacqueline (1991) *The Haunting of Sylvia Plath*, London: Virago.

Rosenthal, M. L. (1967) *The New Poets*, New York: Oxford University Press.

Sagar, Keith (1972) *Ted Hughes*, Harlow: Longman for the British Council.

——(1975; second edition 1978) *The Art of Ted Hughes*, Cambridge: Cambridge University Press.

——(1981) *Ted Hughes*, Windsor: Profile Books.

——(ed.) (1983) *The Achievement of Ted Hughes*, Manchester: Manchester University Press.

——(ed.) (1994) *The Challenge of Ted Hughes*, London: Macmillan.

——(2006; first edition 2000) *The Laughter of Foxes*, Liverpool: Liverpool University Press.

——(2004) 'Ted Hughes', *Dictionary of National Biography*, Vol 28, Oxford: Oxford University Press.

——(2005) *Literature and the Crime Against Nature*, London: Chaucer Press.

Sagar, Keith and Stephen Tabor (1998) *Ted Hughes: A Bibliography 1946–1995*, London: Mansell.

Schmidt, Michael and Grevel Lindop (eds) (1972) *British Poetry Since 1960*, Chatham: W. & J. Mackay.

Schuchard, Ronald (ed.) (2006) *Fixed Stars Govern a Life*, Atlanta, GA: Academic Exchange, Emory University.

Scigaj, Leonard M. (1986) *Ted Hughes: Form and Imagination*, Iowa City: University of Iowa Press.

——(1991) *Ted Hughes*, Boston, MA: Twayne.

——(ed.) (1992) *Critical Essays on Ted Hughes*, New York: G. K. Hall.

——(2004) 'The Deterministic Ghost in the Machine of *Birthday Letters*' in Joanny Moulin (ed.), *Ted Hughes: Alternative Horizons*, London: Routledge.

Sewell, Brocard (ed.) (1980) *Henry Williamson: The Man, The Writings – A Symposium*, Padstow: Tabb House.

Seymour-Smith, Martin (1973) *Guide to Modern World Literature*, London: Macmillan.

Skea, Ann (1994) *Ted Hughes: The Poetic Quest*, Armidale, NSW: University of New England Press.

Smith, A. C. H. (1972) *Orghast at Persepolis*, London: Methuen.

Stevenson, Anne (1989) *Bitter Fame*, London: Viking.

Tennant, Emma (1999) *Burnt Diaries*, Edinburgh: Canongate.

Thurley, Geoffrey (1974) *The Ironic Harvest*, London: Arnold.

Uroff, Margaret Dickie (1979) *Sylvia Plath and Ted Hughes*, Chicago: University of Illinois Press.

Usha, V. T. (1998) *Modern English Literature. The Real and the Imagined: The Poetic World of Ted Hughes*, Jaipur: Mangal Deep Publications.

——(1999) 'Remembering Ted Hughes', *Journal of Literature and Aesthetics*, 7 (2): 81–84.

Wagner, Erica (2000) *Ariel's Gift: Ted Hughes, Sylvia Plath and the Story of Birthday Letters*, London: Faber & Faber.

Weissbort, Daniel (ed.) (1989) *Translating Poetry: The Double Labyrinth*, Basingstoke: Palgrave Macmillan.

—— (2002) *Letters to Ted*, London: Anvil.

—— (ed.) (2006) *Ted Hughes: Selected Translations*, London: Faber and Faber.

Weissbort, Daniel and Astradur Eysteinsson (eds) (2006) *Translation – Theory and Practice: A Historical Reader*, Oxford: Oxford University Press.

Winterson, Jeanette (2008) 'Foreword', *Great Poets of the 20th Century: Ted Hughes*, London: *Guardian*.

Wright, Carolyn (1999) 'What Happens in the Heart', *Poetry Review*, 89(3): 3–9.

Wurst, Gayle (2004) 'Words to "Patch the Havoc": The Imagination of Ted Hughes in the Poetry of Sylvia Plath' in Joanny Moulin (ed.), *Ted Hughes: Alternative Horizons*, London: Routledge.

Index

THE NEW CRITICAL IDIOM

Series Editor: John Drakakis, University of Stirling

The New Critical Idiom is an invaluable series of introductory guides to today's critical terminology. Each book:

- provides a handy, explanatory guide to the use (and abuse) of the term
- offers an original and distinctive overview by a leading literary and cultural critic
- relates the term to the larger field of cultural representation

With a strong emphasis on clarity, lively debate and the widest possible breadth of examples, *The New Critical Idiom* is an indispensable approach to key topics in literary studies.

'*The New Critical Idiom* is a constant resource — essential reading for all students.'
Tom Paulin, University of Oxford

"Easily the most informative and wide-ranging series of its kind, so packed with bright ideas that it has become an indispensable resource for students of literature.'
Terry Eagleton, University of Manchester

For further information on individual books in the series, visit:
www.routledgeliterature.com